Going to Live in Paris

Going to Live in Paris

Your practical guide to living and

working in France's capital
2nd edition

ALAN HART

howtobooks

Published How To Books Ltd,
3 Newtec Place, Magdalen Road,
Oxford OX4 1RE. United Kingdom.
Tel: (01865) 793806. Fax: (01865) 248780.
email: info@howtobooks.co.uk
http://www.howtobooks.co.uk

First edition 2003
Second edition 2004

British Library Cataloguing in Publication Data
A catalogue record for this book is available from the British
Library

Cover design by Baseline Arts Ltd, Oxford
Produced for How To Books by Deer Park Productions,
Tavistock
Typeset by PDQ Typesetting, Newcastle-under-Lyme, Staffs.
Printed and bound by Cromwell Press, Trowbridge, Wiltshire

NOTE: The material contained in this book is set out in good
faith for general guidance and no liability can be accepted
for loss or expense incurred as a result of relying in particular
circumstances on statements made in the book. The laws and
regulations are complex and liable to change, and readers should
check the current position with the relevant authorities before

Contents

x / GOING TO LIVE IN PARIS

List of illustrations

Preface

This new revised edition of *Going to Live in Paris* coincides with the centenary of the **Entente Cordiale** signed between France and Great Britain in 1904. By a curious twist of fate, this book has been written in a room with a view directly onto the apartment of the French Foreign Minister responsible for this fundamental act of Franco-British friendship, André Delcassé. Whilst it was a highly political treaty designed to settle political tensions (even then), it was also a *de facto* recognition of the love affair between Paris and the English-speaking world, which began with the *milords* lovingly mocked by French nineteenth-century popular folklore and later by Edith Piaf, and which was epitomised by the fun-loving Francophile, King Edward VII.

Following on from the blue bloods came the 'everyday folk', including most famously the British jockeys and stable boys, the dancers, nannies, and latterly the au pairs; but also railway workers and even the founder of one of Paris's best restaurants! With the Universal Exhibitions at the end of the nineteenth century came a huge influx of British workers, but also the first large-scale American arrival, whose heyday was the 'Lost Generation' of *les années folles*, between the two wars.

Paris is a city which has always known how to guard its mystique. Even other French people sneer at Parisian 'snobbery' and perceived coldness. The aim of this book is to help you realise that whatever your preconceptions are of Paris and the Parisians, there is very definitely a place here for you, and that there is no reason at all why your stay in Paris should not be happy and successful. This book is designed to be what everybody needs to really feel at home in a new town or city – a companion to accompany you, to inform you, to support you, and hopefully to reassure you as you find your own path to Parisian happiness, and unravel the mysteries of *la vie parisienne*.

Paris in 2004 is radically different from the city of a century ago, and has undergone many changes even since the first edition of this book was published. This new edition has taken into consideration a wide variety of lifestyles and budgets, and also imagines that there will be change in your life as settle and grow into your new life. A book like this can only ever be a thumbnail sketch of what you need to know to settle in quickly. It is up to you to add your local colour.

This book is dedicated once again with love and gratitude to all those who have helped me make my home in Paris. As ever, I am also deeply grateful to Nikki Read and all the How To Books team for their enduring support, and for their tolerance of what P. G. Wodehouse called that certain *je ne sais pas quoi* (a Parisian type of madness?) in me, which I hope you will soon acquire as a dedicated, convinced and confirmed Parisian!

Alan Hart

1

Introducing 21st Century Paris

There are hundreds, if not thousands, of books which recount the fascinating origins of Paris and the Parisians. Hardly any stone in Paris is turned without revealing something of the flamboyant city's bloody and glorious history. Reading one or more of these histories and exploring the ancient monuments and sites will thoroughly enrich the experience of any visitor or newcomer to the city. But it will also provide the backdrop for the passions which still run high in present-day Paris.

In 1999, the population of Paris was 2,147,857 **Parisiens**. Almost one third of these had moved to Paris since 1990, and half of the population was in the 25–39-year-old age range. The number of under-15s had declined, the over-60s had already started to move on, and foreign residents accounted for about 14.5% of the population, a decline of 10% since 1990. Nonetheless, Paris still vies with London as the most visited tourist city in the world. All of these figures only take into account the population of the 20 **arrondissements** which form the city of Paris. If you take into account all eight **départements** which form the greater Paris area, the **Île de France**, then the total number of **Franciliens** is around 12 million. Roughly 19% of the French population live in the 12,072 km^2 of the Île de France, which includes 2,400 km^2 of forest.

Disparities between different **communes** in the Paris region in terms of age and nationality or ethnic origin are very high. The theme of **mixité sociale**, seeking to create a social equilibrium, is one of the most contentious on-going sagas of French society and politics. Everybody talks about it, but the reality is that Parisians are just as tribal as other human beings, and like attracts like. However, there have been serious population shifts in the last 15 years which have upset the age-old political and social pattern of Paris. Whilst the first of these signs seemed positive, with the renewal and 'gentrification' of former run-down ghettos, latterly all the signs are that the soaring property prices are squeezing young families, and especially the middle classes, out of the city.

VOUS ÊTES PARISIEN?
Depending on who asks you this question and in what context, it could be taken as a compliment or an insult! Residents of the French capital are the ones that the other French nationals love to hate, either because they are jealous, or because they have had a bad experience at the

hands of the cosmopolitan and sometimes cunning and callous capital-dwellers.

Ask Parisians how they define themselves, and you will receive any number of answers. The authors of the perennially popular *Paris Insiders Guide* defined Parisiniasm as, 'a form of snobbery not automatically accessible to those living in Paris, or born in Paris ... a way of thinking, of having a good time, of laughing, and of being well-up on everything, which only exists in Paris'. (*Paris Insiders Guide*, International Welcome to Paris, 2000). What everyone is agreed upon, however, is that to be Parisian is to possess that certain *je ne sais pas quoi* which tantalises the rest of the world.

Parisians are big-city dwellers like any others. If you are a happy Londoner or New Yorker, you will soon get the hang of the city. You will learn the knacks and pick up the habits fairly rapidly, and start to form your own, all of which will allow you to settle comfortably into the city. Paris is no less friendly than any comparable city, and is indeed a lot friendlier than some other major French cities where foreigners can feel frozen out. Paris is so cosmopolitan that it is always possible to find your niche eventually. But to make the city work for you, you have to make an effort to be open to new ways and styles. Don't try to turn the tide, but go with the flow. With a city as diverse as Paris, there are always several 'flows' to go with, so you should be able to feel at home.

UNDERSTANDING THE FRENCH PEOPLE
If you are coming to live in Paris, you will be surrounded

by one of the most complex peoples on the face of the earth. The essential problem with understanding the French is that they are 'neither fish nor fowl', neither Latin nor Anglo-Saxon, but a mix of the two cultures. From the former they take their romanticism, a large part of their looks, their religion, their love of intrigue and a tendency to corruption and lawlessness. From the Anglo-Saxons they have acquired the other half of their looks, much of their culture, and commercial brilliance hampered by their innate need to argue about everything.

The French themselves agree on their own bizarre character. At the beginning of the presidential election campaign in France in 2002 *L'Express* (3 January 2002) wrote: 'There is a French magic, a particular temperament which mixes the indomitable defensiveness of an Asterix, the personification of our "exception", and the mad energy of a Popeye ... who always fights to maintain an eminent place in the world, and to seduce', echoing Paris's first-ever Green Party mayor. The new mayor of the Second Arrondissement Jacques Boutault, said of his own party: 'The Greens are Gauls! As soon as they are together, they cannot stop themselves from arguing amongst themselves, but when they are under attack from the exterior, they band together.' (*Le Parisien,* 25 March 2001).

'Asterix contra mundi'

The fact that Asterix has an enduring appeal to the French may perhaps explain the popularity of the anti-globalisation (**mondialisation**) campaigner José Bové, who bears more than a mild physical similarity to the fictional character. Bové's popularity explains much about the

French character which otherwise remains incomprehensible to foreigners and especially to Anglo-Saxons. The problem that France has with Europe, and indeed with the rest of the world, has a number of origins.

Firstly, it is due to the fact that the French believe passionately in **l'exception française**, the French exception in politics and culture. The general impression is that they have lessons to teach the rest of the world, without necessarily having anything to learn. The French often display a sense of superiority which can grate on foreign nerves. This all explains why, for instance, the French have more court rulings outstanding against them for infringements of European law than any other EU state. France sees the European Union not so much as a coalition of states reaching consensus on various issues, but as the alignment of Europe to the French model.

However, this belief in exceptions is frequently the cause of problems for those on the outside looking in, expecting France to take the 'logical' path when in fact she reverts to Gallic independence to keep the peace amongst her infighting factions. As the right-wing *Figaro* (29 June 2002) grumbled, 'as a result of her "exceptions", nobody understands France: her 35 hours, her incessant strikes, her simultaneous records of growth and unemployment, the inability of successive governments to impose indispensable reforms ... and her overall richness which jumps out and hits you between the eyes.'

Secondly, it stems from a sense of 'victimisation' from the English-speaking nations and their common language.

The French rightly complain that English is too dominant as a language in the world; but have yet to produce a convincing argument why their language should replace it. José Bové's attacks on multinationals touch his fellow citizens precisely because he stands for the individualism they cherish in the face of multinational companies. Following the EU ruling in July 2002 that all food product labels in Europe should be in English, *Le Figaro* (10 August 2002) declared, 'we would say that [France's] table and her language are in the sights of Brussels!'. There is nothing more likely to irritate a Frenchman than attacks on either his language or his **cuisine**.

The third reason for the seeming arrogance of the French is their fear of foreigners. Part of this fear derives simply from the perfectionist French anxiety about making a fool of themselves in front of foreigners. But according to a survey in October 2000, 60% of the French population thought that there were too many foreigners in France, and 43% consider themselves to be 'a little' racist.

Read in isolation these comments might seem alarming; but read in the context of the other comments above, they go a long way to identifying the complexity of the French character. After all, one half of the population dreams of moving to Paris, and after a few years in the city, they dream of moving out and buying a home in the places they originally wanted to escape from, as the 1999 census figures prove. How can you reason with a mentality like that? The answer is that you cannot. You simply have to take it all in your stride, make allowances, and try to be sensitive. In so doing you will disarm the French who do take time to get to know and accept newcomers, French or foreigners alike. You will overcome their reticence, their *froideur*, and their apparent arrogance. But first you have to learn the rules of the game, and then play to win.

DISCOVERING PARIS BY NUMBERS

The city of Paris is divided into 20 districts known as arrondissements (see Figure 1), described in the following chapters. Arrondissements are most often simply referred to by their number, for example, le seizième (16ème). Certain **quartiers** of Paris (eg, Les Halles, the Marais, or St Germain) spread over more than one arrondissement. Other quartiers (eg, la Butte Montmartre, la Butte aux Cailles, or Batignolles) are pockets in individual arrondissements.

The arrondissements of Paris curl out from the original city centre on the river banks (**rives**), islands (**îles**), marshes (**marais**) and fields (**près**) to a first city limit (the 1st–6th arrondissements), then spread east beyond the Bastille, and west into the 7th and 8th arrondissements. The sick and the infidels – Protestants, Arabs or Jews, or simply non-French – were kept to the outer lying districts of the 9th and 10th arrondissements beyond what became the Grands Boulevards.

The villages of Montmartre, Batignolles, and Belleville to the north, Autueil, Chaillot and Passy to the west, and the Butte aux Cailles to the south, were gradually pulled into the city limits following the urban expansion of areas such as Montparnasse. Whilst the south and west became generally calm areas favoured by the bourgeoisie and the

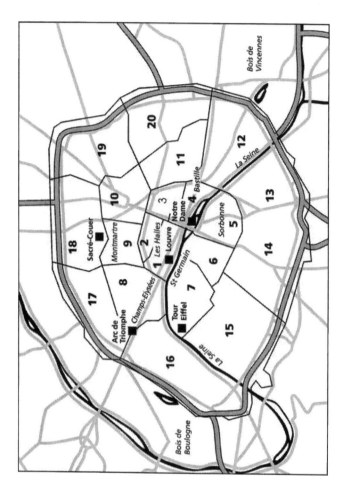

Figure 1. The Paris arrondissements.

aristocracy nearer the centre, the 'red' arrondissements of the north and east – the 13th, 18th, 19th and 20th – were villages transformed into the first dormitory towns (**cités dortoirs**), which became hotbeds of political radicalism for the working classes expelled from the renovated city centre.

These defining lines are still largely operational today, with the current Socialist mayor being elected from the **populaire** 18th arrondissement, having beaten his predecessor from the luxurious 5th. Despite its transport network and much talk, Paris remains a socially disjointed city, although urban renewal is levelling the differences. Paris is bursting at its neatly stitched seam, the **périphérique** ring road, which separates it from the good, the bad, and the ugly suburbs which may yet be absorbed into 21st and 22nd arrondissements. This road has today replaced the ancient city walls to illustrate the truth that Victor Hugo uttered a century ago: 'le mur murant Paris rend Paris murmurant' (the wall which walls in Paris makes Paris murmur).

UNDERSTANDING HOW PARIS WORKS

Paris is rather like a very large French residential building owned in **copropriété** (see Chapter 10). The individual owners (the arrondissements) are responsible for a share of the overall costs according to the size of their share, plus their own expenses such as local crèches, cultural centres or sporting facilities. The copropriété (the **Mairie de Paris**, or city hall) looks after maintaining the **parties communes**: the lighting, the cleaning, city-owned and subsidised housing, and some of the most well-known monuments.

Parisians elect their local councillors and ultimately their city council every six years, and the most recent elections were in March 2001. The electoral system provides a two-round race, unless an electoral list gains 50% or more of the vote in the first round. After the second vote, the winners gain 50% of the seats, and the rest are distributed proportionally to parties which have gained 5% or more. In the second round, only parties which have gained 10% in the first round can go forward, but make-shift political alliances are common. The 163 municipal councillors are drawn from the winning electoral lists, and it is these councillors who ultimately vote in the mayor of Paris, a post created in 1977 and held by Jacques Chirac until his election as president in 1995.

The **Conseil de Paris**, presided over by the mayor, sets the city budget and agenda, leads attempts to attract events such as the Olympic Games, organises major festivities, and distributes millions of euros of grants to associations and projects. The local mayors of each arrondissement (directly elected by the voters, or resulting from political coalitions) and local councils are responsible for providing and administering local facilities. They also have some control over the vast but insufficient number of social priority housing (known as **HLMs**), but the City of Paris retains overall control of these, including many highly sought-after 'grace and favour' residences.

The Chirac regime and that of his successor, Jean Tiberi, transformed Paris into a huge fund-raising machine for the defunct RPR party. The result has been an explosive series of corruption scandals involving a large number of

France's leading politicians who also had electoral strongholds on the Paris City Council. In 2001, Parisians made clear that they wanted a mayor who concentrated less on the national arena, and more on the city and its needs. For the first time since 1871, control of Paris fell to the Socialists, led by Bertrand Delanoë. He has proved a highly popular and charismatic mayor, and the city is being transformed by his Socialist and Green Party administration. Ironically, he is now considered as a future presidential candidate. The Socialists' hold over the whole Île de France region was confirmed in 2004 when they were re-elected to the regional presidency (**Conseil Régional**), which coordinates regional initiatives similar to those of the Conseil de Paris.

Voting in Paris

European Union nationals resident in France are entitled and encouraged to vote in municipal and European elections. They can even be elected as local councillors (and have been outside of Paris), as long as they are not elected politicians at the same time in their home country. The procedure for electoral registration is surprisingly simple for a country which adores complicated paperwork:

1. You must register before 31 December prior to the election at your local town hall (**mairie**).

2. Take along a valid **carte de séjour** (residence permit).

3. Take along either a rent receipt (**quittance de loyer**) or a telephone or EDF bill with your name and address.

4. Officially, you should provide a written document stating that you have not been banned from voting in

your home country. In practice, you simply sign the appropriate form **sur l'honneur** (in good faith).

5. If you are living **chez** somebody else, you will have to provide a signed statement from that person stating that you are living there.

6. Electoral cards (**cartes d'électeur**) are sent out a few weeks before the election, and you need to take these along with you (plus your carte de séjour), in order to vote.

In April 2001 Delanoë created an advisory Council for Foreign Residents of Paris. He also introduced a series of annual public meetings in each Paris mairie, to allow Parisians to give him their opinions directly.

THE CHANGING FACE OF PARIS

The mayoral election campaign of 2000–2001 revealed a number of priorities for voters. The main issues that were raised were security, transport, the environment, housing, and educational facilities. In each of these areas, the Socialist-Green Party coalition has already taken major steps, with varying degrees of success.

The right-wing UMP (Union pour un mouvement populaire) government has also made serious attempts to combat street crime, with some success. The out-of-sight-out-of-mind concrete towers (**cités**) relied on by a previous generation of urban planners have provided a bad harvest of excluded, ghettoised, and often violent young people from the poorest, principally immigrant, communities. Violent crime was and still is a reality in central Paris where the pickings are easy. This is not Rio or the Bronx, but you should still adopt a streetwise attitude to deal with situations which take much longer to recover from than to occur. Nonetheless, government crackdowns are having a positive effect, even if the methods are sometimes contested (as always in France!).

Everybody agreed in principle on the idea of a new tramway around the outer edge of Paris. Delanoë, supported by the Green Party, has launched the project, with the first portion due to run from Balard to Porte d'Italie. Once again, the method has been contested, but it is as much out of shock that something was actually done rather than talked about. For the time being, the giant roadworks are not having the desired effect in the areas concerned, but the intention to continue is clear.

The environmental problems of crowded Paris were an increasing cause for concern, even before the murderous heat-wave (**canicule**) of 2003. Bike and bus lanes have been installed across the city, to the ire of the Parisians addicted to their cars. The banks of the Seine and the Canal St Martin are regularly shut to traffic to allow rollerbladers, cyclists and pedestrians to enjoy at least summer weekends in peace. Plans to cover the railway tracks of the large northern stations are still under discussion, but new flower-filled renovations of the main streets are also gradually advancing across the capital.

Delanoë proposed a minor revolution in French education by organising a poll on changing the Paris school week to a regular Monday–Friday, and leaving weekends free for families. This was rejected by conservative parents and teachers unions, who voted in favour retaining the traditional Saturday morning classes with Wednesday afternoons free. Students are now reaping the benefits of the new university site in the 13th arrondissement, behind the Bibliothèque Nationale, but little else has changed in the political minefield of French education.

Housing remains the thorn in Paris's side. House prices have leapt astronomically in Paris, largely due to foreign purchasers. Rents rose on average 3.6% in the majority private rental market in 2003, and 10.6% in the case of a new lease. The result is a strong urban drift away from centre to the suburbs. This has had another knock-on effect of pushing the poorer population further afield, as the middle classes are pushed out of the centre into the nearer suburbs. Many Parisians have simply given up on Paris, its problems and its cost. From 1990–1999, 570,000 people left Paris for the **provinces**, and this urban drift could reach 1 million by 2010. To solve this Gordian knot, Delanoë has floated two unthinkable ideas. One is to extend the Paris city limits to incorporate the neighbouring suburbs. The other is to build new good quality highrise tower blocks in a city which abhors them.

TRACING POPULATION PATTERNS

The squeeze on the Paris property market, and generally across the Île de France, has accelerated the growth of the new trendy regenerated areas, the **quartiers branchés**. The mayoral election result in March 2001 confirmed the ebb of the traditional Catholic bourgeoisie in western Paris, and their replacement by the rising tide of the 'Bobo' generation in north and east Paris. This has been seen as a battle between the traditional Bourgeoisie of the western arrondissements under right-wing UMP control, and new bourgeoisies of the eastern and northern arrondissements under Socialist control.

'Bobos' have been described as the 'bohemian middle class ... the merger of the artistic and intellectual worlds and the business world ... Individualistic, multicultural, environmentally concerned, addicted to liberal values, ... more concerned about questions of lifestyle and quality of life ... but still displaying typical right-wing concerns about taxation and crime' (Christophe Guilley, *Libération*, 8 January 2001).

It is these groups which have invested the former working-class districts of the north and eastern Paris in search of cheaper property, more space, and the 'authentic common touch', to add a little rough to their smooth. In so doing, they have changed the face of Paris for decades to come. Whilst the 5th–8th, 15th, 16th and western 17th arrondissements tend to house the traditional family units, the Bobo couples and families have colonised the 11th–14th arrondissements, the 17th in the Batignolles district, the 18th from the Mairie to Pigalle, and the 19th and 20th arrondissements.

Figures released in 2000 for the PACS (the civil contract for both heterosexual and homosexual couples) revealed that the largest numbers of PACS were recorded in the 11th and 18th arrondissements, with their significant young professional and gay communities. The 1st–4th arrondissements, with similar populations and high property prices, tend to draw those who are happy to pay more for less space, without family constraints. However, they do contain excellent schools and draw those families which can afford the financial sacrifice. The 9th arrondissement is a Bobo heartland from Trinité to Pigalle, and also the 10th close to the Canal St Martin.

Ethnic Paris

The American, British, Irish and other European Union communities are not concentrated in any particular area of Paris, with the exception of a strong Portuguese community in the 14th arrondissement. Estate agents have noticed recently, however, a strong number of British purchases on the **Rive Gauche** in the 5th, 6th, upper 13th and upper 15th arrondissements. The western suburbs are also considered as an Anglo-Saxon 'stronghold' (see Chapter 6).

The African, and especially North African (**maghrébin**) communities are most strongly concentrated in the poorer areas of the 10th, the northern halves of the 17th and 18th, and the further extremities of the 19th and 20th arrondissements. The Chinese and Vietnamese communities are heavily concentrated in the 13th near the Place d'Italie, in the 19th near Belleville, in the 3rd near rue du Temple, and now also in the 11th near to rue Popincourt. The traditional Jewish quarter is based on the rue des Rosiers in the 4th, and also in the 9th around rue du Faubourg Montmartre. However, all these communities are well represented across all the arrondissements.

This thumbnail sketch of social distribution in Paris may well explain why you have fewer facilities for your kids than your neighbours in a different arrondissement, where the focus may be less on young childless professionals or 'alternative lifestyles' and more on families. The aim of these comments is not to reinforce social ghettos but to help you settle quickly into an area that best reflects your personal culture.

RECLAIMING THE CITY – THE NEW *QUARTIERS*

For many people, Paris is an 'eternal' city in the same way as other European masterpieces such as Florence or Rome. But the truth is that it is, in the words of T. S. Elliott, 'still, and still moving'; beautifully preserved but constantly renewing its skyline, horizon and perspectives. Paris is a city on the move, and you may well find yourself drawn to different areas at stages in your Parisian life.

Following the pharaonic constructions which marked the Mitterrand years – the Grande Arche at La Défense, the Pyramids at the Louvre, the Porte de la Villette complex, and the Opéra-Bastille and the neighbouring 'Arts Viaduct' – it is fitting that his final memorial should be the four great towers of the **Bibliothèque Nationale François Mitterrand** on the Left Bank of the Seine, built to resemble four open books. This stands at the heart of one of the **ZAC (zone d'aménagement concerté)** renovation sites which have transformed Paris.

This previously lifeless stretch of the river around the former warehouses and railway tracks has been transformed. The railway tracks have been covered, and above them stand some of the most sought-after social priority and private-sector housing apartments in Paris, a new university site, and new offices. The trendiest and most avant-garde art galleries congregate in the area, and nightclubs float on the Seine. Line 14 of the métro has further opened up the area, whisking passengers from one side of Paris to the other in less than half an hour, and the extension of the line to Tolbiac is having the same effect further south. The whole project is due to be crowned in 2006 by a swimming pool floating on the Seine itself in front of the library.

On the opposite bank, behind another Mitterrand development, the gigantic Finance Ministry at **Bercy**, the former wine warehouses of the defunct Bercy station have been transformed from area where nobody chose to go, but everybody now wants to be. There are even more luxurious apartments, a trendy shopping and cinema complex, more offices, and a beautiful park leading up to the Bercy sporting arenas. The former American Centre in Paris is also under renovation as a new Cinema Museum and Centre.

The closure and sale of hospitals, barracks and government office sites will create many new possibilities in the next few years. These will be some of the most interesting opportunities for possible purchases, as the city adapts the newly released resources to the population's needs. In 2004, the mayor launched a mass survey of the Parisians to decide on the urban planning priorities for the next decade for the city. He also put on public display the projects of the four finalists for a massive redevelopment plan for the **Forum des Halles** in central Paris.

This is a massive project to flatten the existing structure and re-landscape the 15 hectare site, with the first sector due for completion in 2007. The Forum receives 41 million visitors a year, 800,000 commuters per day who use its three RER and five metro lines, not to mention the 8,000 shops and offices, 23 cinema screens and the most highly used swimming pool in Paris. The final choice has not yet been made, and is seen as a highly political decision given that the previous plan was chosen by Jacques Chirac himself. But in keeping with his style, Delanoë is taking into close consideration the views of the 7,000 local residents who will be the most affected.

To the north, everybody is watching carefully to see precisely when the long talked-of renovation of the tough **Château Rouge** quartier will really begin, bordering on the **Goutte d'Or**. These are two of the most squalid corners of Paris, synonymous with violence, theft and drugs. It will take some time to clean these areas up, so if you do buy here your return on investment will be long-term. Some initial attempts have been made to clean up the rue de la Goutte d'Or, and the magnificent ruined 1930s cinema at **Barbès-Rochechouart** has been designated as a future cultural centre close to the pioneering Virgin Megastore nearby. Meanwhile, the mayor is turning his attention to transforming yet more redundant railway lines and neighbouring areas on the border of the 18th and 19th arrondissements. Priority here will certainly be on social priority housing and local amenities. A projected high-speed Roissy-Gare de l'Est rail link is also under serious consideration.

Another set of tracks that many people would like to see covered are those leading away from St Lazare, in the 17th arrondissement. Even the local right-wing council supports the idea of covering the tracks with a suspended garden, as at Montparnasse. The only snag is that nobody wants to pay. However the **Porte d'Asnières** further along the tracks at the north-west edge city limits has for some years now been exciting attention. Plans were announced in 2000 for a large-scale development, but little advance has been made on the disinfection of the former industrial site. However, this might suddenly be seen as priority if Paris wins the 2012 Olympic Games bid. For this is the site ear-marked for the Olympic Village, to be transformed subsequently into a mix of public and private housing. No matter what the outcome of the bid, necessity will no doubt soon push the planners into action on the site. The advice here is, 'watch this space'.

Finally, the other principal area of development lies between Paris and EuroDisney, to the east of the capital. Long gone are the days of the isolated pink castle surrounded by empty fields. The **Val d'Europe** development of shops and offices is a prime area of urban development. With easy access by road and rail to the capital, the airports, and the rest of France, the new housing developments are proving highly popular with young families. Further to the South, in the **Essonne** department, the new town of **Sénart** is also set to be the centre of a major urban expansion. To the north, the hoped-for renewal of **St Denis** centred on the **Stade de France** has been slow in coming, but property prices are increasing rapidly in what is still a hard-core urban priority area. However, the property professionals now advise that this will soon be the place to be, as Parisian money filters down to its renewable reserves of space and property, only 10 minutes by RER from Chatelete and the banks of the Seine.

FINDING OUT MORE
Conseil Régional d'Île de France, *www.iledefrance.fr*
Mairie de Paris, *www.paris.fr*

2

Making a Successful Move to France

To make a success of your move to France, plan as much as possible. Remembering to bring the right papers with you, and then to take them to the right appointment in France in your earliest days can and will save you many headaches later on. A successful move falls into three categories: before and during your arrival, which are considered in this chapter, and immediately after your arrival which is considered later.

Four important points to remember are:

1. Moving home is reckoned to be one of the most stressful experiences known to humans. You will have

a hiccup or two somewhere along the line even if you plan well. Try to retain what the French most admire in foreigners – their sense of humour!

2. To the French, bureaucracy is not a means to an end but a way of life. A French civil servant really could not care less how many times you have turned up at his or her counter. They literally have all day to sit there. Correct preparation will allow you to get off the 'roundabout' as quickly as possible.

3. Losing your temper is on the whole very counter-productive with the French administration. Stay calm; try to smile even if you are developing a deep personal loathing for the person across the counter, and avoid screaming fits.

4. Take a good supply of reading material and always arrive early at French administrative centres.

PREPARING BEFORE YOUR DEPARTURE

Preparing the paperwork

Passports
Under internal arrangements (the Schengen Agreement) within the European Union (EU), citizens of the Union can enter France with just a National Identity Card. However, **British citizens need a valid British passport in order to enter France** (or indeed any other country covered by the Schengen Agreement), as the United Kingdom does not adhere to the Agreement.

Commonwealth citizens with residency rights in the UK are not recognised as British citizens under EU regulations. You will therefore be subject to entry requirements related to your country of origin. **Channel Islanders** and **Manx citizens** are not included either in the EU provisions, unless they, or a parent or grandparent were born in the UK, or they have been resident in the UK for five years.

Visas and residence permits

EU citizens do not require visas in order to enter France. Regulations for visas for non-EU citizens vary, and you will need to check current regulations with the French Embassy or Consulate nearest to you. For non-EU citizens, a number of different visas are available:

- **Visa de transit**. Allows three days travel across France by train.

- **Visa de circulation**. This is often given to business people. This allows several stays of up to 90 days, with a maximum of 180 days in any one year. This visa is normally valid for three years.

- **Visa de court-séjour**. A short-stay visa valid for up to 90 days, permitting re-entry to France during that period.

- **Visa de long-séjour**. A long-stay visa for those studying, working or living in France for more than 90 days. You must already have this visa if you decide to stay for a longer period than originally intended. Otherwise, you will be obliged to return to your home country in order to apply for this visa.

Minimum requirements for Americans seeking visas to live and work in France include a valid passport; several passport-size black and white photographs; proof of your financial means and ability to support yourself during your stay in France and also support any dependants you may have; your work contract with French Labour Ministry approval. Full details are given later in Chapter 3]. American tourists can enter and stay in France for up to 90 days without a visa.

> **All non-EU citizens intending to reside in France for more than three months must obtain a residence permit (carte de séjour). Temporary residence permits for non-EU nationals are normally valid for up to one year.**

Driving papers
You are obliged to carry your papers with you whenever you are driving a vehicle in France. Failure to produce them can lead to a fine. You can bring a car into France for up to six months in any one year without having to complete customs formalities. See Chapter 15 (pages 345–351) for further details on licences, car importation and car registration.

Professional papers
Take with you all relevant professional certificates, diplomas, etc, which may be required if you are setting up your own business. You will also need to enquire at your nearest French Consulate about the **carte de commerçant** required in some cases by those seeking to create their own business.

Personal papers

You should bring with you copies of income tax documents for the last four years, and of any documents relating to investments and stocks and bonds. Receipts for your moving expenses, if they are not reimbursed by your employer, may be needed for tax purposes.

Documents checklist

Check that you have all the following papers ready as you prepare for your departure:

◆ Valid passport.

◆ Valid visa for non-EU citizens.

◆ Full certified copies of your birth certificate, that of your spouse, and those of your children.

◆ Full certified copy of your marriage certificate.

◆ Valid driving licence.

◆ Car registration and insurance papers.

◆ Carte de commerçant if this is required and professional certificates.

◆ Au pairs need their **Déclaration d'Engagement** from their employer. Non-EU citizens will also be asked for a medical certificate.

◆ Students should bring with them evidence of admission to a study course.

◆ Bank statements, tax declarations and other financial documents. Proof of your financial resources may be demanded before you are granted a residence permit, depending on your nationality and occupation.

◆ Vaccination certificates for your pets.

DECIDING WHAT TO TAKE WITH YOU

French kitchens are normally smaller than British kitchens, and you would probably be safer buying large kitchen machines and appliances within France. British electrical appliances do work in France. However, you must remember to either change the plug, or buy adapters. Foreign televisions and video recorders will not work in France, and these will need to be purchased or rented locally.

Self-assembly furniture stores readily exist in France, and buying furniture does not need to cost a fortune. You will need to decide if it is cheaper to buy furniture in France or to ship your own furniture. Furniture storage represents an extra cost. French beds come in three standard sizes: single, small double, and large double. Whilst your sheets and bedding will almost certainly fit these sizes, remember that standard French pillows are square.

You will need a fair share of winter and summer clothing if you are moving to France for a prolonged period. Clothes can be bought reasonably cheaply in France in high street stores such as Monoprix or Prisunic, or from catalogues (some of which have stores) such as La Redoute if both your budget and your storage facilities are limited.

Import rules and regulations

> **Detailed rules about the importation of household goods should be discussed with the customs sections of the French consulate.**

If you use a professional moving firm, they should also be able to inform you about necessary customs formalities.

- ◆ For EU citizens, goods on which you have already paid VAT in another EU member country are exempt from VAT payments when imported into France. This should be specified on the CMR form provided by a professional removal firm. If you have receipts which show that VAT has already been paid, it is wise to have these available for inspection if required. You should also prepare an itemised inventory of your effects, both for customs inspection, and in case of an insurance claim.

- ◆ Non-EU citizens are also exempt from VAT payments on their belongings, *providing that* they have been in their possession more than six months, *and* that VAT has been paid in another EU country. You will be required by the French customs officials to produce receipts to this effect. Items purchased less than six months before your arrival, and outside of the EU area, will be subject to VAT payment. You have one year from the date of your arrival in France to import your possessions before they become subject to VAT payment. You must obtain a stamped **Certificat de Changement de Domicile** from your 'home' French

Consulate, and your detailed inventory must also be stamped by the same consular authorities. Restrictions on what is considered duty-free should be checked with the French Consular services concerning which of your personal effects and possessions may be subject to tax upon importation.

◆ Arrangements for the importation of vehicles are given in Chapter 15.

◆ There are restrictions on which plants can be imported into France (particular varieties of herbs and pot plants are not appreciated), although a limited number of plants can be included amongst your personal effects. If in doubt, contact the Service de la Protection des Végétaux, 175 rue de Chevaleret, 75646 Paris Cedex 13. Tel: 01 45 84 13 13.

◆ Works of art and collectors' items may require special import licences, as will firearms and ammunition. Medicines and medical products, except for prescribed drugs, may also be subject to special regulations. For all of these items, you must contact the French Consulate for further information. You can also contact the French customs office at the Centre Renseignement des Douanes, 238 quai de Bercy, 75572 Paris Cedex 12. Tel: 01 40 01 02 06.

Bringing your pets
You can bring up to three cats and dogs with you into France, including only one puppy or kitten (3–6 months). For British dogs and cats there are two categories:

- ◆ **Pets vaccinated against rabies**. The animals must travel with their vaccination certificate from a licensed vet issued between 1–5 days before their entry into France; and the animal must not show any signs of contagious disease. The animals should be identified by a tattoo or microchip, which should be mentioned in the certificate.

For any other information regarding the importation of pets, contact the Pet Department of the Agriculture Ministry: Tel: 00 33 (0)1 49 55 84 83. Fax: 00 33 (0)1 49 55 83 14.

PREPARING FINANCIALLY

It can cost a lot of money to set up your new home in France. If you rent an apartment or house, you will have to pay two months' rent in advance as a deposit (and up to three months for commercial premises), and also the rent for the first month – ie, three months' rent in advance.

If you use an agency to find your new home, there will also be their fee to pay, normally equivalent to one month's rent. You will then have the cost of electricity and gas connections, and the rental of a telephone line to pay as well.

It can be difficult to secure a rental contract from French landlords especially if you are a foreigner. Even young French couples are asked for written guarantees, either from their parents or their employers, as a precaution against unpaid rent and bills. Make sure that you bring a significant sum of money with you to cover both these initial expenses, and day-to-day living expenses.

PREPARING CULTURALLY

Many people come to France specifically to improve their French, or quite simply to learn the language for the first time. You will find that a grasp of the most basic phrases and words will help you enormously when you arrive. Do not count on 'everybody speaking English' to you; many can, but not everybody will. You will certainly need to understand what is being said to you when you apply for your residence permit, for example. You will also integrate more rapidly and increase your own personal standing if the French see that you are trying your best to communicate with them in their own language.

You should also try to find out something about the country to which you are moving. There are plenty of excellent introductions to French history and culture available from bookshops. The varied and generally very good French press is also widely available. Reading articles on current life in France will not only help you understand your new environment, but will also improve your language skills.

MAKING THE BASIC MOVES

Registering at your embassy
British citizens are not required to register at the Embassy or the nearest Consulate-General. However, if you use the consular services for other reasons (eg, information purposes), it may be as well to register.

American citizens are not obliged to register at their Paris Embassy but are strongly advised to do so. This will not only help establish your rights as a US citizen in France, but will also make it easier to deal later with the reissue of passports, emergency situations which may occur which involve contacting your family in the USA, and also ease the registration of any children born in France with US citizenship.

Obtaining your residence permit

Citizens of a member country of one of the original EU countries are no longer required to apply for a residence permit. You must have a full British passport to qualify for this exemption. EU Citizenship rights are not granted to Australians with British residency rights and there are certain restrictions on inhabitants of the Channel Islands and the Isle of Man.

Citizens of one of the new member countries which joined the EU in 2004 are still required to apply for a carte de séjour if they wish to have an 'economic activity' ie you wish to work or open your own business, the law goes on to state that you do still require a **carte de séjour**. This situation will probably continue until c.2006.

Citizens of non-Eu countries need a long-term visa (visa de long séjour) before arrival in France. Residence permits will not be issued without the appropriate visas. Americans and Canadians do not need entry visas for France, but Australians do need entry visas. **In Paris** you will need to ask your Consulate which police centre (**centre d'acceuil des étrangers**) you need to apply to. The centre will be different according to where you live. **Outside Paris**, you should initially apply to the local town hall (mairie) who may refer you to a **Préfecture** (police head-quarters) for that département. For Americans who are moving to work in Paris, you should refer to Chapter 3 for a more detailed explanation of the process you need to follow.

The bureaucracy you encounter to obtain your carte can be agony. It is advisable to take several copies of all your documents with you, a good book, and allow plenty of time. You will receive a temporary carte (**récipissé de demande de carte de séjour**) initially, proving you have applied and valid for three months. This will be eventually be replaced by your permanent carte.

Checklist: Documents needed to obtain a carte de séjour
The following is a list of documents which are usually required no matter what your nationality or status. **Regulations often change, so check the precise requirements with your local préfecture or mairie**.

♦ Your full birth certificate (a 'certified' copy).

♦ Your passport.

♦ Four passport sized black-and-white photographs.

♦ Either the rental contract on your apartment; or a bill from France Telecom or Electricté de France (EDF) in your name showing your address; or a **certificat d'hébergèment** from the person who is lodging you dated in the last three months plus a copy of their **carte d'identité** or carte de séjour (if they are also non-French).

- If you are in paid employment, either: two copies of your **lettre d'embauche** (job offer) on headed paper from your employer; or your original contract plus a copy and three most recent pay slips if you have already begun work.

- For various categories of independent workers, you will be required to provide proof that you have taken the correct administrative steps to establish your business legally in France. Take advice upon this point.

- If you are retired you must be able to prove your financial ability to support yourself and your dependants. You must also prove that you have sufficient health cover.

"*Cartes de séjour* are normally limited to the length of your 'guaranteed' stay (ie the length of your employment contract) in France. Within Paris, refer to your own Embassy for details of your local permit centre. Outside Paris, you should ask at your local **mairie** (town hall) where you may be referred to a main **commissarait** (police station)."

Student cartes de séjours are normally limited to one year, and are renewable. Further details are given for applications for student cartes de séjours in Chapter 13 (see page 284).

MANAGING YOUR MONEY

Currency exchange offices are located in airports, railway stations and most banks. If you have the time and the

choice, compare exchange rates to find the most favour-
able rate, and also check to see how much commission
you will be charged. In central Paris, you will find many
currency exchanges centred on the rue Scribe and the
Place de l'Opéra near the bus stops for Roissy airport.

Introducing the euro €

France is a founder member of the single European
currency, the euro:

◆ Notes (or bills): 5, 10, 20, 50, 100, 200, and 500 euros.
   Any remaining French Francs notes can be exchanged
   for euros at the Banque de France until 1 January 2012.

◆ Coins: 1 and 2 euros, and 1, 2, 5, 10, 20, 50 cents
   (equivalent to centimes, representing one hundredths
   of euros). French cents are marked 'RF' to show they
   were issued in France.

**The euro (€) is valid in all countries which participate in the
European Monetary Union scheme,** including Germany,
the Benelux countries, Italy, Portugal and Spain. The
scheme allows for other countries to join the system when
they meet certain economic criteria.

FINDING OUT MORE

French embassies and consulates

◆ In the UK: *www.ambfrance.org.uk*. The French
   Embassy, 58 Knightsbridge, London SW7; The
   French Consulate-General, Visas and Immigration
   services, 6a Cromwell Place, London SW7. Tel: (020)
   7838 2050.

- In the USA: *www.france-consulat.org.* The French Embassy, Consular Services, 4101 Reservoir Road NW, Washington DC. Tel: 202 944 6195; New York: 934 Fifth Avenue, New York NY 10021. Tel: 212 606 36 89, *www.franceconsulatny.org.* Consulates in Atlanta, Boston, Chicago, Houston, New Orleans, Los Angeles, Miami and San Francisco.

Foreign embassies and consulates in France

- **The American Embassy**. The Paris Consulate is at 2 rue St Florentin, 75008 Paris. M° Concorde. Tel: 01 44 96 14 88. *www.amb-usa.fr.*

- **The British Embassy**. The Paris Consulate is at 18bis, rue d'Anjou, 75008 Paris. M° Concorde. Tel: 01 44 51 31 00. *www.amb-grandebretagne.fr.*

- **The Canadian Embassy**. The Embassy is at 35 avenue Montaigne, 75008 Paris. M° Alma-Marceau. Tel: 01 44 43 29 00. *www.amb-canada.fr.*

- **The Irish Embassy**, 4 rue Rude, 75116 Paris. M° Etoile. Tel: 01 44 17 67 00.

- The **French Government** web portal (*www.service-public.fr.*), which will orientate you to all government websites. Some of these are in English. Click on the British flag to obtain a quick list.

- **Official French website** (with a section in English for students), outlining procedures for obtaining your carte de séjour. *www.prefecture-de-paris.interieurgouv.fr.*

- **L'Institut Français in London**. 17 Queensberry Place, London SW7 2DT. Tel: 0207 838 2144.

www.institu.ambafrance.org.uk Tube: South Kensington. Buses: 14, 45a, 49, 70, 74, C1. Open Monday–Friday 10h00–21h30, Saturday 12h00–21h30. For anybody seriously considering moving to France, or finding out about the French language, culture or lifestyle, a visit to the French Institute is a must.

◆ **The French Travel Centre**. 178 Piccadilly, London W1V OAL. Tel: 0891 244123. Fax: 020 7493 6594. *www.franceguide.com*. Open Monday–Friday 10h00–18h00, Saturday 10h00–17h00 and French Railways Ltd, The Rail Europe Travel Centre, 179 Piccadilly. Tube: Green Park or Piccadilly Circus – French Government tourist centre.

3

Finding Employment

Despite varying efforts of both the Socialist and right-wing UMP governments, unemployment continues to stagnate in France at about 9.8%, roughly the same as for the last five years or so. The government under Prime Minister Jean-Pierre Raffarin, and Finance Minister Nicolas Sarkozy, has announced a cautious liberalisation of the French economy under extreme pressure from the European Union. This provoked a fierce back-lash from the unions and a large section of the population generally, who rejected reforms of pensions, unemployment benefits, and now social security. The result was a severe sanction of the government in the regional elections in 2004, when they lost control of all but one out of 22 regional councils.

Symbolic industries such as Air France and EDF are due for measures of full or partial privatisation, and this is further increasing tensions. The unexpectedly fierce dispute with the performing arts professions also continues to rumble on. A long series of delocalisations and plant closures in the private sector has provoked bitter protests, and much hand-wringing from government.

The Île de France represents about 21% of the working population, and the half a million or so companies produce about 29% of France's Gross Domestic Product. The most important districts are Paris and La Défense. Some major companies have chosen to relocate their principal activities on the cheaper outskirts of the city, bringing new life to poorer areas. About 8,000 foreign companies are established in France, of which approximately 1,800 are British.

FOREIGN WORKERS IN FRANCE

Citizens of European Union (EU) member states are entitled to take any position in the private sector providing that security clearance is not required (which you may be granted in any case); but you are generally excluded from positions in **la fonction publique**, with possible exceptions for the health and education sectors. Certain other areas are open to foreigners, but think twice about entering all-French preserves, as French unions do not tend to welcome what are perceived as neo-liberal-Anglo-Saxon subversive interlopers in national (ie French-only) territory.

Commonwealth citizens with residency rights in the UK should note that those rights are only valid in the UK, and do not exempt them from meeting French requirements for citizens of their own country. Residents of the Channel Islands and the Isle of Man should also note that these British dependencies are not full members of the European Union, and different rules also apply. Check with the British Consulate in Paris or the French Consulate in London for details.

US citizens face a major struggle with French bureaucracy similar to the reverse process for a European moving to the States. If you are planning to stay more than 90 days or for purposes other than tourism then you must have a visa de long séjour (long-stay). If you do obtain one of these visas, you must apply for your carte de séjour within *one week of arrival.*

The basic rule for all visa applications – both employment and residential – is that you must start from the outside and work you way in. **You cannot avoid returning to your point of origin outside of France in order to successfully apply for your visas. You cannot convert a tourist visa into a long-term visa once in France. This applies to all non-EU nationals.**

The US Embassy in Paris (*www.amb-usa.fr*) states very clearly in all its documentation that it cannot intervene with the French authorities on behalf of US citizens seeking visa exemptions and work permits after arrival. Wannabee Hemingways and fake Fitzgeralds take note.

US citizens who wish to take a full-time position in France are dependent upon the French employer to take initial steps towards securing both residence and work permits. The basic rule which you have to remember is that a successful application by your employer for a work permit should normally lead to a successful visa application, after which you must complete the process by applying for your residence permit once you have arrived in France.

Authorisations for Americans to work in France rests with the **Service de la Main d'Ouevre Etrangère** of the Ministry of Labour (127, boulevard de la Villette, 75010 Paris. Tel: 01 44 84 42 86). However, you do have a vital part to play in your own application. Figure 2 shows the parallel processes for your work permit and visa applications once you have found a potential employer.

Once you have passed all the hurdles outlined above, you will be issued with a **carte de séjour temporaire salarié**, valid for one year. It will specify in which départements the permit is valid and the professional activity in which you are employed. This card can be renewed two months before the expiry date or upon presentation of a new work contract.

Three years continued residence in France allows a US citizen to apply for a **carte de résident** valid for 10 years and automatically renewable and valid for all professional activities. Spouses of French citizens are entitled to the carte de résident.

Employer/French government departments	Employee
1. Applies to French Ministry of Labour for permission to employ an American citizen. The authorisation will be sent to the chosen French consulate in the USA.	1. Informs the employer of which French Consulate in the USA will receive the visa application in order to receive the Ministry of Labour approval.

2. Provides a copy of the signed employment contract to the French Ministry of Labour for approval.	2. Provides documents required for French visa. The minimum requirements for a French visa are:
	a) a valid passport
	b) several passport-size photographs
	c) proof of financial resources to support the applicant and his or her dependants during their stay in France. This can be:
	  – bank statements
	  – written confirmation of regular transfers of funds from a US bank account to a French bank account
	  – letters from family or friends guaranteeing regular support
	  – a certificat d'hébergément (housing certificate) from a French family or friends with whom the applicant will be staying in France.
	All documents need to be notarised including official translations into French of the documents supplied.

3. If the contract is approved, the Ministry of Labour forwards a copy to the **Office des Migrations Internationales** (**OMI**) who transmit it to the designated French Consulate in the USA.	3. Once you receive your visa and enter France, you must apply at the Préfecture de Police for your residence permit (carte de séjour) within one week of arrival.
4. **When the French Consulate receives approval from the OMI, the applicant will be informed and can proceed with the visa application (2).**	4. The visa formalities are not completed until the candidate and family have undergone a medical examination by the doctors designated by the OMI.

Figure 2. Administrative procedures for Americans intending to work in France.

LOOKING FOR WORK

Using job centres

The state-run job centres are the **Agence Nationale Pour l'Emploi**, (**ANPE**). If you do register, you must do so in person. Written applications will not be accepted. Proof of permanent residence in France (eg carte de séjour) will be required, and they may also ask to see your passport. Job advertisements are displayed in the centres, and workshops, counselling and personal interviews are available. **APEC** is the equivalent to the ANPE for **cadres** positions, open to both cadre and non-cadre applicants, although it specialises in candidates with cadre experience or profiles. There is no set moment when you can expect to be made cadre; it may happen immediately, or it may happen after some years. Further explanations are given below, but do not be afraid to explore cadre positions. You do not have to be registered in order to reply to advertisements at these centres.

Using employment agencies

Although employers are obliged to inform the ANPE of vacancies in their companies, they are much more likely to seek the help of recruitment agencies (**conseil de recruitment**) and headhunters (**chasseurs de têtes**) to fill vacancies. Most agencies are accessible only by appointment. You therefore need to prepare and send your CV and covering letter (see the section on applying for jobs later in this chapter) in order to open these doors. There are now several agencies in Paris which specialise in bilingual appointments, particularly for secretarial and administrative work. Providing that you do have a good working

knowledge of French, your greatest immediate asset in the
search for work will be that you are English mother-
tongue.

Using newspapers and magazines

The most important newspaper for job advertisements in
France is *Le Figaro* every Monday. The separate
'**économie**' section normally carries a wide variety of
jobs of all levels and areas. These are repeated every
Wednesday in the job newspaper *Carrières et Emplois*,
which also includes jobs advertised in *Le Parisien*, and
sometimes advertisements from *The International Herald
Tribune*. *Le Monde* on Mondays and Tuesdays carries a
selection of well-paid jobs, and the business newspapers
Les Echos and *La Tribune* also carry similar job
advertisements. *Les Echos* has a reciprocal agreement
with *The Financial Times*. This means that you may be
able to start your job-search even before you move to
France.

Libération also has a small but developing jobs section
each Monday, and magazines such as *L'Express* and *Le
Nouvel Observateur* also carry a variety of job advertisements. Regional newspapers are also an important source
of opportunities.

In Paris two free magazines, *France-USA Contacts*
(*www.fusac.fr*) also known as FUSAC, and *The Paris
Voice* (*www.parisvoice.com*) have job sections of great
interest to English-speakers, with advertisements and
contact details for all the major bilingual appointment
agencies.

Sending unsolicited applications

Candidatures spontanées, comprising your CV and a general covering letter, are the most important method of filling vacancies in France and accounts for 70% of appointments. This fits in with the general 'networking' approach which is highly prevalent. A well-presented CV and letter, followed up by a phone call, can secure you at least a first interview for a post that nobody else knew was even vacant.

Using the Internet

Many agencies and firms now accept applications by Internet, allowing you the chance to avoid the otherwise obligatory handwritten letter with the almost inevitable spelling error(s). There is a vast choice of Internet sites to choose from in France. Five of the best are:

- *www.anpe.fr* (extremely well-designed and informative job-centre site with access to all offers)
- *www.apec.fr* (the cadre job-centre site with access to their regular published magazine)
- *www.cadremploi.fr*
- *www.monster.fr*
- *www.keljob.com.*

Looking at advertisements on these sites before you leave for France will help you to start to understand the jargon, requirements and offers being made.

Using professional associations

Certain professions in France have very restrictive rules over practice, such as lawyers, accountants, and the medical professions. **Before leaving your home country** contact your own professional association to enquire if they have any information to offer you or corresponding associations in France who could offer you guidance on the work available to foreign professionals in a particular field. They may also have contacts with foreign nationals who have already integrated into the French system and who may be willing to offer advice or even a position.

Using chambers of commerce

The Franco-British Chamber of Commerce and Industry (FBCCI) is the oldest foreign chamber of commerce in Paris. The American, Australian, Irish, and South African chambers are all also very active, and each chamber offers a wide selection of information and services. Contact details for these chambers can be found in Chapter 5 (pages 93–95). Each chamber organises regular social events to help new arrivals network with each other and with established members of the expatriate communities. The Franco-American Chamber of Commerce at *www.amchamfrance.org*, and the Franco-British Chamber of Commerce and Industry at *www.franco britishchamber.com* both provide full details of the services offered to job-seekers and new arrivals by both chambers.

REPLYING TO JOB ADVERTISEMENTS

Job advertisements come in a wide variety of shapes and word forms. Figure 3 contains a number of standard terms. The explanation given beneath Figure 3 will help you decode precisely what is being offered.

Importante société internationale de prêt-à-porter en
pleine expansion recherche

Vendeurs/Vendeuses confirmées
pour ses boutiques sur la Région Parisienne.

Jeune et dynamique, vous avez les sens du contact, une
première expérience professionnelle réussite dans ce
domaine, et vous cherchez maintenant à évoluer dans
votre carrière.

Envoyez votre candidature (lettre, CV, photo et
prétentions) à DRH, Wear-Well S.A.,
Service Recrutement, 19, rue Eugene Leblanc,
92300 Levallois-Perret, sous réf. 24679.

Figure 3. A typical job advertisement.

The basic format is to indicate the name of the company
and/or its activity first, then to indicate the post that is
being offered, followed by a brief description of the
candidate profile the company is seeking. It is important
to understand this brief profile, no matter how standard
or banal it may seem, in order to compose the correct
application letter indicating your suitability for the job.

Two common specifications given in job advertisements
are the level of education required of applicants, and
whether the position is cadre or non-cadre. Both of these
require explanation.

- **Bac + 3** or **Bac + 4** etc. This indicates that graduates are being sought who have at least the level of **baccalauréat** (A-levels), plus three years of further education, or whatever number is indicated. Bac + 5, for instance, would require an initial higher education degree, plus perhaps a master's degree. A further specialised **cycle** may also be required for certain jobs. **Niveau bac** means A-level education is the minimum.

- **Cadre**. This is basically an executive post, unique to France. Advantages include better salaries (in general) and better social security benefits later in life, and a certain 'snob' value. Disadvantages include long hours for no extra-pay. Cadres are not normally paid over-time, unlike non-cadres.

Decoding the final part of the advertisement is crucial. For the sample advertisement in Figure 3, your complete application must include the following items:

- **Lettre d'accompagnement**. This **must** be handwritten in impeccable French, well-presented, and no more than one side of A4 paper. Standard forms of letter suitably adapted are perfectly acceptable, but typed letters will simply be ignored. Many firms in France still use graphology as a selection test for candidates, especially for more important jobs.

- **CV**. Your curriculum vitae (CV) or resumé must be neatly typed and easy to read, in the French format, and no more than one side of A4 paper. Bring out the most important and relevant elements in your experi-ence which suit you for the job for which you are applying. On average, most recruiters spend about two minutes reading what has taken hours to prepare. They need to see your suitability right away.

◆ Salary/**Prétentions**. Some advertisements clearly state salary, some give a salary range according to experience (eg, €40–45K = €40,000–45,000), and some advertisements ask for your prétentions, as in Figure 3. Basically, this is asking you to state what you are willing to accept as a salary – which is a tricky business! You therefore need to know what the 'average' salary is for someone of your experience, and for such a position. Looking at similar advertisements can help. **Only include your prétentions if you are asked for them**, or in certain cases when you make a candidature **spontanée**. Otherwise, prétentions will have a much more English meaning!

◆ **Photo**. Despite being the land of *liberté, égalité et fraternité*, the French still tend to pre-select their candidates to a large extent on a rather superficial basis. On the other hand, as in the case of the advertisement in Figure 3, appearance is important. As with prétentions, only send a photo when you are asked to do so. Do not use a photo taken in a photo booth at a railway station, etc. Go to a photo shop and arrange to have a set of four black and white passport-size photos taken in which you are dressed well and appropriately for the position for which you are applying. This should only cost about €6, and is money well spent. One photo should then be stapled to the top right-hand corner of your CV.

PREPARING YOUR FRENCH CV

Preparing your French CV can be heart-rending, especially if you have spent your university career 'collecting
CV points'. You only have one side of A4 on which to
cram in the information in a relevant, readable, and eye-
catching manner. There is therefore no point in telling
potential employers how you captained a cricket team
(which the French don't even understand), if it means
sacrificing space.

Figure 4 shows you the basic format for preparing your
CV. There are many excellent guides available in France
that will help you to choose one of the variations on this
theme which best suits your experience. Contrary to
popular opinion, there is no one 'correct' way to present a
CV in France. But what is definitely wrong is to produce
the kind of detailed CV common in the United Kingdom.

Points to remember are:

1. Your **état civil** (name, address, telephone number(s),
   marital status and number of children) always comes
   in a neat little section at the top of the page. Leave
   space on the right-hand side for a photo if necessary.

2. Start with the most recent/current employment and
   work backwards. Arguably you should adopt the same
   practice with your education.

3. Referees are not normally included on a French CV.
   They may be called for subsequently, but are not
   normally asked for in advance.

4. Companies and consultants receive thousands of CVs.

Paul Williams
75, rue Aristide Briant,
75019 Paris
Tél. 01 47 97 14 39 (Dom.)

Etat civil
Situation de famille: Célibataire
Nationalité: Britannique
Né le 15 mars 1973 à Bristol (Grande-Bretagne)

Formation
1991 – 'A Levels' (équivalent du baccalauréat) en géographie, français et histoire contemporain.
1995 – 'Bachelor of Arts Honours Degree', University of Warwick (Licence d'Histoire Contemporaine en 3 ans).

Langues
Anglais (langue maternelle)
Français (parlé et écrit couramment)
Allemand (connaissances de base)

Expérience professionnelle
Depuis septembre 2000: Manager du département prêt-à-porter masculin auprès du Buyright Limited, Manchester, Angleterre.

– Responsable d'une équipe de cinque vendeurs dans un important magasin en plein coeur d'une des plus grandes villes d'Angleterre.
– Responsable de la commande des stocks.
– Participation à l'élaboration du plan général du management du magasin.

1999 – 2000: Assistant au directeur d'exportation auprès du Woolbridge Products Limited, Manchester, Angleterre.

- Réceptions et suivi des commandes (y compris les clients à l'étranger) et grande expérience du service facturation.

1996 – 1998: Vendeur, Woolbridge Products, Manchester, Angleterre.
1995 – 1996: Vendeur auprès du Riley Products, Sydney, Australie

Autres expériences
1991 – 1992: Voyages en divers pays de l'Afrique du sud.
1995 – 1996: Séjour en Australie et Nouvelle Zealand.
1993 – 94: Président du 'History Society' à l'Université de Warwick.
Permis de conduire

Fig. 4. An example of a French CV.

To succeed, yours must stand out. Use a good quality paper, and if possible a similar envelope. Ask French friends to check your spelling, grammar and punctuation. The French are very picky indeed about such things.

'Converting' your qualifications

If you or a potential employer has any doubt over the level of degrees that you hold, a **lettre d'équivalence** can be requested from the Ministère de l'Enseignment et de la Recherche equating your degree to a French degree level.

Writing your application letter

Even if you have the perfect CV and are amply qualified for the job, you may well fall foul of a recruiter with a badly written or badly presented letter. Standard form letters are acceptable. However, it is much better to take the standard form and adapt it to the job for which you are applying, bringing out the major points in favour of your application. The letter should not be simply a repetition of your CV. Figure 5 is an example of a typical lettre d'accompagnement in response to the advertisement in Figure 3. Examples of standard letters can not only be found in CV guides, but also in many good French-English dictionaries, such as Le Robert.

Points to remember are:

1. The letter must never exceed one side of A4 paper.

2. Begin by stating that you are replying to the advertisement in X newspaper, and give the date of the advertisement. If a **réf.** (**référence**) is given in the

75 rue Aristide Briant
75019 Paris

Wear-Well S.A.
19, rue Eugene

Leblanc

92300 Levallois

Perret

Paris, le 3 avril

2000X

Monsieur,

Votre offre d'emploi pour un poste de vendeur auprès du Wear-Well parue dans Le Figaro économie du 30 mars, (réf. 24679), m'a beaucoup intéressé.

De nationalité britannique, et doté d'une forte expérience du domaine de prêt-à-porter, je suis actuellement à la recherche d'un poste en France qui me permettrait d'évoluer dans ma vie professionnelle.

Vous trouverez dans le curriculum vitae ci-joint le détail de mes études et de mes activités professionnelles. Le montant de mes prétentions s'élève à €1600 brut par mois.

Je suis à votre disposition pour vous fournir toute information complémentaire. Dans l'attente d'un entretien à cet effet, je vous prie d'agréer, Monsieur, l'expression de mes salutations distingueés.

Paul Williams

P.J.: Curriculum vitae

Fig. 5. A lettre d'accompagnement.

advertisement, remember that it must appear in both the letter and on the envelope.

3. If the name of the person and their gender is not given, begin simply by '**Monsieur**'. Do not write '**Cher Monsieur**', as this would imply a degree of intimacy.

4. As with the CV, the letter must be impeccably written, on good quality stationery.

5. Finish the letter with a standard formula. Generally, men assure their correspondents of their '**salutations distinguées**', whilst women send their '**sentiments distinguées**'.

GOING TO THE INTERVIEW

When you reach the interview stage, the same basic rules apply in France as anywhere else. Dress appropriately and smartly, arrive in good time, shake hands on meeting your interviewer, and smile.

As a foreigner newly-arrived in France, you can expect to be asked about your motivation for moving to France, as well as your experience. Prepare yourself as much in advance as possible for the questioning, as your language abilities will be under scrutiny. Allowances will be made for the fact that you are a foreigner, but you must understand at least 95% of what is being talked about.

FINDING OUT MORE

♦ Regulations concerning visas, etc tend to vary from time to time. For up-to-date detailed information for Americans applying for employment in France, check the Consular section of the American Embassy website at *www.amb-usa.fr,* and also the French Embassy at the USA websites, *www.consulfrance-washington.org,* and *www.ambafrance-us.org.*

Almost all the newspapers listed in this chapter have websites which can be found by searching by name. You will be able to access the employment sections via the websites.

LOOKING AT EMPLOYMENT CONTRACTS

The two principal forms of contract for legal employment in France are the fixed-term contract, and the indefinite contract.

- **Contrats à durée déterminée (CDD)** – fixed-term contracts. These can only be applied in certain circumstances, such as a sudden increase in business; or for seasonal work (eg, at Christmas); or to cover pregnancy or sick leave; or to replace an employee in a position which is being cut, or for which the new employee cannot yet take up the permanent position. They may not exceed nine months, but can be renewed a maximum of twice. After two renewals, the company is obliged to offer you a permanent contract. CDDs are increasingly common in France.

◆ **Contrats à durée indéterminée (CDI)** – indefinite contracts. These are the most common form of contract in France. They are also the most preferable form of contract for foreigners moving to France, as they will provide you with longer-term residency rights.

There is no standard model for a contract in France, and surprisingly, there does not even have to be a written contract. However, the following points should normally appear in a written contract:

◆ Name and address of both parties.

◆ Job title and description of duties.

◆ Place of work.

◆ Rate of pay and bonuses, etc.

◆ Hours of work per week.

◆ Notice period required by either employer or employee.

◆ Trial period, normally from one to three months, can be renewed once by the employer. Both sides can terminate without notice during this period.

◆ Holiday entitlement.

◆ Collective agreement (**conventions collective**) applicable to the position or company. This is important as it may modify standard working practices.

◆ Details of where employer social security payments are made and of complementary retirement fund centres may also be included.

Your acceptance for a position is also subject to a general medical examination (**visite médicale**) by the firm's independent doctor and being declared **apte** for the position.

You may be in a position of either having to accept a part-time of fixed-term contract when you first arrive. For example, you may have a working spouse via whom you will acquire residency and social security rights and access to the property market; or you may be offered a long fixed-term contract of up to nine months, which will provide you with a chance to sample Parisian life (if you are an EU national).

For part-time and fixed-term contracts, the elements shown in Figure 6 must also be included in your contract by law.

SALARY

The minimum hourly wage in France is usually known by the initials **SMIC (Salaire Minimum Interprofessionnel de Croissance)**. It is currently €7.19 before social security contributions, making a salary of €1,127.57/month for those firms still operating a 39-hour week, or €1,090.48/month for those operating the 35-hour week. The SMIC is linked to the cost of living index, which is reviewed every six months. When this index rises by 2% or more, the level of the SMIC is raised. Pay reviews must take place

CDI part time	CDD full time
1. Your qualification(s). 2. Pay. 3. Number of hours **either** per week **or** per month **or** annually, depending on how your job is organised. 4. Method for changing work hours. 5. Number of complementary hours which the employer can request. This is generally limited to one tenth of the time stated in the contract, and cannot bring the total over the legal limits. **NB:** This is not overtime (**heures supplementaires**).	1. The *precise* reason for the CDD. This does not allow the employer to force you into a CDD because 'there is too much work at the moment', etc. 2. If you are replacing somebody, the name and qualifications of that person. 3. Date limit of the contract, renewal date and deadline for renewal. 4. Minimum period if no fixed date is defined ie at least three months. 5. All of the general elements outlined above must be included.

Figure 6. French employment contracts.

once a year by law. However, salaries above the SMIC do not have to be increased, even if the cost of living has increased.

Salaries are normally quoted in contracts as a total annual figure before social security deductions, but may also be quoted on a monthly or hourly basis. Salaries are usually paid monthly, on around the 26th day of each month. This is to allow the transfer of money to your account to settle bills due at the beginning of the month (notably rent). Payment is normally by standing order to your bank account, except for lower salaries which may be paid by cheque.

BONUSES

Most French firms offer bonuses of a 13th month's pay (**13éme mois**). This is normally paid as one lump sum at one point in the year, usually in December. Bonuses are not, however, obligatory. Other companies offer profit-sharing schemes (**participation des salariés aux résultats de l'entreprise**), which is an obligation in companies with more than 100 employees. Both of these, and any similar benefits, are normally mentioned in your contract. You should note that pay rises are not obligatory. Stock-options in France are still a limited commodity for the happy few.

If you are employed under a CDD, you are entitled to an end of contract bonus (**indemnité de fin de contrat**). This is equivalent to 6% of your salary, and in addition to any other bonuses. CDD employees do not generally receive other bonuses.

WORKING HOURS

Your general working hours should be marked in your contract. Cadres only have a notional working week to some extent and are expected to work the hours that it takes to get the job done without extra pay. Non-cadres employees should also note that in certain large firms, such as law firms, the lawyers will be classed as **collaborateurs** as they are officially self-employed, so that even if an office has a staff of 50, only 20 may be employees. This could have a significant effect on the length of your working week.

In the year 2000 new legislation transformed the French legal working week of 39 hours to 35 hours over a five-day period paid at the same rate as 39 hours. By October 2000, almost half of private sector employees had seen their working week cut to 35 hours. On 1 January 2002, the 35-hour week became law for all companies no matter what their size.

However, the introduction of the 35-hour working week is still causing major problems in France because of both the financial and the human resource implications, forcing companies to create new positions. The problem is how to fit a financial square peg into a round hole.

The Socialist government was faced with Hobson's choice, of both reducing charges paid by companies in order to persuade the employers to accept the reform, and reducing working hours and unemployment, but also increasing the amount that each employee must pay in social charges. Both the unions and the business leaders association (the MEDEF) opposed these aspects of the 35-hour week legislation, and by 2002 only about half of companies in France had actually implemented the legislation. Ironically, the worst offender for non-application was France's main employer – the government.

Further confusion has been introduced into the picture by measures from the current right-wing government which have essentially stalled and probably 'killed' the 35-hour week, except for those companies and industries where agreements have already been reached. This has created a two-tier working week in France. The number of authorised overtime hours per year has been increased from 130 back to 180 hours, but at inferior rates, and effectively paving the way to a return to the 39-hour week. You should enquire if a firm operates a 35-hour working week when you find out more about a position.

The traditional long French lunch is rarer in Paris than the provinces. However, government offices still observe a total shutdown between 12h00 and 14h00.

HOLIDAY ENTITLEMENT, LEAVE OF ABSENCE AND RTT

Holiday entitlement is gradually built up on the basis of 2.5 days per month worked, to a total of five weeks annual paid leave. This does not include public holidays. Normally this is taken in segments over the course of the year: one week in winter and spring, and a longer break in the summer months. Some companies still observe the traditional total shut-down in August, when seemingly the whole of France and his wife head for the hills, the coast, or the airports. Extra days off may be allowed under the terms of conventions collectives (see below) for close family bereavements, weddings, or moving house.

Any existing holiday arrangements are normally honoured when you join a company, but be careful to check this. The 'holiday calendar year' normally runs from 1 May to 30 April. Some companies allow you to carry over some holiday entitlement, but you must be careful not to lose holiday time not taken.

One important side effect of the 35-hour week legislation has been the introduction of the **RTT (récupération du**

temps de travail). These are days off each month in order to bring employees into line with the principle of the 35-hour working week. The method used varies from company to company, some insisting on long weekends whilst others are strictly limiting the amount of accumulated RTTs which can be taken at any one time so as not to disrupt office time.

INSURANCE AND PENSIONS

In addition to the regular contributions you will make to the state schemes, you will probably find deductions on your pay slips for complementary health insurance via the **mutuelle** to which the firm subscribes, and to a complementary pension scheme.

These contributions, if they are levied, are obligatory. However they are very worthwhile, and will cover most if not all of the shortfall in state reimbursements for medical treatment. Ask your personnel department or your colleagues how to apply to the mutuelle for supplementary reimbursement. Unemployment insurance (**allocation d'assurance chômage**) is automatically included in your social security contributions.

In 2000, the Socialist government launched a long-awaited reform which offered savings plans (**épargnes**) including plans for what look suspiciously like pension funds. These already exist in many shapes and forms, from simple savings plans topped up by employers, to share schemes for employees.

COLLECTIVE AGREEMENTS

Conventions collectives, as they are known, exist in many varied professions. They cover everything from compassionate leave to the right to union membership, as well as complementary health rights, loans and rates of pay. They may substantially alter the general conditions of work, and you should note if mention is made of a convention in your contract.

FOOD AND TRAVEL

Many French firms offer either a luncheon voucher scheme (**ticket restaurant**), or a canteen facility. In Paris, the firm will normally reimburse half of the cost of your **Carte Orange** (travel pass) each month. This will be paid directly with your salary, and will be indicated on your pay slip (**fiche de paie**).

PROFESSIONAL TRAINING

French firms with more than 10 employees are obliged to set aside 1.2% of their gross annual payroll for **formation continueé**. This may be used for advanced training, but also for basic language training. In both cases it could be of great interest to you. However, the allocation is entirely at the discretion of the employer.

WORKER REPRESENTATION TO THE MANAGEMENT

There are three levels of worker representation, all of which may apply in the same company. This depends upon the number of employees.

Déléguées du personnel (employee delegates). Any company with more than 10 employees must have déléguées, with the number of déléguées increasing in proportion to the size of the workforce. They present employee concerns to the management over individual and collective working conditions, job roles, wages, and application of employment laws.

Comité d'entreprise (work council). Both the déléguées du personnel and the members of the comité d'entreprise are elected by the employees, by secret ballot, with representatives for the cadres and non-cadres in a company. There must be more than 50 employees on the payroll for a company to have a comité d'entreprise. The comité normally also includes a senior management member, and a member of the personnel department. The comité discusses in more general terms the same concerns as the déléguées. However, it should also be informed of firm's general policies before they are implemented, and is entitled to view the company accounts annually. The comité normally has a budget of its own linked to the number of employees, which is used to enable employees and their families to undertake cultural and leisure pursuits at reduced rates. You may also find that your comité has offers available on the purchase of tickets for new shows etc.

UNION MEMBERSHIP
French unions are numerous but union membership, at about 20%, is among the lowest in Europe. The presence of unions is rarer in the private sector, and under the terms of certain conventions collectives, simply not allowed. If union membership is allowed, the right to

strike is guaranteed under French law (and freely exercised!), except for certain essential public employees.

The main unions

The **Confédération Générale du Travail (CGT)** and **Force Ouvrière (FO)** are the largest and most belligerent unions, with strongholds in the public sector, transport and industry. The **Confédération Française Démocratique du Travail (CFDT)** is the most moderate of the main unions, mainly representing workers in the metallurgical, gas and chemical industries.

Most unions are closely related to political parties. The principal unions are mainly, but not exclusively, concerned with workers in the former national or nationalised industries. They are vociferous opponents to privatisation, and in defence of their **acquis sociaux** (basically this means 'perks'). To a very large extent the unions consider themselves to be 'the Fourth Estate' politically, and to have the right to issue political demands – ultimately backed by strike action – to any government.

UNREST AND PROTEST

It seems that scarcely a day goes by without some form of strike (**grève**, sometimes also called a **mouvement social**), protest, demonstration (**manifestation** or **manif'** for short), one-day stoppage or embargo taking place in France. Cynics have commented that ever since 1789, it has been mob rule that has prevailed in France. A quick glance at the country's history suggest that there might actually be some truth in that jibe. The unwritten French commandment seems to be 'Strike, and thou shalt receive'. However, the French generally prefer to see this as another form of liberty of expression.

Dealing with conflicts at work

If at all possible, it is best to try to contain a problem before it gets out of hand. Speak to the personnel department, and if they cannot or will not help, then try your déléguée du personnel.

Questions raised by the déléguées during their confidential meetings with the management are recorded and viewed annually by the work inspectors (**inspection du travail**), who have the right to pursue an enquiry if they think it necessary. This may also help you in more serious disciplinary cases, or worst of all, in the case of dismissal.

Companies are obliged by law to display the address of the nearest inspection du travail, and a telephone number. You can go to them for free confidential advice. You can also find their telephone numbers in the *Pages Jaunes* (*Yellow Pages*).

DISMISSAL

Firing someone in France is almost as difficult for the employer as it is for the employee to find a job in the first place! Nonetheless, it does happen. Strict procedures must be followed, including written warnings. If the procedures are not adhered to, you have a strong case for compensation, especially if you have not been paid your full share of holiday pay, etc.

The two grounds for dismissal are **faute grave** (gross misconduct or incompetence), or economic, in which case you are entitled to 'first refusal' if your job is recreated subsequently. If you intend to contest your dismissal, you can take your employer to an industrial tribunal (**conseil des Prud'hommes**). Winning your case would entitle you to compensation but not reinstatement. Most companies prefer to settle out of court.

Legal aid does exist in France (**l'aide juridictionnelle**) for those on low incomes, including the income of your spouse or partner. For further information, contact your local mairie.

LOOKING AT CROSS-CULTURAL ISSUES

One phrase that often creeps into both French office conversation and job advertisements is '**culture générale**', which can be translated quite literally. Quite apart from points such as hand-shaking on arriving and leaving, linguistic problems and so forth, one of the main differences between British and French culture for instance is the emphasis you place upon the role and importance of your work.

One French immigrant manager in the UK said recently, '[In the UK] The assumption is that you'll be more productive if you work longer hours but I doubt it. People in France put work in a different place in their lives. It's important, but not central. We take our lunch breaks, for example, and even at a business lunch nobody talks about business. You talk about the food because food is also an important part of life.' (*The Observer*, 2 July 2000). Whilst this is a little exaggerated, it is generally true.

Both the French and the British place vital importance on the development of the working relationship, but they have different ways of going about it. The British prefer to call you by your first name, but the French prefer to talk to you about your last holidays. The French are also renowned for talking about their personal lives in the office and their business lives at home, whereas the British are perhaps too prone to compartmentalise their lives.

The dangers of riding roughshod over local sensitivities have been firmly displayed in France in recent years. Foreigners will notice that the French government and press are quick to turn foreign companies in France into the scapegoats when French companies start to adopt similar courses of actions. All the more reason, therefore, to take cultural sensitivity seriously.

The French are not keen, however, on out-of-office socialising such as you might find in the UK or USA, and the stalwarts of the local bar or office softball team are normally Anglo-Saxons. This reflects the fact that whilst the British in particular are considered too independent and individualistic in their professional practices, the French are once again notoriously individualistic in their own private lives and private work domains. This difference might therefore be summed up as:

- French = obedient and conformist in public life, policy and method, but highly individual in private.
- British = generally conformist but still highly individual in public life, but greater team spirit in private.

PAYING TAX IN FRANCE

> The general advice given in this section is based on information available at the time of writing. If you have any doubt about your tax liability in France, you should seek professional advice.

You are liable for tax in France if you reside more than 183 days in France in any one calendar year. A double taxation agreement between France and the UK prevents those who still have tax liabilities in the UK from being taxed twice on the same element of income. This is the *Convention for the Avoidance of Double Taxation and the Prevention of Fiscal Evasion with respect to Taxes on Income.*

If you continue to pay tax in your home country (eg, in the UK where you are taxed at source), then if you have taxable income you should declare the amount of tax you have paid on and from what source of income, on your French tax declaration. **Take professional advice on this topic**, as some sources of revenue are more highly taxed in one country than in France and vice versa. You might therefore find yourself owing the French tax service an additional sum as they will consider you have not fully acquitted your obligations.

A similar double-taxation agreement exists between France and the USA. **US citizens** are required to declare their earnings throughout the world on their Federal income tax returns, and living outside the USA does not remove your obligation to file a tax return. However, living overseas can lead to deductions, exclusions and credits. The US Embassy in Paris offers advice on tax matters at the IRS office at 2 rue St Florentin, 75001. Open: 09h00–12h00. You can also call 01 43 12 22 22 from 13h30–15h30 or fax 01 43 12 47 52. Information can also be found on the Embassy website *www.amb.usa.fr*, or the IRS website *www.irs.ustreas.gov*.

Making your declaration

Income tax (**impôt sur le revenu**) is paid in arrears. You will be required to complete a tax declaration, sent directly to your home, in March each year. This will be for the preceding tax year, which in France runs from 1 January to 31 December. If you send a late declaration, you risk a fine equivalent to a surcharge of an extra 10% of your allotted tax bill.

If you do not reach your tax threshold by the end of the calendar year (eg, you start work in September), you will be exempted from income tax for your first year in France. However, you must prepare yourself for your first tax bill when it does arrive, as you will be required to pay this in one lump sum. This is normally in about October or November, and is roughly equivalent to one month's salary. It is advisable to open a deposit account at the bank to prepare for this.

After the first lump sum payment, you will have the choice of paying monthly (**mensuelle**), quarterly (**trimestrielle**), or annually (in one lump sum). You will also have the chance of paying by standing order, which the tax office will regulate, or by cheque.

The new tax demand will come into effect in January each year. In effect, you will be paying tax each year on the basis of your earnings two years previous to the current calendar year. For example: in March 2005, you declare your revenue for 1 January to 31 December 2004. In the summer or early autumn of 2005, (the French tax authorities are known for their sense of timing; they generally wait until the return from the summer vacations to tell you your new tax bill), you will receive a new **avis d'imposition**, based on the 2004 total, which will take effect in January 2006. If you have opted to pay monthly, your payments will be automatically adjusted over the last few months of the year to take into consideration your new monthly bill.

It is important to bear in mind that you will therefore still have income tax to pay in France even if you leave France, for a limited period after your departure. As and when you do leave France, you should visit the tax office to 'sign off' their registers, and make the appropriate arrangements.

Working out your declaration

1. On your December payslip for the year ending before the March declaration date (ie, December 2004 for the March 2005 declaration), you will see a figure supplied by your employer marked **Net imposable**. This is the sum total to declare for the period you have been employed by this company. If you change employers during the year, you will need to take your December payslip figure and the same figure mentioned on your final payslip from your previous employer(s), and add all of these together.

2. Make sure you check all **personal details** recorded on your declaration, eg, marital status, number of children, etc. This will determine the number of '**parts**' you will have and the attendant reductions.

3. If you have savings accounts or shares at the **bank**, they should supply you with a statement ready prepared stating what you owe and in which category on the form this belongs. Certain savings accounts are tax exempt as long as you keep to the terms of the account.

4. If you receive **shares** as part of your salary remuneration, you will be taxed not only on the dividends from the shares but also on the value of the shares at the date you received them. For stock-options, you must take professional advice.

5. If you make **donations** to a church or charitable association that is registered under **sous la loi 1901**, they can issue you with a tax receipt which will lead to a 50% rebate on the value of your donation(s). These can be accumulated from several different charities.

Tax bands in France
In 2002 new tax bands came into force which saw tax rates come down for all tax payers, with the lower paid benefiting the most. In total, if President Chirac's election promises are fulfilled, income tax will come down by 30% from 2002–2007.

A variety of rebates and exemptions are granted on gross income which moderate the rate of taxation. Most salaried workers receive not only the standard deduction

Amount declared (€)	Tax rates from 2003
less than 4,262	0
4,263–8,382	6.83%
8,383–14,753	19.14%
14,754–23,888	28.26%
23,889–38,868	37.58%
38,869–47,932	42.62%
more than 47,932	48.09%

Figure 7. French tax bands.

of 10% but also a further deduction of 20%. The lowest paid category must complete a tax return, and will almost certainly be eligible for a reimbursement of the CSG (one of the social contribution payments withdrawn from your monthly salary). Certain building works will also give you tax breaks; and if you have an adult child under a certain age living at home, they can be declared on your declaration if they are studying and you are paying for their general upkeep.

Reducing your tax burden

Generally, families are favoured by the French tax system. 'Le Quotient Familial' means that taxable income is divided into units reflecting the family status of the family. Hence a single person is taxed on their whole income. A married couple is considered as two units, and their joint income will be divided by two. The first two children each count as a half-unit and each additional child is counted as a full unit. Couples who sign a PACS receive the same tax status as a married couple two years after the signature of their PACS.

The Raffarin government has increased the level of tax relief for families who employ (legally) a home help (**aide à domicile**). The tax relief is now 50% of expenditure up to €10,000 (salaries and social charges included). The employees concerned can be cleaners, childminders, tutors, or helpers for the handicapped or elderly. It can be combined with a number of other advantages. Au pairs, music teachers and nurses are not covered. If your child attends a local crèche for which you will pay, you can accumulate this benefit with the **réduction pour garde de jeunes enfants à l'extérieur du domicile**, which is equivalent to 25% of your expenditure up to €2,300 per child.

Wealth tax

Wealth tax (**impôt de solidarité sur la fortune** or **ISF**) must be paid by both French residents and non-French residents who have assets in France of more than a certain value. Currently this figure is set at assets of €720,000 + . Non-resident foreigners who are subject to this tax include those who have their family home or main residence in France; or who exercise their principal professional activity, including a salaried activity in France; and those who have their 'economic centre of interest' in France.

Finding help on taxes

Most banks and the vast majority of newspaper and journals will publish free guides in some shape or form when tax declaration time comes around. The Finance Ministry offer a number of possibilities to help you complete your declaration: either by telephone on 08 91 67 10 10, or on *www.impot.gouv.fr*. You can order tax forms on the Internet, and even making a 'virtual' declaration (although they still need hard copy in any case) on *www.minefi.gouv.fr/services/formulaires*. In the weeks leading up the declaration date-limit, you can also ask for help at your tax office, and also now in many local mairies.

UNEMPLOYMENT IN FRANCE
Unemployment is dealt with by two agencies in France. The ANPE (Agence Nationale pour l'Emploi) (*www.anpe.fr*) is the local job centre, where you must be registered if you are out of work and seeking to claim unemployment benefit. The **ASSEDIC** (*www.assedic.fr*) is the agency which actually pays you unemployment benefit, if you qualify. The unions, government and MEDEF (the 'social partners' or **partenaires sociaux**) are jointly responsible for running the central unemployment funds and for shaping unemployment policy. This is often a source of conflict.

Job seekers from other EU countries
When you arrive, you have the right to seek work in France for three months before you will have officially 'outstayed your welcome'. During that three month period, if you are registered as unemployed in your home country, you will retain your right to receive unemployment benefits from your home country via the ASSEDIC. **However, this can take up to three months to be delivered by the French authorities**.

In order to obtain these benefits, you need to complete and bring with you two EU social security forms:

♦ The **E303** and **UBL22** – you must present these at your local ANPE **within seven days of your arrival**. You must also register at the ANPE at the same time.

♦ The **E119** – this will provide you with full medical cover for the three month period during which you are entitled to stay in France and seek work. To establish your health rights during this period, contact your local **CPAM (Caisse Primaire d'Assurance Maladie** – the local health authority), and ask for details of how to contact the nearest **Service des Relations International**.

Unemployment rights for French residents

If you are employed in France and lose your job, you will start to appreciate the heavy social charges that you paid when you were in employment.

Qualifying for unemployment benefit

1. If you resign without good reason, are dismissed for a faute grave (serious misconduct), or refuse a suitable job offer, you will be refused unemployment benefit on the grounds that you do not wish to work.

2. New laws introduced in 2001 provide cover for entrepreneurs who are setting up new businesses. If that business fails, unemployment benefit is now extended to those who tried and failed, as long as they enrol at the ANPE within three years of the end of their last contract.

3. To qualify for unemployment benefit, you must have worked at least three months in the last year, and for two of the three last years. You must also be under 60.

4. You must register at the local ANPE, and be both capable of work and actively seeking employment.

The **allocation d'assurance chômage** (unemployment benefit) you receive depends upon how much you have paid into the system and over what period of time. For instance, if you have been working for four years on an average wage, you will receive more than if you have been working on the minimum wage for the last two years. Payments may take some time to come through initially, but are back-dated.

Your allocation will diminish with time, as you effectively use up the fund you have created by your and your former employer's contributions during the time you were employed. After eighteen months, your situation will be reassessed and you will receive a reduced allocation. The next stage after that, known as the RMI (revenue minimum d'insertion), is the very basic minimum aid which is given out. It is not currently available to anybody under the age of 25. Once that has been exhausted, you are not entitled to any further benefit.

You must be careful to keep copies of job searches and applications when you are **en chômage** (unemployed). This will be required by the ASSEDIC and the ANPE to justify your benefit payments.

Help for the unemployed
Your social security rights, if they are already established, will remain intact throughout the time that you continue to receive unemployment benefits. Even after you have

used up the right to the RMI, you will have social security rights under the French system for one further year.

The **Service Social** at your local mairie also has a fund at its disposal to help in cases of difficulty and emergency, eg, the electricity is about to be cut off. The amount of aid available depends entirely on your local mairie, and may only be a token contribution towards clearing your debts.

The ANPE offers financial assistance in certain circumstances for travelling expenses incurred to attend interviews, and also for those who accept jobs far from their homes. If you are unemployed and you are forced to move to take up a new position, the ANPE also offers limited financial assistance for moving costs. A new law introduced in 2004 also provides for tax relief if you become unemployed. You will still pay tax, but at a substantially lower rate. Once you re-enter employment, your tax contributions will then be readjusted to allow you to balance your tax requirement.

FINDING OUT MORE

Almost every topic covered in this chapter relates to a French government department. The quickest and easiest way to find out more is to go to *www.service-public.fr*, and chose the appropriate ministry (social security, employment or finance), and refer to the government websites. Most of these are available only in French, but if you click on the English selection first, you will quickly be able to find which sites are bilingual.

5

Self-Employment and Student Employment

SELF-EMPLOYMENT

Being your own boss in France is not as easy – or as cheap – as you might think it ought to be. The Prime Minister, Jean-Pierre Raffarin, was previously Minister for Small and Medium-Size Business (**PMEs**), and has professed a desire to create a France of entrepreneurs. In 2002 he announced a series of measures to ease the process of creating your own business.

Nonetheless, becoming either a **travailleur indépendant**, or a **professionnel non salarié**, or a member of a **profession libéral**, (all of which are in fact the same thing), a

commerçant (independent shopkeeper) or an **artisan** (ie, a craftsman), still involves certain basic and important steps at the outset to avoid pitfalls and nasty shocks.

Planning your business

There is a difference made between what might be termed 'active' and 'reactive' business creations. 'Active' business creations could be defined as an employee who decides to quit their job to start a new business, taking a considerable risk in the process.

'Reactive' business creations could be defined as a person who is spurred into creating their own business by forced unemployment. They have not chosen their situation, but the state is willing to guarantee them a certain level of protection and to offer some form of financial aid to help them back to a reasonable level of prosperity. Although many foreigners may feel that they fall into the category of forced inactivity because they have moved to France with their employed spouses, it is unlikely that the state authorities would accept applications for state aid from individual foreigners who have not already been working in France and contributed to social security and unemployment funds.

Professional restrictions

Certain professions – most notably lawyers and doctors, but also accountants and architects for example – may not simply open up their own business in France without the agreement of the appropriate professional order. Contact your own professional association before moving to France to find out if you fall into one of these categories.

You should also note that certain professions, including accountants and doctors, are not allowed to advertise their services under French law. Any breach of this law can have very serious consequences. This may affect your ability to establish your own practice upon arrival. Even if your natural instinct is to work independently, you need to establish a good reputation and a client base to make a success of your business. You need to think carefully about how you are going to do this. To start with, the simplest and easiest option is to use somebody else's client base!

Finally, you need to be sure that you have the correct qualifications to operate and succeed professionally in France. This is particularly true for English teachers. You must hold one of the official teaching certificates for teaching English as a foreign language (TEFL). Courses for these certificates are offered very widely in Paris. Without one of these certificates, you will be hindering yourself considerably in a very over-subscribed market.

Budgeting for your business

For the first two years after establishing your business, you will be assessed for social charges on the basis of set figures for health insurance, pensions and family allowance contributions. Your **CSG (Contribution sociale généralisée)** and **RDS (Recouvrement de la Dette Sociale)** payments are also included in the set figures for the first two years of operating.

In the third year of operating, you will suddenly find that you are facing higher social charges, and a significant separate CSG and RDS contribution. Since your contributions are based on your net profit from the previous two years, you may find yourself heavily out of pocket if you do suffer a sudden downturn in business.

You must take all of these factors into account when you are preparing your business plan as you search for funds for your new business. You must also bear this in mind even if you do not intend seeking funds because you are not intending to hire premises, etc, and you only intend to stick to a small-scale one-person independent operation.

Finding the funds for your business

There are a number of different means of seeking funding now available to entrepreneurs in France. All of these come with different restrictions and requirements, but all also require you to put together a solid business plan.

The variety of loans also distinguishes between the active and reactive categories explained above. None of the selection of funding possibilities listed below appears to be mutually exclusive, and so it may be possible to accumulate loans from different sources providing you meet the criteria and provide a solid business plan to those concerned.

Loans more appropriate for active creations

♦ **Le prêt à la création d'entreprise (PCE).** These loans are for businesses less than three years old whose total financial needs are less than €45,000. The loans themselves are limited to €3,000–8,000 (over five years) but you are not required to provide guarantees or deposits. More details can be found on *www.bdpme.fr*, or by telephoning 0825 30 12 30.

◆ **Réseau Entreprendre**. A group of local networks of business 'godfathers' backing projects likely to create at least 10 jobs in the long-term, and providing interest-free loans repayable over five years. The full list of the 18 networks can be found on *www.réseau.entreprendre.org*

◆ **Capital Risk investors**. Two useful contacts between business builders and capital risk investors are **AFIC** (**Association française des investisseurs en capital**), tel: 01 47 20 99 09, *www.afic.asso.fr* , and **UNICER (Union des sociétés de capital risque de proximité)**, tel: 03 20 68 35 86, *www.unicer.asso.fr*. See also comments below.

Loans aimed at reactive creations

◆ **ADIE (l'association pour le droit à l'initiative écono-mique)**. A network of local associations providing loans of up to €4,600 reimbursable over two years at market rates, plus deposit. Limited to the unemployed and/or those unable to obtain bank loans. Tel: 01 42 18 57 87, *www.adie.org*.

◆ **Le dispositif Eden**. Destined for the young unemployed (age limits 18–26), but now also for the over-50 age group, this action plan includes exemption from social charges for the first 12 months, a set of free advice session 'vouchers' with designated specialists (**chéqu-iers-conseils**) either just before you launch your business or in the 12 months following the start-up; and reimbursable loans of up to €6,100 for one-person operations, up to €9,100 for a multi-partner project, or up to €76,200 for a group of former employees who buy up their former company should it shut down. The scheme is operated by the ministry of employment (**travail, de l'emploi et de la formation professionnelle**) and you need to contact the local départemental headquarters for further details. A list of their contact details can be found on *www.travail.gouv.fr*.

♦ **Fonds France Active**. Aimed at the same public as the ADIE, the **FFA** will stand guarantee of two thirds of a bank loan for business creation, up to a limit of €22,900. Also provides a network of advice on finding financial and practical support. Tel: 01 53 24 26 26, *www.franceactive.org*.

Other sources

Two further initiatives launched by Jean-Pierre Raffarin could also help you:

♦ **Fonds d'investissement de proximité (FIP)**. Capital risk investors from within your own circle of friends and family will each receive a tax reduction of 25% of the amount invested, up to a limit of €10,000 for a single person, or €20,000 for a couple.

♦ **Tax breaks are also offered to investors** in companies which are not registered on the stock exchange (**non cotée**). This tax break is once again 25% of the sum invested, with a limit of €20,000 for single people, and €40,000 for a couple.

> **NB: When you are planning your business, take professional advice before counting on using any of these measures. They all have restrictions as well as advantages.**

TAKING THE FIRST STEPS

Taking the first steps falls into two different categories – administrative and financial. Some steps are optional but highly advisable, others are obligatory. The administrative steps will mainly be taken care of for you once you have taken the initial step of registering your business. However, these are important steps as they are not only the most costly, but are almost all linked to providing you and your dependants with social protection including healthcare and pensions.

Visiting the local tax office

This is not an obligation, but a wise precautionary measure. The tax inspector (**inspecteur des impôts**) will be able to tell you if you can open your business as a self-employed person. He or she will also set out your financial obligations, including those for VAT (known as **TVA** in France).

Registering your new business

You must register your new business with the appropriate authorities, including the **Union de Recouvrement des Cotisations de Sécurité Sociale et d'Allocations Familiales**, more commonly and easily known as **URSSAF**. To register your business, contact the local **Centre de Formalités des Entreprises (CFE)**. For Paris, the main address is URSSAF, 3 rue Franklin, 93518 Montreuil cedex. Tel: 01 48 51 10 10 or 01 49 20 10 10, fax: 01 49 20 22 04. The **Chambre de Commerce et de l'Industrie de Paris (CCIP)** also offers CFE facilities. They can be contacted by telephone on 01 53 40 48 48, or by fax on 01 53 40 48 88. Their **Foreign Investment Department and Paris**

Development Agency with information in English and business creation information is at 2 rue de Viarmes, 75001 Paris. Tel. 01 55 65 33 93, fax: 01 55 65 33 90. One of the new Raffarin reforms has been to establish an on-line CFE facility via the **Agence pour la création de l'emploi**, *www.apce.com*.

Another Raffarin reform has been to extend the period of time that you can declare your business as based in your home. This has been extended from two years to five years. Over 3,000 French companies now have 'head offices' (**siège social**) outside France in order to pay lower social charges. Whilst this does not contravene EU law, the Finance Ministry is fighting back legally against the evasion of French social charges. No matter where the 'head office' of the company is, it is local French law which applies, just as it will be for services that you draw upon to support you and your dependants.

To avoid paying excess social charges, the best time to register your new business is at the beginning of a quarterly period (eg. 1 April). Once you have made the initial '**déclaration du début d'activité non salariée**' (un-waged activity), the CFE will automatically undertake the next steps for you, which are:

1. The **déclaration d'existence** to the tax inspector, and the enrolment for the **taxe professionnelle.**

2. Your enrolment at the **Caisse d'Allocations Familiales** (family allowance centre), run by URSSAF itself.

3. Your enrolment at the **Caisse d'Assurance Maladie des Professions Libérales** (local health authority for non-

salaried professions). They will offer you a choice of compulsory medical insurance schemes, of which the largest is the Mutuelle de Mans, 18 rue de Londres, 75009 Paris. Tel: 01 40 16 72 72.

4. Your enrolment at the **Caisse d'Assurance Vieillesse** (for pensions). Most professions have their own individual caisse. However, if you do not fall into an established category, you will be enrolled at CIPAV, 21 rue de Berri, 75403 Paris Cedex 08. Tel: 01 45 68 28 90.

5. Your registration at **INSEE** – the national statistical office. Your registration here acts as a form of business registration, which will lead to your business receiving the necessary **SIREN** and **SIRET** (company registration) numbers.

Once you have completed this process, you will receive a **récépissé de création d'entreprise**, valid for one month. This will include your definitive SIREN and SIRET numbers, which will allow you to proceed immediately with you banking matters.

PROTECTING YOURSELF IF YOUR BUSINESS DOES NOT WORK OUT

Two new changes to social legislation became law in 2001. For precise details, enquire at your CFE and at the ASSEDIC (who actually pay out unemployment benefit), *www.assedic.fr*. For the first time they provide continued limited unemployment rights for those who choose to enter self-employment, changing the traditional French approach that resigning your job also meant resigning your right to unemployment benefit.

Every entrepreneur can enrol for unemployment support as long as it is within 36 months of the end of your contract prior to the creation of your business, including those who had not successfully managed to achieve finance for their start-ups. These changes clearly only effect those people who have already been employed in France and have contributed to the French social security system, and so are 'activating' the 'points' they have acquired under the system.

One other advantage which it is possible for employees to apply for, but which is at the discretion of their employers, is the **congé de création d'entreprise** for employees who have worked at least 36 months (not necessarily consecutively) in the same firm. Further details can be found on the employment ministry website, *www.travail.gouv.fr.*

MAKING THE RIGHT FINANCIAL CHOICES

(a) **Registering for TVA at your local tax office**. This is an optional step which you can take at the tax office. Companies will expect you to charge them TVA, and you will be able to reclaim TVA on purchases if you are registered. On the other hand, you are not obliged to charge TVA to individuals – hence you can be more competitive in your pricing policy. You should discuss the pros and cons of this choice with the tax inspector when you first visit the tax office.

(b) **Joining an 'association agréée'**. This is another optional step to take, but very worthwhile. An 'association agréé' offers not only advice and support, but can also offer an important reduction (**abattement fiscal**) in your tax burden. Conditions of membership are simply falling in to one of the self-employed categories, conforming to basic accounting rules, and paying an annual membership fee of around €150.

This abattement fiscal is achieved by having your annual accounts checked and countersigned by the association before your tax declaration. In effect, it is worth 20% of your profit figure, as you will only be assessed on 80% of your profit (if it is less than €106,900) by the tax authorities if your accounts have been countersigned by an association.

(c) **Making banking arrangements**. You must have separate bank accounts for private and business accounts. If a bank is aware that an account is being used for business purposes, you may be required to pay higher bank charges. If necessary, to avoid these higher charges, open your business and personal accounts at different banks.

(d) **Accounting**. You must keep correct accounts which conform to basic French accounting procedures. The easiest way to do this, if you already have a computer, is to buy an inexpensive personal computer program, which will eventually correspond to the standard French tax form (number 2035).

WORKING ALONE OR IN PARTNERSHIP

One consideration you may wish to make is whether to be truly **indépendant** or to work with a business partner (**associé**). This is a complex issue which requires professional advice, as certain investment and tax issues might favour a 'company' partnership of self-employed workers. Certain clients may also prefer the apparent security of dealing with a company rather than an individual. Amongst the options to explore are:

◆ Forming a company without any partners, **une Entreprise Unipersonnelle à Responsabilité Limitée** (or **EURL**). This is an alternative to being a **travailleur indépendent**. The minimum capital for an EURL has been reduced to €1. However bear in mind that the smaller the declared capital, the more difficulties you risk encountering with your suppliers.

◆ The 'means of business' – eg, office premises or furniture, etc – can be placed in common ownership, whilst each **professionnel libéral** maintains their own clientele. There are several ways of achieving this, for which you should seek professional advice.

◆ Associations in France, which are controlled by the law of 1901, can also be of use in making certain economies, as can **Groupement d'Intérêts Economique (GIE)**. It costs nothing to establish an **association 1901**, but in general they are designed to be non-profit making. Any profit will be taxed on the basis of company tax rates. An association 1901 is not allowed to distribute profits amongst its members. Once again, seek professional advice on this point.

None of these steps should be taken without professional advice. A good association agréée should be able to put you in contact with professionals to discuss the best way forward.

'MULTIPLE' EMPLOYMENT

Pluriactivité, as it is known in France, has important implications, which make it a generally unproductive option. This is principally because of the level of social charges.

1. **Several self-employed activities**. This will affect which caisse d'assurance maladie and which **caisse d'assurance vieillesse** you contribute to. If you are chosen to advise a public authority, you contribute to their funds. If you belong to a profession which has an 'order' (eg, doctors or lawyers), you will contribute to their funds. In other cases, you have a fairly free choice according to the areas of activity.

2. **Self-employment and paid employment**. For the first year, an entrepreneur who remains in salaried employment will only pay social charges on the salaried activity. From the second year, you are obliged to make payments to the caisse de vieillesse in both systems, even if your self-employment is a subsidiary activity. However, you will have rights under both systems. The same applies for the caisse d'assurance maladie. But only those services and rights offered by the caisse of your *principal* activity will be available to you.

MAKING THE FINAL DECISION

If you are considering self-employment in France, you are probably already aware of the attractions of such a choice, most notably the entrepreneur's freedom of action. However, listed below are the three main considerations you must make before taking the plunge.

1. **Professional restrictions.** Are you allowed to practise in France, and how will you build up your clientele if you are not allowed to advertise? Do you have the right qualifications to succeed in the French market?

2. **Heavy social charges**. On average, an employee costs a company double what he or she receives in their bank account each month. Being your own boss means paying the boss's share of the bill too. French social charges are among the highest in Europe. Worse still is the fact that after two years of operating, you are assessed on your profit figure of two years ago. If your sales suddenly drop, your difficulties will be increased by social charges which could rise to as much as 90% of your current revenue, at the same time as your sales revenue falls.

3. **Employment v self-employment**. In addition to points 1 and 2, you should also bear in mind that a period of one or two years of paid employment in France will bring with it a considerable number of benefits and safe-guards when you do decide to launch your own business. These include unemployment protection but also market knowledge, professional contacts, and a stronger financial position and credit rating.

FINDING OUT MORE ABOUT SETTING UP A BUSINESS

♦ American Embassy (US Foreign Commercial Service), 2 avenue Gabriel, 75008 Paris. Tel: 01 43 12 25 32, fax: 01 43 12 21 72, *www.amb-usa.fr*.

♦ American Chamber of Commerce, 156 boulevard Haussman, 75008 Paris. Tel: 01 56 43 45 67, fax: 01

56 43 45 60, *www.amchamfrance.org.*

◆ Australian Business in Europe, 4 rue Jean Rey, 75015 Paris. Tel: 01 40 59 34 92/33 00.

◆ British Embassy Commercial Section, 35 rue du Faubourg St Honoré, 75008 Paris. Tel: 01 44 51 31 00, fax: 01 44 51 34 01, *www.amb-grandebretagne.fr.*

◆ Franco-British Chamber of Commerce, 31 rue Boissy d'Anglas, 75008 Paris. Tel: 01 53 30 81 30, fax: 01 53 30 81 35, e-mail: *fbcci@fbcci.com*, *www.francobritish-chamber.com.*

◆ French Embassy in London Economic and Commercial Section, 21/24 Grosvenor Place, London SW1X 7HU. Tel: 0207 235 7080, fax: 0207 235 8598, e-mail: *londres@dree.org*, *www.dree.org/grandebretagne.*

◆ Greffe du Tribunal de Commerce de Paris, *www.greffe-tc-paris.fr* – the Commercial Court of Paris responsible for company registrations offers an excellent bilingual site explaining what you need to do, where, how, and when, and including a free **French-English legal/ commercial dictionary**.

◆ Invest in France/DATAR London agency – same address as the French Embassy commercial section, tel: 0207 823 1895, fax: 0207 235 8453, e-mail: *info@investinfrance.co.uk, www.investinfrance.co.uk.*

◆ DATAR (Délégation à l'Aménagement du Territoire et à l'Action Régionale) promotes foreign investment in France (see above). 1 avenue Charles Floquet, 75343 Paris Cedex 07. Tel: 01 40 65 12 34, fax: 01 43 06 99 01, e-mail: *info@datar.gouv.fr*, *www.datar.gouv.fr*. Check the website for details of the nearest Invest in France office. Branches are found in countries around the world.

◆ APCE (Agence pour la création d'entreprise), the official government agency to aid entrepreneurs in France and to encourage business start-ups, *www.apce.com*.

◆ Paris Chamber of Commerce and Industry, 2 rue de Viarmes, 75040 Paris Cedex 1. Tel: 01 45 08 36 00, fax: 01 45 08 35 80, *www.ccip.fr*. Publications in English available.

◆ Chambre de Commerce Française de Grande-Bretagne, 21 Dartmouth Street, London SW1H 9BP. Tel: 0207 304 4040, fax: 0207 304 7034, e-mail: *ail@ccfgb.-co.uk*. Publishes a guide in English on setting up small business in France.

◆ The French Government web directory, *www.service-public.fr*.

WORKING WHILE YOU ARE STUDYING IN FRANCE

Students are amongst the most sought-after workers on the current French job market. French Government restrictions limit the right to work for both student French nationals and foreign students alike. (See *www.edufrance.com*, in English). Foreign students normally find that a command of English and another foreign language give them a lead over competitors.

Every situation is different, and so it is hard to generalise in this field of work. But the main tendencies to note are:

1. **Hotels and restaurants**. If you can stick the smell and the pace, you will have a good chance of finding a position in this industry. Fifty-one per cent of the employees of the Quick chain of restaurants and up to 65% of employees of Pizza Hut are students with CDI contracts. This contract status is a handy extra when it comes round to applying for apartment rentals, but the fast food environment is hard, and not the most desirable CV material. The hotel industry suffers from a lack of good staff.

2. **Working with temporary agencies**. Working as an **intérimaire** has its advantages as well as its pitfalls. The work on offer will to some extent depend upon your capacities as well as what that agency/ies have to offer. But at least if you find that you really cannot bear where you are working, you know that you can ask your agency to place you somewhere else.

3. **Call centres**. Although the English term has crept into the French language, these are officially known as **centres d'appels**. Advertisements regarding **télémarketing**, **téléopérateurs** or **téléacteurs** will mostly concern call centres. The number of such centres has exploded recently. A limited product training is normally provided, but conditions and contracts vary greatly. You may be offered a **contrat vacataire** which is designed to allow an employer to take on temporary workers to complete a particular project, for example, launching a new product which requires

telephone canvassing or a user hotline. These contracts are pretty basic and swiftly ended by the employer as they please, and pay may be by the hour and/or linked to the number of calls you deal with. It should be noted that contrats vacataires do not contribute towards securing residence rights for new arrivals.

4. **Language courses**. Many students offer a few hours of tuition for 'cash in hand' payment. Officially this is illegal, but in reality it is tolerated. The best way to advertise your services is to place small advertisements in the local **boulangeries** and other local shops.

5. **Working on the web**. This is the *luxe* of student employment. You need to be appropriately educated and up to pace to make it in the web world, but if you are, this is where the money is for students: longer contracts, better salaries, and better CV material.

WHO CAN WORK, WHEN, AND FOR HOW LONG?

1. Students registered at language schools are **not** entitled to work.

2. You must be registered and studying at an official French university or Institute of Higher Education which has both obliged and entitled you to be enrolled into the French Social Security system under the special student *régime* (see Chapter 13). This does not mean that you will be exempt from French social charges (**cotisations**) but it does mean that your extra contributions will start to accrue other advantages for you within the social security system.

3. Students must complete the first year of their studies before applying for employment.

4. The student working week is limited to 19.5 hours/week in term time and 35 hours/week in vacations.

5. American students must justify their need to work when applying to the French Ministry of Labour for the **autorisation provisoire de travail**, normally valid for three months and renewable upon production of evidence of continuing studies. Students who receive grants and/or have sufficient financial means are not normally granted a work permit. American students must also produce a valid **carte d'étudiant** and contract from their employer with full personal details and details of working hours and pay. These provisions generally apply to students from non-EU countries, but check with your embassy for precise terms and conditions.

6. Students from EU countries do not require work permits, but are subject to French legal restrictions. Commonwealth citizens should remember that British residency rights do not equate to British citizenship rights within the European Union. You will be governed by the regulations pertaining to your nationality status.

WHERE TO LOOK FOR WORK

Most of the traditional French press options outlined in Chapter 6 also include job offers specifically aimed at students. French students produce their own magazine which is widely available, *L'Etudiant*, which has its own employment service (*www.l'etudiant-emploir.fr*). Other notable sites include *www.supjeune.com*, *www.recrut.com* and *www.net-work.fr*.

A WORD OF WARNING

No matter who you work for in France, you and your employer are subject to French law in France. Your contract and work conditions must conform to French law. Foreign firms have been criticised repeatedly for failing to observe basic French regulations when employing students and temporary workers for seasonal employees and students working through the academic year. The French government website *www.droitsdesjeunes.gouv.fr*, will help you draw the line between working hard for your money and working for next-to-no money at all.

WORKING AS AN AU PAIR

Au pairs and nannies

Nannies have formal qualifications in childcare, and as such are much better paid. Their duties are restricted specifically to childcare, and accommodation is not normally provided. Both nannies and au pairs are often expected to travel with their families.

An au pair is generally a young person with no formal qualification in childcare, who lives as one of the family. The legal age limits are 18–30 years old, and they are paid a small sum of 'pocket money' (normally between €270 and €300/month) in return for looking after the children, *light* housework, and several evenings baby-sitting per week. Accommodation and meals are normally provided by the family. Au pairs normally take a language course during the daytime. This is obligatory for non-EU residence permits.

You must avoid undeclared unofficial positions which leave you open to abuse. Not only are you not covered if you have an accident cleaning an apartment or minding the children, but you are living and working illegally and could face expulsion.

Looking for work

There are a number of agencies which place au pairs and nannies, both in the UK and also in France (principally in Paris). It is possible to find a position before arriving in France, through British magazines such as *The Lady*. In Paris, the magazines *France-USA Contacts* and *The Free Voice* carry regular advertisements. Some agencies which advertise are better than others which will place you with a family, take the fee and never contact you again. Try asking around for the names of the good and bad agencies.

Check notice-boards at the English-speaking churches for small advertisements, and place advertisements seeking work in the same places. There are generally more jobs available than au pairs to fill them, so you should not feel stuck.

Conditions of employment

Au pairing falls within one of the 'grey' areas of French employment. The official title of an au pair in French law is a **stagiaire aide familiale**. There are set guidelines, but making sure that these are applied is not always easy. Establishing a good relationship not only with the children but also with 'Monsieur et Madame' is vital to a successful stay.

Generally, you will be employed from September till June, although you may well be asked to stay and help in the summer holiday months. Your employer *should* make a **Déclaration d'Engagement** to the Social Security office. In reality, few employers will do this voluntarily as they fear paying extra taxes to pay for your statutory rights. If you are an EU citizen, make sure you take E111 form with you to France to cover emergency health care.

Legal requirements for American au pairs are listed below. **Rules and requirements also applying to EU nationals are in bold**:

1. **Age limit of 18–30 years old**.

2. Fair knowledge of French and/or studying French.

3. Minimum stay of three months, maximum 18 months. You can change families during this period but the maximum stay is 18 months.

4. Summer au pairs of one to three months are not required to take French classes but must have completed one year of college-level studies in French.

5. The recognised objective of au pairing is to share in a French family's life and culture. Foreign families are not normally authorised to hire au pairs.

6. **Room and board must be provided, with meals shared with the family and a private bedroom**.

7. **The au pair's daily schedule should not exceed more than five hours work per day, and should be arranged to allow time for study including classes. Au pairs should have one day off a week, and once a month this should be a Sunday. An au pair should never be prevented from attending church on Sunday even if this is a working day.**

8. American citizens must obtain their au pair visa in the US from the French consulate with jurisdiction over their place of residence *before* entering France. You cannot convert tourist visas. This means following the same procedure outlined in Chapter 3 for obtaining a visa de long séjour, with a contract as a stagiaire aide familiale approved by the French Ministry of Labour. Your work permit itself is finally granted once you arrive in France after your contract has been approved by the Ministry of Labour. If a contract is not immediately available, a letter describing the position may be accepted as part of the application process.

You may be required to travel with the family, in which case they should cover your expenses. If you are based in or near Paris, the family may pay half of your travel pass but this is not obligatory.

Au pair contracts
EU nationals from one of the new member states may not stay in France more than three months without a valid residence permit (carte de séjour). To obtain this, you need a formal work contract with social security declarations and contributions.

Americans with student visas can obtain au pair status

after arrival in France after registering at a French university and obtaining a residence permit. Student au pairs still can only work for French families under a valid contract approved by the French Ministry of Labour.

French families and au pair agencies can obtain contracts at the French Ministry of Labour section at the address given in Chapter 3. This needs to be completed and returned accompanied by a medical certificate not more than three months old signed by a doctor, either in French or translated into French. For students planning to work as au pairs you must either produce your student card if you are already studying in France, or produce evidence of your student status if you are applying in the US for your visa. Completed applications including these documents will be approved and stamped by the Foreign Workers section, and one copy stays with the family and one with the au pair.

The American au pair must provide the stamped copy together with evidence of registration at a French language school (**NB:** evening classes are not acceptable) together with all other documentation required in order to obtain the carte de séjour within eight days of arrival in France. Once the carte de séjour has been obtained, and following a final visit to the Foreign Workers section, you will be granted a renewable temporary work permit of six months.

SEASONAL WORK

The major department stores normally advertise for extra help throughout the traditional busy periods up to and after Christmas and during the sales (**soldes**). Every year, the CIDJ organises a two-day summer recruitment fair to help students find a summer job. The term **job** is used now in French, but normally implies low/minimum pay for low calibre work. At the 2001 job fair 25% of the jobs were in the lower end of the hotel and restaurant industries, and 21% were in the commercial sector.

You need to start early on the summer job search if you are planning to work. For more information on this area and all areas of student employment, call in at the **CIDJ (Centre de l'information de la jeunesse)** of your university *www.cidj.asso.fr*. The CIDJ also offers advice on regulations for the employment of students from outside the European Union.

Non-EU students will still be subject to visa formalities but work for up to three months during the summer vacation period is generally accessible. The Council on International Educational Exchange (CIEE) has negotiated reciprocal rights between France and the USA allowing students in full-time American university education or study abroad programmes to obtain temporary work permits. Further details can be obtained from the following addresses:

- ◆ Work Abroad, CIEE, 205 East 42nd Street, New York NY10017. Tel: 212 661 1414.
- ◆ Work in France, CIEE, 1 place de l'Odéon, 75006 Paris. Tel: 01 44 41 74 74.

6

Deciding Where to Live

Deciding where to live in Paris will involve balancing professional, family and perhaps educational obligations, and personal preferences. Think about the following points when you decide where to live:

- **Size**. Do you prefer to have a larger home in a less popular but cheaper area, or a smaller home in a more central and/or expensive area?

- **Facilities**. Which facilities do you want to be nearest – shops, schools, entertainment, your workplace?

- **Transport**. What public transport facilities are there nearby? Do you need parking space?

- **Safety**. How safe is the area you have chosen? Is it really as safe, or as dangerous, as you have been told ?

◆ If you have the opportunity it is a good idea to briefly visit the quartier (district) where you are considering living. Bear in mind the points above, be observant when you visit the quartier, and decide on your priorities before taking a decision. Moving is expensive, time-consuming and unsettling.

There are three basic points to remember when you begin your home search:

1. Furnished rented accommodation is generally more expensive than unfurnished accommodation.

2. The suburbs are generally less expensive than the city centre, although everything depends on location.

3. Weigh up a larger home in a more distant location against increased travelling time and monthly cost, as well as perhaps inferior amenities – although that calculation can work in both directions.

LOCAL CONSIDERATIONS

Each arrondissement has its own mayor and local council, and state-run services from education to taxation are operated on the basis of sub-divisions of the arrondissements. This can have varying degrees of importance at different stages of your Parisian life. For instance:

◆ Your chances of finding a place in a municipal **crèche** for your child. The number of places available varies greatly from arrondissement to arrondissement.

◆ Your children will be assigned to state schools according to the arrondissement you live in, and the sub-divisions become crucial when it comes to entering your child into one of the élite Parisian **lycées**, or being faced with sending them to one of their much poorer 'cousins'.

♦ Your local housing tax (**taxe d'habitation**) will vary according to not only the size of your apartment or house, but also to its last official listed valuation by the local authorities, which will take into account average market prices per square metre at the time of the valuation. However, in the suburbs surrounding Paris in particular, the presence of large businesses or factories can have a very beneficial effect for local residents in terms of their taxe d'habitation. For instance, both Boulogne-Billancourt and exclusive Neuilly sur Seine on the western edge of Paris' city centre, ideally placed and offering good quality housing, have substantially lower taxes d'habitation than neighbouring communes because of a strong corporate presence.

♦ Local authorities rival each other on the quality of services they offer to their residents. Mainly this is part of the party political game, but the results of a sustained programme over a number of years to restore a certain quartier or maintain a general standard of living can make a considerable difference.

ENVIRONMENTAL CONSIDERATIONS

When you do narrow your choices down, it is worth taking a trip to the local mairie to find out what is planned in the area in the near future. If it is planned to move the school a kilometre away, or to cut a new **métro** line under your street, or to build a block of new flats on the site opposite, you may want to reconsider.

You should also be wary in rural areas of the danger of flooding, which has been a particular problem in recent years in France. The Seine also does occasionally reach very high levels which leads to cellar flooding. Village centres are not immune from major problems. When you view a property, ask if the building is in a flood-risk zone (**zone inondable**). Many buildings were constructed in such zones even up until very recent times. The age of a building is no guarantee against the risk of flooding in some areas.

You should also be aware that south-facing apartments can become very uncomfortable in the summer months. The deadly heat wave of August 2003 proved this point very firmly. French apartments and houses are never air-conditioned (**climatisé**). Bear in mind that in the summer months night temperatures can stay as high as 70°F in the city, after reaching 90°F or more during the day. Small apartments high up, such as converted **chambres de bonnes** can prove cold in winter and hot in summer.

AREAS POPULAR WITH EXPATRIATES

There are no particular Anglo-Saxon or European quartiers, but there are areas traditionally associated with the expatriate communities. Generally, these are the more expensive areas of the city. These include the 1st, 4th, 8th, 16th and neighbouring districts of the haut-17th arrondissements, all on the **Rive Droite**. Property specia-lists have also noticed a strong British interest in recent years in the most expensive areas of the **Rive Gauche**, in the Gobelins district of the 13th, 6th, 7th and northern 15th arrondissements.

In the suburbs, there is a strong English-speaking presence in the western suburbs, mainly because of the American, British and international schools in Croisy sur Seine, St Cloud, Sèvres, and St Germain en Laye. Once again these are expensive areas. Maisons-Lafitte and Versailles in the west, and Chantilly in the north, are historically connected to the British community also. To the east, the EuroDisney development has brought many foreigners to the area, and those who have stayed have often tended to profit from the new cheaper housing near the Val d'Europe development. To the south near Fontainebleau, the INSEAD business school acts as another international community centre.

LOOKING AT BASIC HOUSING TERMS

It is difficult to generalise, but the following basic terms will give you an idea of what to expect when you turn up to visit a property:

- **boulevard** or **avenue** normally suggests a wide tree-lined main street

- **rue** is simply the French word for 'street', anything from 5 to 500 metres in length

- **impasse, cité** or **villa** suggests a small cul-de-sac. Depending where they are and on a host of other 'historical' factors about the area, this could be an exclusive residential area or former workshops converted into apartments

- ◆ **cité** is also used to describe down-at-heel and rough high-rise blocks, so be careful according to which area you are visiting, especially in the suburbs

- ◆ an **HLM** is Paris-speak for municipally-owned social priority housing

- ◆ **passage** translates quite easily, but as with cités, these can be pretty and fun depending on where and how they have been converted

- ◆ **voie privée** means private street, with gates preventing access to passers-by

- ◆ **pavillon** is the French for a detached house normally found in the suburbs; **hôtel particulier** indicates that this whole building was originally the private residence of one family alone, and normally indicates a high-quality building; **maison de ville** or **maison de maître** would indicate a smaller middle-class house, now much sought-after in certain areas of Paris, dating from the nineteenth-century expansion of Paris. A **résidence** is a block of privately-owned apartments normally of superior quality.

- ◆ **pierre de taille** indicates a good quality stone building, probably dating from the nineteenth or twentieth centuries.

UNDERSTANDING MICRO-MARKETS

In the following chapters, you will find tables giving a selection of indicative prices for good quality apartments, averaged out for a whole town or arrondissement. However, there are many large variations within each

___

local market according to fashion, facilities, and the age and quality of the property on offer. For instance: in the 18th arrondissement of Paris, in the exclusive avenue Junot close to Sacré Coeur prices average over €7,000/m, whilst the overall arrondissement average is less than half that price.

UNDERSTANDING AVERAGE PROPERTY PRICES

A favoured French obsession is surveying property prices with varying results. As an example, the table below was composed on the basis of figures published at the beginning of March 2004. The official average price per square metre in Paris was €3,850/m^2. The *Nouvel Observateur* nonetheless published a real average price of €4,150/m^2.

By the end of April 2004, *Le Point* published an average price of €3,989/m^2, and agreed more or less to the majority of the increases shown, with a couple of exceptions. Estimating prices is not an exact science, and this table and the tables in the following chapters are only intended to give you an idea of the evolution of property prices over recent years. **You must make your own assessment** of your investment based on comparative studies and by talking to several agents, in order to establish the real market value of any property.

Arrondissement	Challenges March 2001 Average	Price ranking 2001	Nouvel Observateur Average March 04	Price ranking 2004	Nouvel Observateur March 04 Estimated real price increase in 2003 for good quality apartments	L'Express December 02 'Quality of life' ranking
Paris 1	23,900FF = €3,643	7	€4,745	7	7.8%	2
Paris 2	19,350FF = €2,949	11	€4,093	11	17.7%	14
Paris 3	18,400FF = €2,805	13=	€4,392	8	12.9%	18
Paris 4	29,267FF = €4,461	3	€4,844	5	8%	3
Paris 5	25,033FF = €3,816	5	€5,100	3	11.9%	1
Paris 6	32,033FF = €4,883	2	€5,957	1	8.1%	5
Paris 7	32,066FF = €4,888	1	€5,846	2	10.5%	6
Paris 8	24,867FF = €3,790	6	€4,872	4	16.4%	8
Paris 9	18,993FF = €2,895	12	€3,699	13	12.1%	9
Paris 10	16,166FF = €2,464	20	€3,036	17	15.3%	19
Paris 11	18,333FF = €2,794	15	€3,461	16	12.9%	13
Paris 12	18,400FF = €2,805	13=	€3,600	15	14%	4
Paris 13	17,833FF = €2,718	16	€3,638	14	13.5%	7
Paris 14	21,000FF = €3,201	10	€4,144	10	12.8%	10
Paris 15	21,800FF = €3,323	8	€4,239	9	12.8%	11
Paris 16	25,300FF = €3,857	4	€4,832	6	9.9%	12
Paris 17	21,700FF = €3,308	9	€3,830	12	10.6%	17
Paris 18	17,733FF = €2,703	18	€2,927	19	16.7%	20
Paris 19	16,766FF = €2,556	19	€2,755	20	13.5%	15
Paris 20	17,767FF = €2,709	17	€2,990	18	16.5%	16
Average for Paris	€3,298		(€3,850*) €4,150			

*The official average figure from Chamber des notaires Paris–Île de France is €3850/m² (Nouvel Observateur 18/03/04). Overall property prices are estimated to have risen in Paris from around 55–60% in the period 1992–2004 (Challenges (04/03/04, and by 11% per square metre in 2003 (Le Point 29/04/04).

Figure 8. Comparative table of purchase prices per square metre (m²) published in the French press for apartments in central Paris.

Sources: as noted. 2001 figures in French Francs converted to euros at official bank rates.

7

Living in the City – La Rive Droite

In Paris, 67.5% of the population live in the 14 arrondissements of the Right Bank, stretching from the luxurious west to the up-and-coming east via the colourful and sometimes difficult northern arrondissements, and including the historic and fashionable heart of Paris.

Couched between the two green lungs of Paris, the **Bois de Boulogne** and the **Bois de Vincennes**, the heart is composed of the ancient royal and noble districts which are still renowned for luxury shopping and art galleries, fine apartments and vibrant nightlife. Stretching out to the west along the former rural playground of the Champs-Elysées is the most important business district in France (leading out to the second most important in La Défense). To the north, the former villages of Batignolles, la Butte Montmartre, Belleville, la Butte-Chaumont, Ménilmontant and Charonne still mix working-class sentiments with trendy artistic revolutionaries.

THE 1ST ARRONDISSEMENT

According to one local resident interviewed by *Le Figaro* (10 February 2001), 'The real problem with the arrondissement is that it ... runs length-wise, a cut-through, with few residents, monopolised in the west by a rich population – French and foreign – ... [whilst] in the east, near the Forum, it is much more working-class'.

The reasons for the geographical layout and social divides are mainly historical in this busy and elegant area in the heart of Paris. Unlike the majority of central Parisian arrondissements which complain of lack of open green spaces, the 1st is dominated by the **Jardin des Tuileries**, all that remains of the missing third royal palace which once filled this area. The original palace and fortress was the **Louvre**, and the oldest exposed sections of the great palace can now be found underground in the newest additions, the Carrousel du Louvre. The Sun King Louis XIV left his mark on the Cour Carrée even though he removed the court to Versailles, and it was Napoléon and his successors who added the great long wings running down to the Tuileries, with the finishing touch of the pyramids added by President Mitterrand. Just next door stands the **Palais-Royal**, originally built for the powerful Cardinal Richelieu. The tranquil gardens of what is now the French Culture Ministry were the scene of revolutionary ferment when this was the residence of the Orléans branch of the royal family in the years leading up to 1789. The end result of that ferment was the final demise of the lost palace of the Tuileries which stood at the end of the gardens, razed to the ground by the mob in 1870 after the fall of Napoléon III. Now all that rests of the palace are **Orangerie** with its collection of Monet paintings, and Napoléon III's tennis court **Jeu de Paume**, now a contemporary art museum.

Linking the right bank and fortress of the Louvre to the Île de la Cité and the Cathedral of Notre-Dame and royal palace on the island (now the **Palais de Justice**, with just the **Sainte-Chapelle** as a reminder of bygone days), is Paris's oldest bridge, confusingly named the **Pont Neuf**, which is old French for the New Bridge. The medieval city grew up behind the Louvre, and the maze of tiny streets beside the **Samaritaine** department is a reminder of this medieval heritage. The royal churches were St Germain L'Auxerrois, and the majestic St-Eustache beyond the great market district of **Les Halles**.

Les Halles was a vast covered market, and the rival of the old Covent Garden in London. Like its British counter-part, the market activities were exiled to a distant suburb, and the markets were flattened to build the subterranean **Forum des Halles** shopping and entertainment centre, with gardens at ground level. Beside the market district and still in proximity to the Louvre and the river, a commercial district grew up in what is now the area known as **Châtelet**, where street names mark the former activities of each street.

The wealth of the merchants and nobles drawn to this area led to the expansion west towards the city limits along the **rue St Honoré** of fine seventeenth and eighteenth century town houses, now converted into offices, shops and apartments. The splendid Eglise St Roch is the church which features heavily in the original version of *Les Liaisons Dangereuses*, and in its vaults lie many of the French aristocracy. The exclusive **Place Vendôme**, home to the Ritz and most of the world's leading jewellers, is a showpiece of the wealth of this area.

The polarity of the 1st is indeed very remarkable, with the *haute-couture* fashion industry concentrated at the western end in addition to many trendy interior design shops. However, the more central zone is also showing clear signs of luxury living. The area around Palais-Royal with its flower-filled gardens and border of covered galleries is one of the most expensive in Paris for good accommodation, and the area nearer the Seine saw a 52% rise in prices in 2001–2002! (*La Vie Financière*, April 2003). In addition, there is a dearth of ordinary shops where you can simply by your groceries and life's little necessities. The overall effect has been an exodus of 30% of the population in the last 25 years. Paradoxically, as for the 4th arrondissement, this has created a high level of childcare and education opportunities which, under other circumstances, would draw families to the area.

With a bottle-neck medieval street plan and eighteenth century streets designed for horse-drawn traffic, and the great rue de Rivoli and main Paris thorough-fare on the river-banks (**quais**) of the Seine, the area also suffers from the traffic and pollution problems common to all the central arrondissements. The Forum des Halles RER station (the busiest such station in Europe) drains the outlying suburbs, many of which are much less than pleasant. Les Halles is a highly nocturnal quartier, and the night-buses (**noctambus**) leave and arrive at the Place du Châtelet. But the result of this activity is that Les Halles and the gardens of the Forum are unsafe areas at night, although the upside is that this is the cheaper part of the 1st arrondissement. Plans for the giant renovation of the Forum and its gardens will probably not be completed until at least 2008.

Yet with its impressive number of theatres (notably the **Comédie-Française** and the **Théâtre du Châtelet**), concerts, museums and monuments, the 1st arrondissement is the cultural as well as the geographical heart of Paris. The Les Halles redevelopment has breathed new life into an old quartier, and brought one of the most fashionable swimming pools and one of Paris's major multi-screen cinema complexes (the **UGC-Ciné Cité**) to the heart of the city. No matter where you live in it, the 1st arrondissement does not offer you a quiet life, but it certainly does offer you a good one if you have the means to support it.

THE 2ND ARRONDISSEMENT

Covering only one square kilometre and with about 20,000 inhabitants, the smallest arrondissement of Paris is a rich collection of contrasting communities, which ensures that the most densely populated arrondissement is anything but a ghetto of one group or another. Nestling between the Grands Boulevards to the north, the gracious

1st arrondissement and the gardens of Les Halles to the south, and the Marais to the east, the area contains elements of all its neighbours as well as a tangle of calmer streets in the centre around the old **Bibliothéque Nationale**.

The western half of the arrondissement, beginning almost at La Madeleine and stretching to the rue du Quatre-Septembre, is one of the most prestigious commercial districts of Paris. The **rue de la Paix** leading from the Place Vendôme to the Place de l'Opéra has for generations been associated with the world's leading jewellers. The **avenue de l'Opéra** is the headquarters of Paris's travel industry, and also to be found in this area is one Paris's main banking districts. Apartments in this area are scarcer than elsewhere in the 2nd, and essentially this is luxury living at commensurate prices. Between the boulevard des Italiens and the rue du Quatre-Septembre is essentially a business area, leading down to the Paris Stock Exchange at **Place de la Bourse**. For opera fans, the 2nd is almost paradise, with the great **Opéra-Garnier** at one corner (now mainly used for ballet), and the renowned **Opéra-Comique** at place Boïeldieu a few minutes up the road.

Beneath the Bourse area and the rue du Louvre, is an area of elegant apartments and shops centred around the old Bibliothèque Nationale. Just beyond, the grand **Place des Victoires** announces the proximity of the Palais-Royal. The Place des Victoires, a seventeenth century gem, is also the gateway to the fashion designer district which has firmly taken up residence in the 2nd arrondissement. Between the rue Montmartre and the Boulevard de

Sebastopol, the most sought-after section of the 2nd can be found in the restored pedestrian district centred on the **rue Montorgueil** market. The influence of the fashion industry is heavily felt on this street, which often seems to be one long catwalk. Trendsetters of all styles have moved in here, and there is a large community of gays and childless couples in the area. Rents are high here, and families are unlikely to find value for their money in this area.

The Grands Boulevards lining the north of the arrondissement are filled with shops and theatres, and feeding off these are the charming and characteristic covered shopping galleries, the passages. The Grands Boulevards were originally conceived as places of amusement and promenades, but the proximity of music halls soon attracted some of the less desirable forms of entertainment industry in the nineteenth century. Wandering through the passage des Panoramas at dusk in winter, when the great lamps are half-lit and the galleries are emptying, allows you to catch something of the *demi-monde* atmosphere that once lingered over the area. Today, the Grands Boulevards live up to their original intent even if they are less elegant than before and attract the masses each weekend. The nightclubs here on the 2nd side of the road are amongst the most popular in Paris. **Le Rex Cinema** near the eastern end of the 2nd is one of the great 1930's picture palace cinemas of Paris, attracting large crowds especially for the children's matinees at the weekends. Beyond the Rex is the more unsavoury Strasbourg St-Denis. Take care here especially at night.

This northern area of the arrondissement contains the **populaire** element of the 2nd and cheaper apartments. Directly above Montorgeuil, **Sentier,** also now known as 'Silicon Sentier'. Traditionally a bastion of sweat-shop clothing factories in the extensive attics of dilapidated yet essentially interesting eighteenth-century buildings, the area became the centre of the **nouvelle économie**, Internet start-ups, drawn to cheap rents and the close proximity of the Bourse with its high-speed Internet access. The clothes industry has far from disappeared, but the two dynamic industries happily cohabit in this crowded area of Paris. The streets surrounding **rue St Denis** are increasingly becoming an anomaly. On the one hand, the rue St Denis is one of the sleaziest streets in Paris, certainly at the upper end. On the other hand, lack of space and the attraction of 'like to like' have drawn more reputable fashion victims than those of Sentier to move into the area and renovate the apartments. However, do take care in the St Denis area.

A lack of local amenities and open spaces is offset by the fact that transport is so easy in this area that you can soon get to a park or a pool. The biggest problems that the 2nd arrondissement face are property prices; traffic and parking in the crowded narrow streets which nonetheless provide much of the charm of the area; and crime. The 2nd suffers because it is couched between the Forum des Halles and Strasbourg St Denis, both known for drug-dealing and racketeering of all kinds. Add the prostitutes on the rue St Denis, and you have a lot of problems for one square kilometre.

The 2nd arrondissement is probably not the best adapted area for families, although it has a very socially mixed environment and young families are said to be moving back to the area. But the area's enduring popularity is proof of the greatest claim to fame of the 2nd, that it successfully combines fashion, finance and fine housing in such a small area, demonstrating that in the heart of Paris 'small can be beautiful'.

THE 3RD ARRONDISSEMENT

In comparison to its larger richer neighbour and quartier partner the 4th arrondissement, the northern half of the Marais which forms the 3rd arrondissement appears at first to be a poorer deal. You can almost imagine 'the mother of the Marais' saying that her other daughter got the talents and the looks, and that the 3rd arrondissement is such a difficult child; a far from fair judgement, even if the 3rd does have its geographical 'moments'. But given the history of this part of Paris, it is almost unsurprising that the area is like no other.

The history is written in street names and in stone in this popular part of Paris, with the **rue du Temple, rue des Archives** and **rue Vieille du Temple** providing the principal arteries from the river bank to the **Place de La République**, passing via the Square du Temple, all revealing that this was the site of the Paris headquarters of the mysterious Order of the Knights Templars. In the seventeenth and eighteenth centuries, the noble mansion-building campaigns (recalled by street names such as the rue de Montmorency) pushed further north into the area that is now the 3rd and merchant, and the southern parts of the arrondissement contain some of the finest examples in the Marais. The **Musée Carnavelet**, the magnificent palace that now houses the museum of Paris and the **Hôtel de Saint-Aignan** (the brand new **Museum of Jewish Life and Culture**) restored to its eighteenth century splendour, both attest to this golden era of the 3rd arrondissement.

Despite being small, the 3rd arrondissement falls into roughly five different sectors. The south-west corner is centred on the **quartier de l'Horloge**, a gloomy modern development. In this area you will pay less to live on one of the busy main thoroughfares which criss-cross the arrondissement, such as the **rue Beaubourg**, the **rue de Turbigo** or the **rue Réaumur** than on one of the grid of smaller side streets containing ancient oak-beamed apartments built around spacious courtyards originally planned for horses and carriages, even if the streets themselves are narrow. At the junction of the rue de Turbigo and rue Beaubourg is **Arts et Métiers** métro, and the heart of a popular and (relatively) cheaper district – close to the centre, but also close to the shops of rue de Bretagne and République. The area takes its name from the renowned engineering institute housed in an ancient abbey which was originally beyond the city walls.

Leading down from Arts et Métiers, along the rue du Temple in particular, is what was Paris's first 'Chinatown' in the 1920s. The street is still dominated by Chinese and Arab wholesalers, and a small rag trade which has also made its home in the northern part of the arrondissement, sturdily resisting all attempts to move them. The result is a breath of more working-class air in the otherwise rarified Marais atmosphere, but at the cost of traffic congestion. To the east of the **rue des Archives** is probably the most pleasant part of the 3rd, leading across to the **boulevard des Filles du Calvaire**, and the **boulevard Beaumarchais**. Running from the rue du Temple in this direction is the **rue de Bretagne** market street, and the whole area is a comfortable relaxed mix between Marais style and good practical living, with an interesting selection of apartments in the **rue Charlot** (currently the height of fashion) and the streets surrounding the **rue de Turenne**. The sector from the rue **Vieille du Temple** along the **rue des Francs-Bourgeois** is the chicest part of the 3rd, with the **Musée Picasso** and other cultural centres behind the busy commercial street and centred around the tranquil **rue du Parc-Royal**.

What then makes the 3rd 'a difficult child'? Although the area has a very cosmopolitan feel to it, with Arab, Chinese, and Jewish communities, a large gay community drawn into the Marais orbit, and a rich influential community of the fashion and arts world together with leading business people, the communities do not all seem to appreciate each other. In addition, social priority housing is virtually non-existent, adding to the social imbalance in the area. Crime also soared in the area in recent years, but this is probably more an indicator of the success of the area and its population than anything else.

Property prices in the 3rd are also among the highest in Paris, and as a result the 3rd is experiencing the same population drift from young families to rich, childless households as the 4th arrondissement. Finally, if property prices were not enough to ward off potential young families from the area, the waiting lists for a place in a municipal crèche in the 3rd is over 300. Endless traffic jams, the lack of green open spaces and a lack of local supermarkets all detract from the area's charm. Yet in spite of all these problems, the 3rd with its oak-beamed, character-filled apartments remains one of the most attractive areas of Paris, especially for young couples or single people, who enjoy the mix of populations.

THE 4TH ARRONDISSEMENT

The 4th is most often referred to under its quartier name, the **Marais**, even though that name also applies to the 3rd arrondissement next door. The Marais, originally the marshlands bordering the river-bank and the original Parisian settlements on the Île de la Cité which also falls within the 4th arrondissement, was a popular area of settlement from the earliest days of Parisian urban expansion. The splendid eighteenth-century high-cei-linged mansions besides earlier medieval and Renaissance buildings attest to a long residential tradition on this site. The Île St Louis behind the Île de la Cité was in fact a speculative seventeenth-century property development on a mudflat, which explains the homo-genous date of many of the fine structures. As you will see when you wander around the streets of the tiny island, St Louis quickly became the favoured residence of courtiers and artists, and to some large extent it remains the favoured residence of similar groups today. Prices are currently very high, more akin to the 16th, and many foreigners have chosen to make this neighbourhood their Parisian home.

So much which represents Paris – the cathedral of Notre-Dame, the Centre Pompidou, the City Hall (**Hôtel de Ville**) itself – all falls within the 4th arrondissement, that it is sometimes difficult to remember or imagine that the area has a life of its own. Yet the 4th remains one of the most enduringly popular areas of the city in which to live, with a number of different mini-quartiers making up the urban puzzle. On the eastern edge, bordering on the 1st arrondissement and Les Halles and spreading into the 3rd arrondissement, is Paris's answer to London's Soho, the gay village centred on **rue des Archives, rue St Croix de la Bretonnerie**, and **rue du Vieille du Temple**. Lively and bustling, open almost all hours in many cases, the bars, restaurants, shops, and cafés have transformed the quartier. Just as the 'pink pound' saved Soho, so the 'pink franc' brought new life to what was a dilapidated quartier. Gallery owners and designers are keen to move in, as the **branché** (trendy) heterosexual population follows the gay lead into the Marais.

Surprisingly, cheek-by-jowl with this community lives one of the city's most well-known Jewish communities, now centred on the **rue des Rosiers** and its tributaries. The result of a successful and lively coexistence of these two areas is that on Sundays, the area is packed with shoppers, not simply munching on a **falafel** (Jewish sandwich), but visiting the interior design shops and clothes shops of the rue des Francs-Bourgeois leading down to the third area of the 4th arrondissement, the aristocratic village St-Paul. In this section of the Marais, centred on the beautiful **Place des Vosges** (an arcaded garden-filled former royal square), the apartments in the restored noble palaces are expensive. From beyond the Place des Vosges to Bastille, and between the rues St Antoine and de Rivoli (one and the same but with a name-change at St Paul), and the river bank, apartments are still expensive but a little more affordable.

The islands do both offer accommodation, even if the Île de la Cité is principally the administrative headquarters for Paris, with the cathedral, the Préfecture (police headquarters), the Palais de Justice (Supreme Court of Paris), and all their attendant buildings, plus one of Paris's oldest hospitals, the Hôtel-Dieu. The Île St Louis has beautiful seventeenth-century apartments, but does betray its origins when the Seine rises and occasionally floods, and residents find their expensive wine collections floating in their flooded cellars.

The 4th almost overflows with cultural and creative life, and with the rue de Rivoli running straight through the middle of the arrondissement, the area certainly does not lack for shops either. The **Bazaar de l'Hotel de Ville (BHV)** manages to meet most requirements, and in the small streets behind you will find everything associated with the diverse communities which inhabit the 4th. The main market street is on the **rue Rambuteau**, although supermarkets are pretty scarce unsurprisingly.

Statistically the 4th has a high level of crime, but the figures are exaggerated by pick-pocketing and handbag snatching concentrated around the Place Beaubourg. Parking is notoriously difficult in the Marais at any time, but especially at the weekends and in the evenings.

But probably the main problem with the 4th arrondissement is that even the cheapest apartments are very expensive, with property prices among the highest in Paris. The cultural richness of the area, its geographical location, the quality of the apartments on offer and the general desirability of the area, and the wealth that certain sections of the gay community concentrated here possess, all combine to make the 4th arrondissement an expensive choice for a family-sized apartment.

Ironically though, the 4th is one of the arrondissements with the highest number of crèche places and school class sizes in Paris, and local initiatives have been linked to developing facilities for children and young families.

The essential problem is one of creating housing at a reasonable price in order to re-equilibrate the social mix of the arrondissement. As it stands, the 4th arrondissement is a highly desirable choice as a place to live – central, varied, and fun with a large stock of excellent apartments and good schools including the renowned **Lycée Charlemagne**. But for the time being, it remains a life-style choice until property prices start to fall or your income rises to the necessary heights.

THE 8TH ARRONDISSEMENT

When the medieval city of Paris could no longer offer the nobles the space, distraction and peace that they required for their town houses, they breached the city walls into the surrounding fields, the so-called 'Elysian Fields' or **Champs-Elysées**, towards the outlying villages and hamlets. The palaces on the **Faubourg St Honoré** prolonged the rue St Honoré, and the American and British embassies and the presidential Elysée Palace are the most magnificent examples on the Faubourg of the new prestige of these villas. The great **Place de la Concorde**, with the matching splendours of the Hôtel Crillon and the Navy Ministry, attested to the glory of the Sun King's descendants – until the day that the revolting locals placed a large and overly-efficient head-chopping device patented by Dr Guillotine in the middle of the place and experimented on the royal family, his court, and then each other.

In some respects, little has changed today (although the guillotine has been replaced by an obelisk). The area remains extremely fashionable, and one of the great centres of nightlife, not to mention of course shopping. The Faubourg is *the* Fashion House address in Paris, whilst the Champs-Elysées remains the centre of France's most important business district. After a lengthy restoration, nightlife returned in force to the Champs, not only with a number of the most famous nightclubs on the avenue itself, but in streets such as **rue Marbeuf** leading down to the fashion house headquarters on ultra-chic **avenue George V** and its luxury hotels. This area, bordered by the 16th arrondissement at avenue Marceau, the riverbank, and the **Grand et Petit Palais** exhibition complex, is one of the most expensive areas of Paris in terms of accommodation, within the **Triangle d'Or** – as chic as the 16th but more lively nonetheless because of the luxury shopping and nightlife. It is also known for being an area favoured by foreign buyers. Slicing across this area is the **avenue Montiagne**, another luxury fashion paradise.

Whilst the southern side of the Champs-Elysées has become the headquarters of luxury living, the north side, including the continuation of the Faubourg St Honoré is an area of galleries and offices. This is the real residential 8th, up to the northern border on the boulevards de Courcelles and Batignolles. In the rue Daru, the **Russian Orthodox cathedral** (featured in the film *Doctor Zhivago*) overflows during the Orthodox Easter. In the neighbouring streets surrounding the small but eternally-popular **Parc Monceau** apartments are highly sought after near **St Augustin** and **Villiers,** which have the sort of shops which make you feel that you are living in the real world rather than peering out of an expensive shop window. But the descent towards the **Madeleine** returns you to luxury shopping. You may well decide to take advantage of **Hédiard** or **Fauchon** beside the Madeleine, but you would be ill-advised to do your weekly shop at these stores.

The north-eastern quarter of the 8th offers the most affordable residential accommodation in the **quartier d'Europe**, centred on the place of the same name behind the **Gare St Lazare**. Unusually for areas surrounding major train stations, this is a calm and bourgeois grid of streets bearing the names of major European cities. The area is popular for its solid well-built apartments and proximity to both central Paris and the livelier 17th arrondissement. Traditionally this area attracts young professional families.

With some of the best museums in Paris such as the **Jacquemart-André**, or again the best nightclubs from the extravagant **Queen** to the exclusive **VIP Room** or **Manray,** and more fashion houses than anyone can shop at in a single day, the 8th is bursting with attractions. Add to this solid, grand apartments and a fast track to Normandy and the coast from St Lazare, and the 8th appears to be an excellent choice for slick city living. However the downside is a lack of amenities such as parks and sports facilities, and scarcity of schools. A large part of the arrondissement also lacks regular food stores or reasonably priced high street stores, which has created a sort of 'Midas Touch' effect for this pleasant area of Paris.

THE 9TH ARRONDISSEMENT

Stretching from the ultra-chic of **La Madeleine** to the hippy chic of **Pigalle**, the 9th is one of the most sought-after arrondissements in Paris, offering something for everyone and drawing everyone into its midst. It is a mixture of a shopper's paradise yet still replete with offices and company headquarters. Consequently, the 9th is charged daily with a significant number of Paris's more than 1.2 million suburban commuters, using either public or private transport. One of the principal complaints of its inhabitants is the level of traffic using the main thoroughfares on the boulevards, the **rue Lafayette** and the **rue de Châteaudun**. The arrondissement also suffers from a lack of open spaces and waterways, with neither the Seine nor the canals passing through the arrondissement. This is not, therefore, an area for claustrophobics.

What then makes it so enticing? Firstly, it is precisely the centrality and accessibility of the 9th which is one of its attractions. In the quaint streets of the **village St-Georges** centred on the **place St-Georges**, the **rue des Martyrs** and

rue Notre Dame-de Lorette, and the **place Goustouve-Toudoze**, the apartments are large and well built, having first been constructed by nineteenth-century bankers working in the principal banking district around the **Opéra-Garnier** at the southern limit of the 9th.

The **rue des Martyrs** is a bustling market street, in an area of Paris that has drawn many showbusiness and fashion celebrities as neighbours to the bankers and young middle-classes in a truly village atmosphere. Several recent surveys have noted the strong presence of both publishers and editors, for instance. The street is a popular venue for **brocantes** (open-air antique markets), and the locals have turned it into a pedestrian reserve on Sundays. The proximity to Pigalle and a young wealthy local community has also led an increasing number of trendy clothing and interior design shops to open in the streets between the rue des Martyrs and the **place Gustave-Toudoze**. New restaurants have also opened up in the place of market traders, and the street is now livelier in the evenings than before. The **avenue Trudaine** at the top of the rue des Martyrs is a sought-after spacious tree-lined street more reminiscent of the 7th arrondissement, quite simply offering the best of both worlds.

The fact that the area is favoured by many showbiz celebrities is hardly surprising given the number of theatres in the area. The 9th has always had a reputation as an artist's quarter, and Delacroix, Toulouse-Lautrec, Degas, Bizet, and Berlioz all made their homes here. The **avenue Frochot** was home to the Renoir dynasty, and today is an exclusive enclave for film stars and fashion designers. The area from **Trinité** to the **boulevard de Clichy**, was known as the '**Nouvelle Athenes**' – the New Athens of the nineteenth-century intellectual élite. The Museum of the Romantic Life (**Musée de la Vie Romantique**) in the rue Chaptal is the former home of Georges Sands where she received her lover Chopin.

The eastern and western extremities of the 9th bring you to calmer more bourgeois areas. To the west is the **quartier d'Europe**, shared with the 8th arrondissement, behind the Gare St Lazare. The eastern limits of the arrondissement bring you to the market street of rue **Cadet** and the **square Montholon**. Bordering on the 10th and only minutes away from the Gare du Nord, this area too has a bourgeois calm about it.

The 9th arrondissement is bound north and south by boulevards. To the north lie the **boulevards de Rochechouart** and **de Clichy**, with music and sex industries vying for shop space beneath artists' **ateliers** converted to sought-after loft apartments facing north to the Sacré-Coeur. To the south, the **Grand Boulevards**, offer a non-stop parade of shopping and entertainment. The boulevards between **La Madeleine** and the **Opéra** offer the chicest shopping, whilst the great Parisian department stores of **Galeries Lafayettes** and **Printemps** are on **boulevard Haussman**.

Cinemas are concentrated on **boulevard des Italiens**, whilst the **boulevards Montmartre** and **Poissonière** still play home to many theatres and night-clubs which make this a frantic part of Paris at the weekends. In the **Faubourg**

Montmartre, a significant Jewish community is based in the streets between the boulevards, the rue de Provence, and the **Folies-Bergères**. In contrast, the quiet **rue Drouot** is the headquarters of the main Paris auction houses and stamp-collectors. Weaving their way between the two streets and the boulevards, a series of covered shopping galleries or passages offer an enticing taste of nineteenth-century Paris.

Perhaps the greatest advantage of the 9th is that to go out and enjoy yourself, you need never be very far from home. The world of entertainment and all the major shops are at your doorstep, whilst you have the chance to live in generally spacious apartments in either neat calm contentment or a livelier more haphazard village atmosphere.

THE 10TH ARRONDISSEMENT

It took me almost ten years to finally become reconciled to the 10th arrondissement of Paris. Up until then, my view of the 10th was mainly limited to visits to the Gare du Nord, and occasional peripheral views of this arrondissement as I willed the taxi driver to get me out of this part of town as quickly as possible. And yet I now find myself being drawn back again and again by the charm of an up-and-coming quartier which mixes almost sublime romanticism with the ridiculously squalid.

For all the improvements that have been made, squalor does remain an overriding problem in this arrondissement with an extremely high immigrant population, legal and otherwise; a renowned crime problem which cannot and should not be ignored when considering living in this area; and a fair dose of less salubrious 'under-life' which tends to congregate around major railway stations. With the dominant neighbouring railway stations and tracks, the area is curiously reminiscent of north-central London – Kings Cross and St Pancras together with a dash of Euston and lower Camden – with similar kinds of problems and moves towards urban renewal.

What then draws me back to the 10th? The most important reason is the **Canal St Martin**, where *Amélie from Montmartre* came to skim her stones, running through the 10th from Stalingrad to Republique where it disappears from view underground to Bastille. The car-free quais are popular on Sundays with bladers, cyclists and strollers drawn to the beautifully restored waterway, and the various bridges criss-crossing the canal lead to a fine selection of shops which mark the complete regeneration of this industrial thoroughfare; from **Balmain** to **Lacroix**, to the pastel shades of the '**Antoine et Lili**' emporium at the wonderful Pont aux Grange des Belles. The Canal St Martin has the air of a number of successful similar restorations, such as Canal Street in Manchester, or the upper, less frenetic regions of Camden Lock.

But the 10th has much more to offer than simply the canal. On the southern edge stand the two magnificent restored triumphal arches of Louis XIV, the **Porte St Martin** and the **Porte St Denis**. You should take care at both portes, especially St Denis which was the heart of drug-dealing in Paris, Strasbourg St-Denis. The two arches marked the original city limits, and the seventeenth-century **Hôpital St**

Louis was built beyond the city walls to keep the pestilent at bay. Beside the **Gare de l'Est** the derelict eighteenth-century convent-turned-hospital **Villemin** was abandoned from 1968. It has now been restored and partially rebuilt to create a splendid cultural centre and artists' residence. The gardens just behind it are already open to the public, offering a rare haven of green open space. Just across from the Gare de l'Est and the Villemin Hospital stands the hidden medieval gem of the **Eglise St Laurent**.

In terms of culinary opportunities, the high immigrant population has left its mark on the arrondissement. The **Passage Brady** off Faubourg St Denis is the well-known capital of Indian cooking in Paris, and a little Bombay seemingly frozen in time since the 1950s. The **Marché St Quentin** on boulevard Magenta offers a choice of fresh produce in a nineteenth-century covered market. Trendy restaurants and cafés are creeping along the canal and the Grands Boulevards to the south, although cheap Kurd cafés still abound. If you enjoy *choucroute*, Alsatian wines, and other delicacies from eastern France, then head for the clutch of restaurants opposite the Gare de l'Est, the gateway to Alsace.

There is little doubt that things are only going to get better in the 10th arrondissement (cynics would say, given that in certain areas they could not have got any worse ...), and it is one of the few central Paris arrondissements to still offer the opportunity to purchase real lofts in Paris in former warehouses. New transport plans will further increase the attraction of the area, and a high-speed link to Roissy is being discussed at the moment. Advertising companies and Internet start-ups are moving in beside the fashion houses, alongside the immigrant sandwich shops and cheap clothing stores in what is already being called Paris's answer to New York's So Ho.

The 10th was everybody's 'hot tip' for purchasing three years ago, and the prices are rising even if they still rest reasonable away from the canal. The continual renewal will ensure some of the best inner-city living when or if the basic problem of insecurity is overcome. No matter what happens, for those willing to take a little rough with their smooth, the 10th is still a very good bet.

THE 11TH ARRONDISSEMENT

The 11th is an area of Parisian paradox, both highly successful in many respects and yet failing in other areas. This is best seen in its population figures, for the most densely populated arrondissement of Paris also has the highest rate of population decline. The population of the 11th is a rich social mix from the traditional *bourgeoisie* to the new Parisian Bobos and also a high number of low-income immigrants.

In the northern part of the 11th bordered by the **Faubourg du Temple,** the **boulevards de Belleville** and **de Ménilmontant**, the **boulevard Jules Ferry** and the **rue Jean Pierre Timbaud**, you will find the concentration of the poorer north African immigrant communities, in what was a working-class district of workshops and workers' homes and communities. This area remains one of the cheapest areas of the 11th, although creeping gentrification is leading to higher prices. A further large swathe of the 11th from the upper end of **avenue de la République** to **boulevard Voltaire** and down to **Nation** is deeply residential and frankly not very exciting territory. There are plenty of apartments on offer, but the real excitement in the 11th is in the south-west corner with the exception of **rue Oberkampf**.

The explosion of activity on the **rue Oberkampf**, one of the trendiest in Paris, has spread into the surrounding streets and even up to the métros at Ménilmontant or Belleville, mark the limit of the 'Oberkampf effect' as journalists refer to it. On the rue Oberkampf itself, the cafés are to be found in converted shops which have kept their original shopfronts and used the original names for the bars which are now thronged in the evenings. Around about this street property prices have rocketed. Locals fear the loss of the working-class feel to the area, although this is what everybody is desperately craving, even if they prefer the look to the reality.

The area to the south, bordered by the **boulevard Beaumarchais** (and the Marais) and the **Faubourg St Antoine**, and with the pivotal point of the **place de la Bastille**, offers a mix of excellent apartments (at a price), the best transport links and some of the finest of Paris nightlife from opera to bars to nightclubs. The western boundary boulevards running from République are chic addresses with solid ancient buildings and good apartments. In the **rue Amelot** just behind there is a good mix of styles also, and a fine selection of shops and bars. The garden-filled **boulevard Richard Lenoir** covering the lower section of the Canal St Martin is home to the local market, considered one of the best in Paris.

The **rues Popincourt** and **Sedaine** have become one of the last battlegrounds in the 11th between the newer and older styles of population. Noticeably less well maintained but with good apartments available nonetheless, the area has been subject to a recent Chinese immigrant innovation of wholesalers repeating exactly the same problems as in the 3rd arrondissement.

From the **rue de la Roquette** to the Faubourg St Antoine and bordered by the rue Faidherbe is 'the golden triangle' of the 11th; the *nec plus ultra* in trendy living. Nightlife is centred on the Faubourg, the restored **rue de Lappe**, and the lower end of the **rue de Charonne**, all of which also house designer clothes shops. The **rue Keller** with its bars, galleries, shops and the Paris Lesbian and Gay Centre never lacks for imaginative street theatre.

In some respects both the short **rue de la Forge Royale** and the rue Keller (with a school opposite the Paris Lesbian and Gay Centre) best represents the Parisian paradox of the 11th. At the quieter end leading off **rue Basfroi** the streets seem run down, even menacing at times. At the other end of the street stand trendy nightspots favoured by the **BCBG** (**bon chic bon genre**) upper class youth, surrounded by a clutch of trendy shops and galleries. Beyond the rue Faidherbe, the Faubourg St Antoine slips rapidly into suburban dullness and a seemingly never-ending path to the **Place de la Nation**.

The population problems of the 11th may be explained by

a very short migration from one arrondissement to its neighbour, the 12th, which offers more of the same but more open spaces. It is very much a young person's quartier, and is a popular destination for young singles, couples, and also the gay community, especially in the trendy areas where personal space is a lower priority. But none of these groups are child-producing and so the population level stagnates and declines. Getting the most out of the 11th does require a certain amount of sacrifice in terms of either income or comfort or both, but it does offer many advantages.

THE 12TH ARRONDISSEMENT

Spreading from the **Bastille** to the **Bois de Vincennes**, the 12th is the great success story of Parisian urban regeneration. It has the highest level of population growth of all the arrondissements, and with its forest, parks, promenades and cycle tracks, the Seine waterfront and the Canal St Martin yacht harbour, it is not difficult to understand why the area is now so popular.

The area has undergone several vast renovation projects since the days 25 years ago when it was a dreary industrial backwater covered by railway tracks, most notable for its exits to the south via the Gare de Lyon or the forest in the east. The construction of the great **Opéra** house at Bastille was the signal for the renovation of the area directly adjacent, and around the **rue de Charenton**, the **avenue Ledru-Rollin** and along the south side of the **Faubourg St Antoine** is one of the trendiest districts of Paris, buzzing with designer shops, bars and people, and shared with the neighbouring 11th arrondissement. The exclusive **Port de** l'**Arsenal** on the edge of the Place de la Bastille adds a mini-St Tropez feeling to the whole area, with yachts and pleasure boats bobbing about at the entrance/exit to the Canal St Martin. And just to round off the area, the formerly dull **quai de la Rapeé** is now also acquiring a selection of nightlife similar to the restored banks of the 13th opposite.

At **Faidherbe-Chaligny**, the Faubourg St Antoine seems to calm down into more tranquil and picturesque residential calm, before filtering out into the dull residential mass of the area around **Nation**. **Picpus** is a distinctly upper-class area, with good schools nearby and nearby avenue de Saint Mandé leads into the neighbouring town, a chic suburb nestling between Paris and its eastern forest.

Forming a natural barrier between the 'old' 12th and the 'new' is the **Viaduct des Arts**, running along the **avenue Daumesnil** from just behind the Opéra to the park at Reuilly. The abandoned railway viaduct has now been converted into a selection of superb design shops for both interiors and clothing, and just for good measure you will also find a sprinkling of trendy cafés from which to watch the passing rollerbladers.

The **Gare de Lyon** still dominates its own quartier, with the inimitable **Train Bleu** restaurant in the station forming a romantic railway meeting point. Between the station and the river is the area which has caused the most excitement in recent years following on from the massive construction of the Finance Ministry at Bercy in the 1980s and the great **Palais des Sports**, home to indoor concerts and sporting events.

The smaller disused **Bercy** station and its attendant areas have been almost completely razed, redesigned and reconstructed to provide a highly sought-after series of apartment complexes looking over the beautifully-designed **Parc de Bercy** at the **Cour St Emilion**, which is ideal for children. Beside the park the former wine stores for the produce from the south have been converted into a shopping mall, finished off with a massive multi-screen cinema complex. Unfortunately the architects got so carried away that they forgot to plan a school and any local shops, but this is apparently to be resolved in the near future. In any case, it has not stopped property prices soaring in this new development which symbolises the new wealth of Paris.

At the far end of the avenue Daumesnil before it disappears into the Bois stands the **Porte Dorée**, a relaxed area with direct access to one of the large boating lakes in the Bois, and the popular **Pelouse de Reuilly** where each year the great Paris funfair the **Foire du Trône** takes place. Beside the lake you will also find the Paris Zoo, considered to be the best in France. New plans to bring the Parisian tramway to this part of the 12th, and to redevelop the areas between the **périphérique** and the inner parallel boulevards (**boulevards des maréchaux**) should further develop the attraction of this area.

With all of this so close at hand, it is not hard to see the attraction of the 12th for young families. This has been the real secret of the success of the 12th, and has best

shown the life-style requirements of the new Parisians who
want space, security, and a healthy environment in which
to raise their families. Not unsurprisingly, property prices
have risen steeply in the area but the 12th has successfully
renewed its population to attract the kind of young
professional families who can afford the higher prices.
Many of these families probably could have found
accommodation in their traditional homelands in the
west of Paris, but they have made conscious life-style
choices in moving to the renewed, open, trendier east of
Paris amongst 'their own kind'. The urban addition now
seems to be that the Bastille + Bercy + Bois = *Bobo*,
and the 12th is the tribal homeland *par excellence* of this
new breed.

THE 16TH ARRONDISSEMENT
The rich tree-lined western edge of Paris, equivalent to
London's Kensington and Knightsbridge in population
and style, provides the other, western, 'lung' to the city,
bordering both the péripherique and the **Bois de
Boulogne**. Centred on the three ancient villages of **Auteuil,
Chaillot**, and **Passy**, and stretching out to the **Porte de
Saint-Cloud** and down to the Seine, the arrondissement
encompasses everything west of the 'new town' and is now
the most **huppé** (ultra-chic) area of Paris.

The 16th is a solidly rich, upper-class, and family-
orientated residential area beyond the offices of the
avenues **Kléber, Marceau** and **Victor Hugo**, the shops of
the **rue de Passy**, and the headquarters of Radio France,
and the Organisation for Economic Cooperation and
Development (OECD), the largest but far from only

diplomatic legation in the area. With its grand avenues and discreet leafy **villas** (private streets), the area is popular with film stars, diplomats, the richer expatriate community, and an increasing number of young families. The result is that demand far outstrips supply for places in municipal crèches, even though according to the local mayor, 'In our arrondissement, the family is the principal value' (*L'Express*, 11 January 2001). Given the wealth of many of the residents the lack of crèche places proves less of a problem here than in other areas, as the number of au pairs and domestic staff is higher. However, speaking from experience, for young single people living in the 16th can be a lonely experience if you do not have the appropriate means, even if your accommodation is provided.

The gilded youth of the 16th, who often are the scions of French noble families or captains of industries, will more often than not be educated at the same schools as their parents, such as the excellent **Lycée de Janson de Sailly** in the rue de la Pompe, beside the mairie, where generations of their same family have been educated and inter-married, before themselves settling in the leafy streets nearby. The mayor is right when he says that the family is the principal value of the arrondissement, but he is also talking with his tongue in his cheek. Locally **la jeunesse dorée** of the 16th can be found hanging out in the '**m'as-tu vu?**' ('did you see me?') havens of **La Gare** at **Porte de la Muette** (the former railway station converted into a bar-restaurant) or **Le Duplex**, handily situated at the end of Millionaire's Row on **avenue Foch**.

Strolling through the streets of the 16th, it is not difficult to see what this self-perpetuating group are seeking to preserve for themselves and those whose incomes allow them to join the merry throng. From the **Place du Trocadéro** with its unrivalled views across to the Eiffel Tower, a stroll up the avenue Georges Mandel and a few detours on the left-hand side below rue de la Pompe brings you to the exclusive villas, which would be incentive enough to make anyone want to move in; small leafy mews-style streets such as you find around Eaton Square in London, and some of the most desirable property in Paris. From rue de la Pompe down to rue de Passy, and around Place du Mexico and rue de Longchamps, you are in closest proximity to the local shops. **Auteuil** has retained a sweet village-like atmosphere around the métros and church. But the further west you go, the duller the area becomes, with plenty of property at elevated prices for the sought-after 75016 postcode, but less of the attractions. The apartments along the Seine have the advantage of the views towards the Eiffel Tower, if you are lucky, or simply the disadvantage of views on the high-rise 15th arrondissement coupled with one of Paris's principal highways along the river-bank.

In terms of facilities, the 16th does offer immediate access to the magnificent Bois de Boulogne (the equivalent of Hyde Park or Central Park for Paris), the **Parc des Princes** football and rugby stadium (with the upsides and downsides that offers ...), a large municipal swimming pool, a racing course of its own at Porte d'Auteuil, and the Longchamps racing course and **Roland Garros** tennis club all on its doorstep across the arrondissement border. It also offers Paris's botanical gardens, the **Serres d'Auteuil** opposite Roland-Garros, and museums of note, such as Balzac's former home; the **Musée Guimet** of oriental art; the Museum of Modern Art on avenue Président Wilson (with its café terrace looking on to the river); the Fashion Museum; and the **Musée Marmottan** with its world-renowned collection of Impressionist paintings. But not everything in the 16ème garden is rosy.

Public transport is sparsely distributed over this large arrondissement, which has the highest number of cars per household in Paris, a reflection of both necessity and wealth. Taxis are not always willing to take passengers to the 16th at night because they will not be able to find a return fare from the deadly calm residential streets. Surprisingly the 16th also had until recently the unhappy reputation of the highest number of prostitutes in Paris, from 'regular' female prostitutes to rent boys to transvestites, and the avenue Foch by night still has a regular collection of partner-swappers. Most of the problems were or are concentrated around Porte Dauphine and the Bois. Whilst the 16th appears to be squeaky-clean, there is an uneasy sub-culture which can be both simply annoying for local residents but also dangerous because of kerb-crawlers.

Despite what might sound like alarmist warnings about a very particular sort of crime, the 16th is indisputably one of the best areas of the city. But like marriage which forms its bedrock, it is not to be undertaken lightly, irreverently, or unadvisedly. It is an expensive, conservative, and potentially socially cold climate into which to move if you are not prepared for it, or already in some way 'a member of the club'. Other areas offer similar lifestyles but at a lesser cost and with less restraint for the more independently-minded and younger at heart. But if like-minded security is what you seek, then an apartment in the 16th will be money well-spent.

THE 17TH ARRONDISSEMENT

Covering a large expanse of north-west Paris beyond the original city walls, the 17th contains three distinct geographical sectors and populations between the péripherique and the city centre. To the west, the area between the **Place de l'Etoile** and **Villiers** and from the **Parc Monceau** to **Porte Maillot** is the **haute-17ème**, a quartier huppé as sought after as the 16th arrondissement and Neuilly next door. The commercial vibrancy of the upper end of the **avenue Wagram** and the village-like streets around the **Place des Ternes** and the avenues MacMahon and Carnot soon gives way further down the avenue Wagram and along boulevard de Courcelles and in the streets beside the park to grand mansion apartments and residential calm. The reputed bustling market in **rue Poncelet** echoes to the clack of well-shod ladies stealing surreptitiously into the Central European patisserie **Stübli** for a slice of one of their exquisite cakes.

Between Monceau and the noisy but elegant **Place du Général Catroux**, the 17th starts to start to liven up as you hit **rue Legendre** and the market street of **rue de Lévis**, which provides another excellent market street leading up to Villiers. In the streets leading off **rue de Prony**, such as rue Henri Rochefort, there is an eclectic mix of architecture, apartments, ateliers and offices. If the lower end of the rue Legendre still bears all the hallmarks of the bourgeois population, the middle section leads you into bohemian **Batignolles**, originally a working-class district around the open railway tracks leading down from Pont Cardinet to the Gare St Lazare, centred on the pretty little square des Batignolles and its church.

In the 17th, social standing was always literally defined by being on 'the wrong side of the tracks'. Even before the Batigolles revival, the *Marché bio* on the boulevard des Batignolles with produce on Saturdays was drawing an ecologically lifestyle-conscious crowd to the 17th. But now Batignolles is an area of hot property, as it booms and flourishes unexpectedly into a Bobo paradise centred on the **rues des Dames, des Batignolles** (with its ugly mairie), and **rue Biot**, with the offer of lofts, large apartments and a down-at-heel and rich-in-pocket creativity in a village atmosphere. Property prices have risen steeply in this part of Paris, which was lacklustre and dull until only a few years ago, and which still is more residential than many of the quartiers to which it is often compared.

Beyond Batignolles lies what property agents like to call the **village des Epinettes**, a poorer area with a large immigrant population bordering on the **avenue de Clichy** up to the **Porte de Clichy**. Property prices here are lower, but so is the general standard of living. However, one of the advantages of the eastern edge of the 17th is the proximity to the cinemas at **Place de Clichy**, both the multi-screen complex wrapping round on to the avenue de

Clichy and the art cinemas which host small cinema festivals and a number of art and drama schools. Access to the industrial areas north of Paris is also easy either via public or private transport.

Both the boulevards de Courcelles and Batignolles and the avenue de Clichy are major thoroughfares leading to the suburbs, and the 17th suffers from a drive-through syndrome. Critics also complain about the lack of cultural amenities, open spaces, schools and waterways. Traffic and parking is a major problem, and ironically for the quartier known for its ecological market on boulevard des Batignolles, it has a scarcity of bike lanes in comparison to the rest of Paris. But many locals seem content with their lot, and are attracted by the quality of residential life in an easily-accessible area. The lack of crèches seems to be due more to a lackadaisical local mayor than a lack of children, and certain lycées such as those of the rue Cardinet are sought-after educational establishments. Overall the negative points seem to be accepted with a shrug of the shoulders by laid-back locals happy in their varied but balanced communities.

THE 18TH ARRONDISSEMENT

'Why are they all so worked up about the 18th?', asked the Paris entertainment and life-style guide *Zurban* in a banner headline in December 2000. Those of us who live here already know the beauty and the fun of the trendy bohemian hill-village around the old village centre of Abbesses, rolling down from the Sacré-Coeur to the southern border on the boulevard de Clichy and the Place Pigalle, or to the quieter upmarket lower slopes around the Mairie. Since *Amélie from Montmartre* created a world-wide sensation in 2001, the 18th has been over-whelmed with press and popular interest, and property prices are now as steep and difficult as many of the streets of the happy hill.

Ostensibly, the 18th has little going for it. In a survey in December 2002, the 18th was ranked last out of the 20th arrondissements in a survey of the best to place in Paris by *L'Express* magazine. The cheapest price per square metre for purchasing property in an arrondissement is cancelled out by the highest rate of unemployed residents and the densest population per square kilometre in Paris. Add to this one of the worst crime rates linked to the numbers of tourists plus a virulent drugs trade in a highly volatile area, some of the worst living conditions, a serious lack of schools, and a sizeable chunk of the péripherique as a northern barrier from the insalubrious neighbouring département Seine-St Denis (93); and by now you must be thinking that I am clinically insane to recommend the area to you. And yet ....

... And yet – Parisians and the Parisian literati and glitterati cannot get enough of Montmartre. It all began with a small village on a hill overlooking Paris, the site of the execution of the first Parisian Christian martyrs. Later came the nuns – the Abbesses – and then came the windmills, the farms and the vineyards. The nuns lost their heads in the revolution, the windmills stayed, and the area gradually became a retreat for revolutionaries, exiles, workers, painters, and their whores. By the time that Picasso moved in, urban expansion had already joined the hill to the city below. When Montmartre became home to the music halls such as the **Moulin-Rouge**, it also became a timeless symbol of *la vie Parisienne*.

Today, above and beyond the sex shops of the boulevard de Clichy from **Place Pigalle** to **Place Blanche** you will find one of the most vibrant and cosmopolitan communities in Paris. The bars and shops of the **rue des Abbesses** are a mix of London's Islington and Notting Hill neighbourhoods, a rag-bag of new and established designers and their muses side by side with traditional shops, trendy bars, and a thriving market on the **rue Lepic**. South-facing apartments are bathed in sunlight on sunny days, and the higher you are, the better your view is likely to be, with Paris laid out at your feet. Houses can still be found in both rich and poor areas, from the Villa Léandre in **avenue Junot**, the home to French TV and film personalities, or the villa Poissonière in the rue de la Goutte d'Or. The old farmhouses are still there, but they are now ultra-chic apartments. Two ancient windmills recall the past, and a tiny vineyard which is the excuse for the annual Montmartre Wine Festival complete with traditional wine confraternities, village parade, wine, women and song. Practically any excuse is a good excuse for a party in Montmartre, even a wine that nobody can drink.

In the **rue des Martyrs**, two transvestite revues are amongst the favourite venues for French tourists to the capital for the quality of their shows. The **Divan du Monde** and the **Elysées-Montmartre** regularly host some of the best Paris club nights and most popular concerts, and together with **La Cigale** on boulevard Rochechouart, and **La Loco** and the **Moulin-Rouge** at the **Place Blanche**, ensure that Montmartre remains one of the principal areas of night life in Paris. The **Follies-Pigalle** nightclub dominates the place Pigalle, and remains a temple of Parisian nightlife.

The area of between the cemetery, where many of the famous former residents lie, and the mairie, is a calmer bourgeois enclave centred on the **rue Caluaincourt** and the **rue Lamarck**, with solid apartments and leafy avenues. Around the mairie is popular with young families, but beyond the atmosphere changes rapidly to become much more **populaire**. However with plenty of cheap property and good transport links across the city, these areas are popular choices for first-time buyers.

There is a distinct division between 'the dark side of the hill' – the poor northern areas beyond the cemetery; from **Marx Dormoy** to the péripherique and **La Chapelle**; and the immigrant quartiers of the **Goutte d'Or, Barbés, and Château-Rouge** – and the 'designer darlings' playground of Abbesses, where the worst you can really expect is to be jostled by an inattentive advertising executive or musician glued to their mobile phone. The place Pigalle has been largely renovated, and the renovation of the frantic boulevard de Clichy has begun. Plans are also advancing for a renovation of the quartier around **Barbés**, best known for the giant Tati store where you can buy a wedding dress for €75. In many respects, this latter project represents both the hopes and the fears of the local population.

Local activists fear that with current urban renewal projects, the 18th will gradually lose its working-class mixed nationality roots to become simply a fashion crowd playground, a victim of its own success. Given the state of the Château-Rouge and La Chapelle quartiers it is hard to imagine that this will happen. If it does it will indeed be sad, because for all its faults the joy of the 18th is its ability to absorb everyone into its cosmopolitan village-like system, based on that original village refuge high on a hill overlooking Paris.

THE 19TH ARRONDISSEMENT

The squalid conjunction of the 10th, 18th and 19th arrondissements behind the Gares du Nord and de l'Est along boulevard de la Chappelle has for a long time between one of the eyesores of Paris. But in the same way that urbanists and local communities and their politicians have planned to change these areas in the 10th and 18th, so their counterparts in the 19th arrondissement are now following suit. In many ways, the 19th is a mirror-image of the 18th in almost a butterfly pattern. The area where the 18th ends and the 19th begins forms the central body, a ghetto of essentially North African immigrant poverty. The centre of the 19th is also to be found around a chic and charming hill-village, with less animation but recompensed by a beautiful park, the **Buttes-Chaumont**. Once again like the 18th, the 19th is fringed beyond its Butte by further poorer areas, with a spectacular preponderance of high-rise cités in the 19th, which has already had more than one bite at the urban regeneration with the renovation at **La Villette**.

The Canal St Martin pushes gently north from the 10th, through the 19th with the quaysides neatly cleaned and scrubbed to make pleasant Sunday afternoon strolling territory. But the cafés and shops of the lower section have not spread north, even if the converted loft apartment conversions have begun. The result is that the canal still cuts its way through an urban priority area rather than a renovated quartier, although hope still lingers on that a combination of the cultural mecca of La Villette and the new arrival of major companies on the long grey and ugly avenue de Flandres will kick-start a Bobo revolution. But given that it is ten years since the grand opening of La Villette, and still nothing has happened, it would seem that the area is in line for a long wait although the local mayor plans to liven up the quaysides à la Canal St Martin.

La Villette itself is a definite success. Arriving by métro gives you the worst impression possible – you feel like you are arriving in a underground car park. But save your judgements until you reach the other side of the **Cité des Sciences et l'Industrie**, with the giant **Géode** and its non-stop Zen music, fountains and lawns. Inside the Cité, a succession of exhibitions illustrate scientific themes in English and French, from biology to electricity. Outside, vast lawns and a number of playgrounds make this a popular area for young families. Of note is the fact that is one of the rare areas in Paris where the French suspend their belief that walking or sitting on grass will either kill you, or you will kill it. Walkways allow you to follow the canal and to view the scenes below. Across the canal is the **Cité de la Musique**, and the Grande Halle exhibition centre. Music festivals and the summer open-air cinema complete the official culture complex, whilst the aptly named **Cabaret Sauvage** nearby is a popular alternative nightclub venue.

Beyond the bassin de la Villette, behind the old customs house at **Place Stalingrad**, lies the 'other' 19th. When Haussman banished the working classes to the north of Paris as he rebuilt an imperial capital for Napoléon III, the population shifted to live besides the quarries at the **Butte-Chaumont** which provided much of the required building materials in classy downtown Paris. The remnants of the village of **Belleville** can be found not only on the rue de Belleville itself, but much more interestingly in the area from **Botzaris** métro up to the **Place de Rhin et Danube**. Clinging to the side of the hill and with leafy gardens and high walls protecting them, these are now some of the most sought-after addresses in Paris. Better still, they are beside one of the favourite Parisian parks, created by Haussman on the site of the quarries. Skirting around the park are broad boulevards of fine apartments, but even these do not rival the charm of the original villas.

To some extent the 19th arrondissement is a little bit of Parisian history repeating itself: always working class, beyond the main city, and socially-mixed, with surprise benefits compensating for an industrial use and dormitory-town effect. Whilst the nineteenth century workers were compensated with the Buttes-Chaumont park, their twentieth-century successors were given the Parc de la Villette complex. The **cités** accentuate the sense of insecurity, but flip-side of the coin is a sort of 16ème effect around the park – beautiful, ordered and calm but with a lack of real quartier life, although it is undoubtedly better to stay east of the canal and nearer to the park. The suburban sentiment is reinforced by the fact that the area is principally served by a looping métro branch line and three parallel lines cutting through to the city limits. But the 19th does offer a strong mix of styles which makes it as accommodating to single people, couples or families of all styles.

THE 20TH ARRONDISSEMENT

Originally a collection of annexed villages – **Belleville**, **Charonne** and **Ménilmontant** – saturated by urban expansion and expulsions when Haussman remodelled Paris, the area has in recent years been the subject of endless articles proclaiming the arrival of another example of the 'Oberkampf effect'. But no matter how hard the trend-detectors try, they cannot change the reality of this large left-wing area on the east of Paris with the allure of one of the inner suburbs and the geographical accident of being within the péripherique.

Like the 19th, the 20th was the land of the excluded and most significantly of the famous Parisian dead. The arrondissement is dominated by the renowned **Père Lachaise** cemetery, last resting place of everyone from Oscar Wilde to Jim Morrison to Yves Montand, with many earlier names of note such as most of the Napoleonic Prince-Marshals. Wandering around amongst the extravagant tombs with a map beneath the trees is now one of the great Paris sight-seeing tours.

From Belleville to Ménilmontant along the boulevard you will be certain of finding almost any type of food and hearing almost any language other than French. The area has strong Arab and Jewish communities living side by side, and the rue de Belleville is the high street of the local Chinatown. A few bars have opened up for instance in the lower end of the **rue des Panoyeaux**, but generally this livelier side of the 20th is dominated and animated by the immigrant communities. Ironically in this most unparisian part of Paris, that most Parisian of popular amusements the **guingettes** (music halls) were originally found. Amongst the favourite creations of these guingettes was the fictional character of **milord arsouille**, the eccentric nineteenth-century English aristocrat in Paris later immortalised by Bellevilles' most famous local girl, Edith Piaf.

Behind the Père Lachaise cemetery is the area that 'trendologues' like to pin their hopes on for an urban revival. A handful of charming streets surrounding the medieval village church of St Germain de Charonne, its cemetery, and the upper end of the **rue St Blaise** (avoid the lower part beyond Place des Grés) are rare remainders of the villages that once formed this part of Paris. A few yards away stands what was the end of a lost line of transport (one thing the 20th sorely lacks), the **Petite Ceinture** which surfaces in odd places around the edge of Paris as overgrown, disused and generally attractive railway lines. The old terminus is now the ultra-trendy **Café de la Fléche d'Or**, but it is an isolated beacon in this part of Paris. Nearby, the exquisite enclave of town houses with gardens at Porte de Bagnolet is known as the 'Paris countryside', recalling the days when this was an aristocratic rural retreat – a long, long time ago!

Elsewhere in the 20th other tiny isolated pockets of interesting buildings have survived, but with the exception of the bourgeois buildings around the **Place Gambetta** or the modern apartment blocks along the rue des Pyrénées, the area is most known for the social-priority tower blocks which cover the area like blisters. Fifteen per cent of the total Parisian housing in this category is to be found in the 20th. The middle-range accommodation to be found bordering the 11th at Nation is not as high quality as in the neighbouring 11th and 12th but it is generally better quality than elsewhere in the 20th except around Gambetta.

You may well find good value for money in terms of property surface area in Paris, but the overall quality of life is definitely lower here than elsewhere. What you will find, however, is large selection of accommodation, and especially more recent buildings, to choose from. Given the hilly landscape (the rue de Ménilmontant is not to be walked *up* by the faint-hearted!), a well-chosen apartment at the right level here can offer you the whole of Paris at your feet even if you might lack all the immediate facilities of what you see before you.

Plans for the future in the 20th include a new swimming pool at Belleville and a stretch of the new Parisian tramway. These are bound to have a positive effect on the area, but the real challenge is to integrate a new breed of Parisian alongside the cité-dwellers who make up the majority of the 20th.

8

Living in the City – La Rive Gauche

The Left Bank of Paris, the **Rive Gauche**, has for more than a century inspired visions of languid intellectuals, artists and students associated with the seats of learning and the residential areas around them. But the Rive Gauche also has Paris's most famous monument, the Eiffel Tower, some of the finest museums, and the heart of government with the **Assemblée Nationale** and the **Sénat**. For the everyday Parisian, it is six of the arrondissements of Paris including the largest populations, ranging from the immigrant communities of the 13th to the fashion victims of St Germain, to the respectable bourgeoisie of the 15th.

THE 5TH ARRONDISSEMENT

In many respects the 5th arrondissement is the political and historical alpha and omega of Paris. The arrondissement contains two of the most important Roman sites of the ancient settlement of Lutèce, the Roman baths beneath the **Hôtel de Cluny** at the crossroads of the boulevards St Germain and St Michel, and the amphitheatre (**arènes**), one of the largest known structures of this kind, built in the 1st century AD and abandoned after the first destruction of Lutèce at the end of the 3rd century. When the population withdrew to the Île de la Cité and the city spread on the northern bank, the students of the medieval University of Paris, **La Sorbonne**, moved in and the 5th acquired its nickname as the **Quartier Latin**, due to the fact that university teaching was in Latin. Today about 100,000 students invade the 5th each day.

Ever since the Middle Ages, the 5th has been the heart of French learning, from the exclusive and sought-after **Lycée Henri IV** and **Lycée Louis le Grand**, to the **Sorbonne**, to the specialised faculties and business schools such as the famous **Ecole Polytéchnique**, all of which have formed generations of France's leaders. The huge complex at **Jussieu**, has swelled the student numbers in recent years. Other parts of the decentralised Paris University are also to be found at **Censier-Daubenton**.

As if to confirm that this is where great Frenchmen are made, the great dome of the **Panthéon** on the **Montagne St Génevieve** is the state mausoleum for those deemed good and great by the French state. Originally planned by

Louis XV to rival St Peter's in Rome, the interior is large and lifeless. Of much greater beauty and interest is the tiny church next door **St Etienne du Mont**, where the seventh-century monarchs of France, the Merovingians, are heaped one upon another beneath the shrine of one of Paris's patrons St Genevieve, in a perfect Renaissance church which holds the remains of Pascale and Descartes. The exquisite **St Séverin** church with its open cloister is a popular concert venue in the Latin Quarter, whilst the restored **Val de Grâce** church is stunning example of seventeenth-century Baroque.

Appropriately, the eastern edge of the 5th is dominated in contrast by the great Parisian monuments to Islam, with the **Mosquée de Paris** and the **Institute du Monde Arab**. The former is a real oasis of Arab elegance, and the latter is major cultural and exhibition centre of international importance. Behind the mosque, science and religion rub shoulders with the **Jardin des Plantes** (botanical gardens), offering a variety of exhibition areas, gardens, giant greenhouses, and even a miniature zoo.

The southern edge of the 5th is luxurious calm slipping into the 14th and 13th arrondissements, and is most known for the **Closerie des Lilas** restaurant beloved of the 'lost generation' of Montparnasse literati and present-day politicians. Excitable youth meanwhile diverts itself in the **quartier Contrescarpe** around the **rue Mouffetard** and the **rue Cardinal Lemoine**; or in the cheap Greek restaurants of the Latin Quarter near the Seine; or at the cinemas of the noisy **Place St Michel**.

As if all of this were not enough to make people talk about the 5th, it acquired another notoriety in the 1990s as 'Tiberiland', the fiefdom of the former Mayor of Paris, Jean Tiberi. The quality of life in the 5th arrondissement is now reckoned to be amongst the highest in Paris, as well it should be: in 1999 the average spend per Parisian across Paris was €116, whilst in the 5th it amounted to €420. Nonetheless, with so many churches, schools and a large botanical garden, you might be wondering if there is anywhere to live in this part of Paris. The answer is that it contains some of the most enchanting hidden corners of the capital, but naturally the prices are high. Add to the charm of the area its superb situation on the banks of the Seine at the centre of the city and its generous amenities, and you will understand the attractions of the 5th.

Whilst the Latin Quarter and quartier Contrescarpe offer the charm of hilly streets with a mix of medieval, baroque and rococo buildings, the lower part of the 5th near Val de Grâce, the **Jardin du Luxembourg** and the Jardin des Plantes probably offers the more pleasant lifestyle away from the carousing of students and tourists. However, the most sought addresses are those in the catchment areas of the lycées Louis le Grand and Henri IV beside the Panthéon. Many parents are even willing to rent a small studio in this area in order to be able to join the geographical allocation list for these schools. Yet no matter where you live in the 5th if you make your home here, you will know that you are living in one of the best neighbourhoods in Paris. The *bon-viveur* and bookish President François Mitterrand preferred his apartment here to the Elysée Palace: so if an apartment in the 5th is better than the Presidential Palace, what more is there to say?

THE 6TH ARRONDISSEMENT

The fields (**près**) to the west of the Latin Quarter were turned over to the monks who built Paris's first Christian church on the site of a Roman temple as the centrepiece of a great abbey. Ironically the old village of **St Germain des Près** which grew up in the shadow of the abbey is now the most expensive areas of Paris and the new 'must have' address for fashion houses in an area founded on poverty and sackcloth.

Stretching from the river bank opposite the Louvre to Montparnasse and bordered by the 5th and 7th arrondissements, the 6th is the most sought-after area of Paris, 'the jewel in the Parisian crown'. Amongst current residents are former Prime Minister Lionel Jospin and the current Mayor of Paris Bertrand Delanoë, and a large number of British buyers have also chosen the 6th. Wandering through its streets it is not hard to see why. It has the highest number of cinemas, bookshops and theatres in Paris, some of the best shops, the most famous cafés, bars, and art galleries, and one of the greatest parks. In addition, it has two excellent markets, one of which contains a public swimming pool in the basement. Finally, it contains great Parisian educational institutions, from the Fine Arts school (**Ecole des Beaux-Arts**) to the privately-funded Catholic University (**Institute Catholique**) or the **Alliance Française** language school, all within an enchanting network of medieval streets with beautifully-preserved buildings dating back several centuries.

The best approach to the 6th is from the pedestrian **Pont des Arts** with its wonderful view on to the **Institut de France** where the French language is defined. Once across the bridge, slip through one of the side-passages of the Institut, and you will find yourself in a garden at the top of the **rue de Seine**, an exquisite street of art galleries and cafés where the nearby art students from the Beaux-Art mingle with the gallery owners. During the day the place to be seen is at **La Palette** with its Art Nouveau interior, and the terrace is also packed on warm evenings. Night-owls should turn the corner into **rue Mazarine** to Conran's Paris restaurant-lounge bar in a former music-hall, **L'Alcazar**, where the **tout-Paris** comes to dine, be hip an'cool, and to view and be viewed, before descending to the trendy cellar nightclub, **Le Wagg**.

The **rue de Buci** which intersects with the rue de Seine is a lively market street supplying neighbourhood needs before being transformed into the narrow but charming rue **St André des Arts**, with its cinemas and shops leading up to the Place St Michel and the charming passage cutting through to the cinema and student sprawl of **Place de l'Odéon**, and the great national theatre just behind. If you continue through the tiny streets parallel to **rue Jacob**, you will arrive at the place St Germain des Près, with the abbey church and the now dominant fashion houses. Next to the church you will also find the institutions of the St Germain set, the Cafés **Flore** and **Deux Magots**, and the **Brasserie Lipp** opposite.

Tucked behind the boulevard the great church of **St Sulpice** dominates its own quartier of bookshops, designers and restaurants leading up to Mabillon métro. This lively area has a strong student population, who gravitate towards the great Jardin du Luxembourg, which contains the French upper parliamentary house the Sénat, and the museum attached to it. This was the former palace of Marie de Medici, who, when she was not massacring Protestants or consulting her astrologers to decide who to poison next, built herself a magnificent palace and art collection. The gardens are one of the traditional favoured haunts of Parisians, providing a lung to this overcrowded corner of Paris, with fountains, tennis courts and a children's puppet theatre at the quieter end of the park leading to the Paris observatory.

To the west of the park lies a quieter, more liveable, and very attractive area. To explore it at its best, take the **rue du Cherche Midi** from the **place de la Croix-Rouge** and keep walking. This street is pure St Germain, a mix of clothes and interior designers, trendy little cafés further on, with innovative little twists in every shop window. By now you are pushing towards Montparnasse, an area always preferred by the English-language communities. It is therefore no surprise to find the excellent **Children's English Learning Centre** in **rue de Fleurus**, handily situated next door to the Alliance Française and its language courses.

Cutting across this whole sector, from ultra-chic **Sèvres-Babylone** to more relaxed Montparnasse is the **boulevard Raspail**, a funky highway of designers for humans and houses, and home to an ecological market at odds with the roar of the traffic. As elsewhere in Paris, traffic is one of the major problems of the 6th, with major arteries carving their way through medieval streets which clog with badly-parked cars. But the other major problems of the 6th are both symbolic and symptomatic. For even though the area is bursting with good reasons to live there, the urban drift is away from the 6th with its staggering house prices.

The young people who live there are often single or childless couples and young families are less common than elsewhere on the Left Bank. Ironically the only major crisis the 6th has faced in recent years has ironically been linked to shopping. On the one hand, everyone wails about the invasion of the fashion houses stealing the soul of St Germain. But the 6th does desperately lack practical day-to-day commerce, and is dependent upon neighbouring arrondissements for everyday needs. The fact that you cannot live on designer shopping alone perhaps explains why the 6th is crying out for families yet continues to draw singles or childless couples, as the 6th continues to be a victim of its own fashionable success.

THE 7TH ARRONDISSEMENT

The last of the Poor Little Rich arrondissements nestling on the left bank of the Seine, the 7th is the most aristocratic arrondissement in Paris. Part of this allure comes from the architectural style of the lush avenues built for and still inhabited by the French aristocracy, and part comes from the enormous concentration of power in the quartier, with the Assemblée Nationale and the embassies and government ministries making this the French Westminster and Belgravia rolled into one. But even if the outward appearance is one of ordered calm, the 7th remains an area of paradox. It is also an area which has drawn many British buyers.

On the one hand, this right-wing bastion of family values has unsurprisingly the highest number of **familles nombreuses** (three or more children) in Paris. Yet the arrondissement also has the highest level of urban drift, having lost 9.5% of its population from 1989–99. On the other hand, it occasionally has the appearance of a **quartier populaire** when the concerts, exhibitions and rallies on the **Champ de Mars** at the **Eiffel Tower** are taken into consideration, and the fine weather transforms the lawns in front of **Les Invalides** into an impromptu park and sports ground. Nonetheless it remains one of the most exclusive areas of Paris, reputed for not just being calm but actually stone-cold dead in certain areas dominated by official buildings. Those same lawns which give the 7th its popular veneer are part of a large complex of gardens which make it the most verdant corner of Paris, but probably 60% at least of the gardens are behind high walls in private hands, including those of the church. Finally those same embassies and ministries which are so well guarded by van loads of police that you always feel safe in the 7th are also the targets of demonstrations and marches. So the silver-lined 7th is not without some clouds to spoil the view occasionally.

The real heart of the 7th is the **Gros Cailou** district between the **avenues Bousquet** and **de la Motte-Picquet** and the **rue St Dominique** up to **Invalides**, with the cheerful market street on **rue Cler** where ladies who lunch buy provisions for their friends and families. This is the one area which breaks out of the general 7th mould to demonstrate signs of individuality and local colour, and is an area popular with English-speaking expatriates, many of whom wander down from the **American Church** and community centre on the **quai d'Orsay**. This area is generally the cheaper part of the 7th, and is a real joy to shop or live in; but it does have a distinctly different feel to the areas all around.

Compared to this little oasis, the other parts of the 7th keep themselves in splendid and somewhat ponderous isolation from the rest of Paris. To the west, the 3,000 residents over-looking the Champ de Mars need not be pitied too much for their ringside views of the best concerts and the annual fireworks displays for Bastille Day. They probably are not there, and are more likely to be lounging in a holiday villa on the French coast. The avenues on either side of the Champ de Mars represent the height of exclusive luxury. The **Ecole Militaire** provides a natural dam at the end of the Champ, with UNESCO directly behind, creating an area around **avenue de Breteuil** where you could hear a pin drop.

Les Invalides, founded by Louis XIV as a home for his veterans, today houses the national army museum as well as Napoléon's tomb beneath the golden cupola. It remains an extremely popular tourist site, whilst the lawns in front explode with activity in summer as Parisians stretch out in the sun, play football or softball, and the area takes on a festive feel to match the weather. On the **rue Constantine** overlooking the lawns you will find the **British and Canadian cultural institutes**, which together with the American Church nearby make the 7th a likely venue to meet other English-speakers.

Beyond Les Invalides lies the Foreign Affairs Ministry on the quai d'Orsay, then the residence of the Président of the **Assemblée Nationale** (the Speaker), and then the Assemblée itself. This eastern flank of the 7th, with the concentration of ministries and the Prime Minister's residence at the **Hôtel Matignon**, is the Westminster of Paris, and those embassies and ambassadors who are not to be found near to the President in the 8th will be found here in the magnificent 18th century mansions of the **rue de Grenelle**. Each year in September the **Journées du Patrimoine** allows visitors to cross these hallowed thresholds free of charge for a weekend, but queues for the finest palaces are very long.

On the river bank above, the **Musée d'Orsay** is one of Paris's finest museums. Housed in a converted railway station, it contains a stunning collection of Impressionist art, and hosts major exhibitions. The **Quai Voltaire** (where Rudolf Nureyev lived and died) starts to have some of the allure of the neighbouring 6th, which continues along the rue des Saints-Pères leading down to the **rue du Bac** and the boulevard Raspail.

The great Parisian department store **Le Bon Marché** dominates the eastern edge of the 7th, with the former **Hôpital Laënnec** under redevelopment just behind it. Beside the Bon Marché and its **Grande Epicérie** (equivalent to Harrod's food hall in London) sits the popular shrine of the Miraculous Medal, which also explains the heavy concentration of convents and religious orders in this corner of Paris. Pushing north from Le Bon Marché you are in the heart of St Germain. The tiny **square Recamier** with its luxury apartments overhanging the square and the neighbouring **Espace Electra**, home to the EDF's art foundation in a beautifully converted power station perhaps best mark the point at which the verdant 7th mingles effortlessly into the innovative 6th arrondissement.

Like the neighbouring 6th arrondissement, the 7th is confronted with the urban drift away from the area, with house prices in this area providing a natural filter to those who can afford to join the happy few. The lack of cinemas and bars in the area is a serious handicap to drawing a younger population to the 7th, although both the Gros Cailou and St Germain areas represent the human face of the 7th. The avenue de Breteuil is certainly not for people living on their own, or for anybody who does not understand or aspire to the same ideals (and salaries) as other local residents. The real danger of the 7th is the same ivory-tower effect which overcame the first aristocratic inhabitants, who were so overwhelmed with their walled-in splendour and beauty that they became cut off from reality. The local Socialist challenger for the 2001 elections described the 7th as, 'a museum-piece quartier without life', whilst *L'Express* said in its city survey in January 2001, 'It's not the end of the earth, but it is elsewhere'.

THE 13TH ARRONDISSEMENT

Covering a large expanse of south-east Paris from the Seine behind Notre-Dame to the city limits, the 13th is the fifth largest arrondissement in terms of population (171,000 people in 1999), the same size as the city of Lille. Originally an area of rural cultivation on the edge of the city centred on the **Butte aux Cailles**, the 13th was scarred for decades by the traces of the industries which for centuries had used it as both a convenient base and a dumping-ground. By the late 20th century, the river banks were home to derelict warehouses alongside the open railway tracks of the **Gare d'Austerlitz**, and the 13th was chiefly known for the jungle of concrete towers built in the 1970s to house the influx of Chinese immigrants, amongst others.

However, these industrial and urban scars are now beginning to heal, and new life is returning to an area dominated by one of the largest projects of urban reconstruction in Paris. The ZAC (zone d'aménagement concentré), along the river bank, due for completion in 2006, has covered the railway tracks with a 26 hectare concrete roof, 100m wide and 2.6km long. The new **Bibliothèque Nationale François Mitterrand** on the river bank is the centrepiece of this zone of offices, social priority and private housing, cultural centres including the 14-screen MK2 **Cité de l'Image** (now one of the trendiest in Paris), the new Paris-VII university for 20,000 students designed by the world-renowned French architect Christian de Potzamparc, and a floating swimming pool at the foot of the Bibliothèque Nationale as the final stage.

A crucial factor in the opening up of this part of Paris is the extension of the new **métro ligne 14** via the Bibliotheque to Tolbiac, and a link to the RER ligne C. Previously, the 13th appeared to be little more than a dormitory town for Paris. In 2001, one local politician said that many people choose to live in the 13th because, 'It's nearby'; the sub-text being that it is near to everywhere you would rather be, and the centre of nothing in particular. In the fight to rejuvenate the area, the 13th has gambled on innovation rather than restoration, mixing offices, luxury and social housing, students, intellectuals and artists to transform the 13th into a place to go to, rather than to come from.

So far all the signs are that the gamble is paying off in the northern district, with the ligne 14 creating a cross-river cultural axis with the new Bercy district in the 12th arrondissement. The **rue Louise Weiss** is one of the foremost centres of the contemporary art scene in Paris, and the nightclubs on the **guingettes** (the boats or **péniches** moored in front of the Bibliotheque) are amongst the trendiest in Paris, and the new apartments beside the Bibliotheque are considered very desirable residences. In 2002–2003, property prices increased in the 13th by an estimated 50% in this area.

Further to the west, the renowned intellectual newspaper *Le Monde* has built its new offices on the boulevard Auguste-Blanqui a few minutes from the picturesque **Butte aux Cailles** district, which demonstrates the contrasts of the 13th. Small ivy-covered houses with gardens in narrow twisting streets, create a small oasis of calm cheek-by-jowl with looming concrete towers which were quick to build but are now almost impossible to destroy without flattening the whole neighbourhood. Close by, the charmless **Place d'Italie**, home to the wildly popular rollerblade rallies, the mairie, and bordering on the verdant **Gobelins** district, acts as a melting pot for this multifaceted arrondissement.

The north-west sector of the arrondissement is more like the 5th than the 13th, notably between the **avenue des Gobelins**, and **boulevards Auguste-Blanqui** and **Port-Royal**, another area apparently proving popular with British buyers. The Gobelins tapestry factory is the major museum in the arrondissement, housed in a seventeenth-century complex. A stroll behind the factory brings you to the architectural oddity of the first high-rise tower in the 13th now ageing badly, and a large park at the **square René Le Gall**. Beyond the park lies **rue Corvisart**, and the sought-after town houses and properties which characterise the old 13th. On the eastern end of **boulevard Arago**, towards Gobelins métro, you start to sink into the luxurious 5th. In the direction of the river, at the end of the boulevard St Marcel, stands the **Hôpital Pitié-Salpêtrière**, where the Princess of Wales died. This vast 17th century charity hostel, with its baroque chapel and arcaded courtyards, is surrounded by much-admired gardens which are open to all.

Nothing could prevent a starker contrast to the gentle charm of this quartier than the 13th's other great claim to fame, '**Chinatown**', home to about 30,000 Asian immigrant families settled in the areas around **avenue de**

Choisy. The Chinese New Year Festival here with dancing dragons and parades draws thousands of people each year. The proliferation of restaurants, junk shops, wholesalers and supermarkets, reminiscent of the Chinatowns in London and New York, enliven the seemingly endless avenues which lead to the poorer, cheaper, southern sector bordering the troubled suburbs of **Ivry, Kremlin-Bicêtre** and **Villejuif** beyond the péripherique. The challenge now will be to integrate the industrial and social landscape of these poorer quartiers into the rejuvenation that the chic and happening northern districts are already experiencing.

THE 14TH ARRONDISSEMENT

Fans of the 14th, stretching from Montparnasse to the southern périphérique, often say that it is one of the best kept secrets in Paris, 'the symbol of the art of discretion' (*L'Express*, January 2001).

For Americans in Paris, the 14th is associated with the northern Montparnasse quartier and its mythical mix of writers and painters who moved down from Montmartre in the 1920s. Like any self-respecting artist's quarter, the local Montparnasse Cemetery has its fair share of writers and performers, from Jean-Paul Sartre and his muse Simone de Beauvoir, to the modern French singer-songwriter Serge Gainsbourg, whose English widow Jane Birkin is one of France's favourite 'English Roses'. The ateliers (workshops) of these artists on **boulevard Edgar Quinet** now provide luxury housing in an area which is enjoying a new lease of life as a revived centre for Paris nightlife. The restored nightclub at **La Coupole**, and the desperately trendy nightclubs the **Redlight** and **Amnesia** side by side behind the Montparnasse station, have all brought new life to a quartier that felt tired and jaded. But the Montparnasse of the artists is only one small corner of the 14th, and most of the real artists left a long time ago, even if the **fêtards** (party-goers) are now going strong once again.

Overall, the 14th is now a heavily residential district, even if a few theatres and bars keep the old flame burning, and residential calm now reigns in the area. In the north of the arrondissement, bordering on the 5th lies the Paris **Observatory** founded in the seventeenth century. In the **rue Cassini** directly in front of the Observatory, stand a row of excellent Art Nouveau artists' studios from the beginning of the twentieth century. On the Boulevard St Jacques can be found one of the original eighteenth-century palaces which was moved stone by stone from the former rural playground on the Champs-Elysées, and which is home to the **Société des Gens de Lettres et Théâtre**, a distinguished writers and actors club. On the opposite side of the road is part of one of the 14th's many hospitals; and on the broad sweeping boulevard Arago where artists used to have their ateliers, the reason for the cheap property on this otherwise attractive boulevard becomes clear: a club with a very strict door policy, the **Prison de La Santé**, with its 'celebrity' cells for France's corrupt politicians. Here in a geographical microcosm then, you have the 14th – the learned, the talented, the medics, the famous and the infamous, side by side in calm, discreet surroundings.

Population-wise, the 14th traditionally draws young people starting out in their professional life, without the means to live in more central Paris, and attracted by the security and calm of the area and the more reasonable property prices (although in 2003 price rises were higher in the 14th than the neighbouring 15th). There is certainly no shortage of housing in this area, and perhaps even too much of the same sort of apartments: drab high-rise blocks of municipally-owned social priority housing (**cités**) which reflect the working-class origins of the 14th. The **rue Vercingétorix** with its open spaces is only the most recent attempt at this old formula, leading down from the **Place de la Catalogne** with its expensive modern apartments for the middle and upper classes who generally live in the northern half of the arrondissement near to the best transport connections. Public transport does go out to the further reaches of the 14th, but it is more sparingly distributed along the interior boulevards and on the two métro lines and one RER line piercing the residential mass. What then makes for the best-kept secret in Paris?

Before the restructuring of the Paris hospital sector began in the mid-1990s, the 14th was most well-known for its seven hospitals, six of which are still operational including the psychiatric **hôpital St-Anne** (be careful if anybody suggests that you should try a stay there – it is common parlance for suggesting that you must be mad). Now that Broussais has been closed down in the already saturated social-priority housing area beyond **Plaisance**, new uses have to be found for the vast site which will inevitably include housing. Further restructuring is bound to take place in years to come, but the 14th will probably always maintain its record of the most number of hospital beds per resident. Generally the southern half of the 14th, nearer to péripherique, is where the cheaper property is to be found.

The 14th arrondissement is also one of the first areas to benefit from the new Paris tramway. This controversial initiative means that the 14th is an experimental area where Paris and the inner suburbs start to merge effortlessly into each other, replacing the physical barrier of the Paris ring road. For the time being the 14th has wisely built itself an isolating barrier against the périphérique to the south, with a string of parks and sports stadiums between the boulevards Brune and Jourdan. The **Cité Universitaire** was founded in the 1920s to be a sort of university-level League of Nations, with each country building and maintaining their own house for post-graduates from their country to study together in Paris. The mock-Tudor 'city within the city', has its own sports grounds, theatre, church and hospital. The **Parc Montsouris** opposite is a favourite with Parisians, offering everything parks should in the popular imagination – greenery, a lake, a puppet theatre, and a restaurant. The streets around the park have fine apartments looking over the park, and the **avenue René Coty** provides a quick link back to the real hub of the 14th, the place **Denfert-Rochereau**.

Denfert-Rochereau with its RER station and the Orlybus for Paris's southern airport leads out in all directions, to the commercial heart of the 14th on **avenue du Général**

Leclerc and the cinemas at **Alésia**; to the market street **rue Daguerre** with its collection of renovated trendy cafés nearest to Denfert-Rochereau and a good selection of apartments above the shops and stalls below, running all the way to avenue de Maine; and is also the entrance to the 14th's very own and very particular underground system, the **catacombs** of Paris. Emerging from the catacombs brings you out opposite the kind of accommodation that many people associate with the 14th. The **Passage Montbrun**, or elsewhere the villa Alésia, contain small houses and collections of artists studios which have been converted into loft apartments. Unfortunately, these appear to be scarcer than you may hope for. But perhaps that is the real lesson of the 14th, which makes it a well-kept secret and the height of the art of discretion; that as throughout Paris, the beauty often lies within, beyond the street doors in inner courtyards and inner calm.

THE 15TH ARRONDISSEMENT

Forming a neat south-western corner for Paris from the Eiffel Tower to the périphérique and the **Portes de Sevres** and **Versailles**, this solidly residential monotone middle-class area of Paris in some respects feels like an anchor for Paris. The arrondissement with the highest population (230,000) but a dearth of cultural venues and transport for such a large area is a bastion of family values, acting as a dam to the suburban drifters and keeping Paris's feet on the ground in the face of the trendier individualist quartiers to the east. The arrondissement provides a perfect synthesis between the 7th next door which hogs the local culture, the ultra-chic 16th across the river, and the well-to-do suburbs to the west.

It is difficult to identify real quartiers in the 15th, which has no real history or former villages but instead represents the urban expansion of Paris starting in the 1820s with the 'new' church of **St Jean-Baptiste de Grenelle**. On the eastern borders, the *haute-bourgeoisie*, live comfortably between the **avenue de Suffren** with its access onto the Champ de Mars and the **boulevards de Grenelle** and **Garibaldi** with its métro viaduct forming a natural barrier.

As might be expected from an area of planned dense housing, the 15th is peppered with small squares with public gardens and playgrounds, and municipal benefactors endowed these with bandstands and open air stages such as the **Place Dupleix**, the **Place de Commerce** or the **Square St Lambert**. Unfortunately, these bandstands seem to stand well preserved but forlorn in the parks where the children still play. But perhaps they could be the key to breathing a little life and conviviality. For despite being home to **UNESCO** the 15th is almost devoid of cultural life, and is renowned for being an area which seems to go to bed with a cup of cocoa at 9 o'clock each night.

Ironically for an area that slumbers culturally, two of the best parks in the area which offer a cultural world of their own have resulted from highly original conversions of the 15th's industrial past. At the entrance to the **Parc Georges Brassens** named after a former local resident and renowned French crooner, on the southern city limits, two smiling copper cows (showing no obvious signs of madness) guard the entrance to the site of the former Paris abattoirs. The park is bordered by a school, and this park has areas of cultivation especially reserved for local school children. Along the **rue Brançion** side of the park in the former sheds reserved for condemned horses is now held every weekend the Paris book market for new and second-hand books. A small theatre in the park completes the culture complex in the shadow of the vast looming cités on the outer boulevards.

In the far north of the 15th on the banks of the Seine lies the converted Citroën factory site now known as the **Parc André Citroën**. Surrounded by the state-owned TV stations **France 2** and **FR3** on one side and the privately-owned cable TV channel **Canal +** on the other, the futuristic but beautiful centrepiece park feels more like a botanical garden than a place to relax. Eight giant greenhouses (including one dedicated to the vegetation of Australasia) and colour-coded gardens with nature canalised by concrete and interspersed by controlled waterfalls and fountains give an impression of being in a latter-day Versailles. With so much creativity and wealth concentrated in one corner of the arrondissement, you might expect to find a lively neighbourhood nearby. Instead the **rue Balard** which runs beside the park is deathly quiet. Only the highly popular sports complex at **Aquaboulevard** just beyond gives any indication of human life in this area.

On the river bank between this park and the Eiffel Tower is the quartier **Charles Michels**, a dull jungle of modern apartment blocks. Just behind lies the more animated and pleasant area centred on the **rue de Commerce**, a busy shopping street with a clutch of cafés and bars, most notably the three-storey **Café de Commerce**. This pleasant and lively stretch, feeding off the **avenue de la Motte-Picquet**, is one of the most pleasant corners of the 15th where locals appear to 'come up for air' out of the residential calm. Around the métro **Convention** a similar but lesser effect can also be seen. Interestingly an estimated 20% of buyers in this northern more expensive sector of the 15th (from **rue de la Convention** to **boulevard de Grenelle**) are estimated to be British (*Le Point*, 14 November 2003). The cheaper property once again lies to the south, as in the 14th.

In the eastern corner nearest Montparnasse, not even the proximity of the great train station and Paris's most obvious architectural error the **Tour Montparnasse**, seems to break the monotony of never-ending streets of apartments. The area around **Pasteur** is best known for the Institut Pasteur, a world-renowned medical research institute in the forefront of world breakthroughs. Just nearby the **Hôpital Necker** is France's principal paediatric hospital. Until recently the 15th was as well endowed as the 14th with hospitals, but the restructuring of the Paris hospitals is threatening a number of closures including the Hôpital St Michel. **Boucicault** has already fallen to the financial scalpel, and now the site is the subject of intense speculation. Ironically the hospitals have followed the urban tide to a new super-hospital on the western extremities, the **Hôpital Européen Georges Pompidou**.

The advantage of the 15th is its solid respectability. Apartments abound, and the standard is always at least fair if not very high. There are enough local transport links and shops scattered across the arrondissement to survive comfortably, but nothing more than that. But there are problems associated with the 15th. On the one hand it is a victim of its own success. As the bastion of family life, and home to 10% of Parisians, the number of young children is leading to problems in crèches and schools. The other problem is that it is really rather bland. Criss-crossed by never-ending streets such as the **rue de la Convention** or the **rue de Vaugirard** (Paris's longest street) and devoid of any effort at cultural life, it is a perfect example of the impact of local politicians in shaping the face of the capital. However, given the enduring popularity of the arrondissement, it is perhaps not surprising that the local mayor, supported by his electors, appears to have hung a sign on the 15th arrondissement which reads, 'Do not disturb'.

(9)

Living in the Suburbs

Parisian 'attitude' comes in many forms. City dwellers within the **périphérique** and the twenty arrondissements traditionally rejoice in cursing **banlieusards** (suburban dwellers) for bad driving in the city or overcrowding at favourite nightclubs or restaurants. In so doing, they neatly overlook the fact that some of greater Paris's best addresses are to be found cheek-by-jowl with some of Paris's worst addresses.

Soaring house prices, both for rental and purchase in Paris, have created a new generation of urban drifters. Many of those who once cursed the banlieusards now swell their numbers. More to the point, whilst the new suburban dwellers of the **proches banlieues** are not rich enough to live in Paris, their purchasing power is pushing the poorer sectors of the population further afield into the **grands banlieues**.

One of the greatest physical difficulties Paris faces is breaking down the barrier it constructed in the 1960s and early 1970s with the construction of the **périphérique**. Urban planners built a modern wall around the city to keep out the immigrants who had been allowed in to France to fill the low-calibre low-paid work which the French did not want. Since nobody wants to live next to Europe's busiest ring road especially when it is open air, this was also the obvious place to build high-rise towers to accommodate France's immigrant communities from the former African colonies. Two necessary but undesirable rings were thus placed one upon another, and today 985,000 people live within 800m of the ring road around Paris.

Beyond this cordon lies what is known as the **petite couronne**, **proches banlieues** or the little crown, of inner Parisian suburbs (**banlieues**) the départements 92, 93, and 94, followed by the **grand couronne** of the outer and generally chicer suburbs (77, 78, 91 and 95), which represent what many Parisians aspire to: individual houses, greenery, calm and space, within easy striking distance of the heart of the city. The twenty arrondissements of Paris make up the département 75, but the surrounding départements each are known by their own name and number. Some are surprisingly rural in their composition, whilst others are characterised by concrete rather than cows. The difference between communes is quite marked, and even within communes, so take a good look at the area before deciding where to live.

THE WESTERN SUBURBS

Département 92 – Hauts de Seine

Curling around the western edge of Paris, the département des Hauts de Seine (literally the Upper Seine) has long been one of the most desirable parts of the Paris region. The greatest advantage of the Hauts de Seine is its proximity to Paris, La Défense, and a good transport system, whilst maintaining the advantages of calm, space, individual houses and verdant woods. It is also one of the two départements which has traditionally drawn strong English-speaking communities attracted by the high-quality lifestyle, the business opportunities, and easy access to the American and British schools.

	Average price m^2 beginning 2003 (*Le Point* May 03) €	Average price m^2 end 2003 (*Challenges* and *Nouvel Observateur,* March 04) €	Estimated real price increase in 2003 for good quality apartments (*Nouvel Observateur,* March 03)
Asnières sur Seine	2,091	2,270	18.9%
Boulogne-Billancourt	3,218	3,412	13.6%
Colombes	1,811	1,856	NA
Courbevoie	2,556	2,717	12.8%
Levallois-Perret	3,322	3,494	14.4%
Meudon	2,680	2,759	5.7%
Montrouge	2,356	2,562	17.4%
Nanterre	2,016	2,044	NA
Neuilly-sur-Seine	4,407	4,666	11.6%
Rueil-Malmaison	2,682	2,785	12.1%
St Cloud	3,090	3,270	11.4%
Suresnes	2,556	2,814	15.2%

Figure 9. Hauts de Seine, département 92, increases for apartments.

Amongst the most sought-after areas are those which slip effortlessly into the Parisian city landscape beside the river and the Bois de Boulogne. **Neuilly sur Seine** (not to be confused with Neuilly-Plaisance in the east) is one of *the* Parisian addresses. Served by the métro line, a few minutes from the Arc de Triomphe in one direction and the business district of La Défense in the other, Neuilly exudes luxury living at every street corner. A mix of ancient and modern apartments and houses are home to some of the cream of French society who have spilled over from the 16th next door. Neighbouring **Levallois-Perret** was originally a working-class district, but is now firmly in the upward spiral of gentrification which began quite some time ago. Both suburbs have good transport links, English-speaking hospitals, and rich populations. The living is easy, but definitely more down-beat than life in the city.

The avenue Charles de Gaulle leading up from Paris through Neuilly takes you straight to **La Défense**, the great business centre built on the site of a former defensive fort. A vast array of different towers representing company headquarters built over a vast shopping centre, La Défense only really lives during the daytime and mainly in the week. The shopping centre has, however, proved to be a huge draw, so that Saturdays are also very lively. Apartments are being built all the time to create a local population instead of a commuter population, but it still feels pretty lifeless and sometimes rather sinister after dark. The métro, RER and local SNCF trains all serve La Défense, as does an extensive network of buses.

Neighbouring **Nanterre** is the départemental headquarters. More industrial than its neighbour and definitely not as upbeat, Nanterre is home to a major university. The **Thêatre des Amandiers**, the local theatre, was one of a number of theatres established by President Mitterrand's in the banlieues 'to bring culture to the people'. It offers excellent productions, and occasionally these are in English.

Also beside La Défense, you should check out the towns of **Puteaux** and **Courbevoie** on either side of the business district, and perhaps **Asnières-sur-Seine**. Of the three, Courbevoie is probably the most pleasant, with an extremely attractive selection of houses near to the station off avenue Marceau and rue Barbés, and an ever-increasing selection of new apartments nearer to La Défense itself. Asnières, with its château and world-renowned Pets Cemetery, is a town 'on the up'. You should stick to the river-side areas, as further north and east the quality of life declines.

Puteaux and **Suresnes** offer views across western Paris with a good mix of apartments and houses, and are the 'gateway' to a succession of highly-desirable suburban towns to the west leading out to Versailles. **Rueil-Malmaison**, centred on the château of the Empress Josephine, is another popular choice amongst young families. **St-Cloud** at the end of the métro and also served by the SNCF, is home to the American School of Paris and also one of Paris's chic racecourses. All that remains of the former royal château where Napoléon III held court is the wonderful park overlooking Paris – a mini Bois de Boulogne. **Sèvres** is renowned for its porcelain factory and museum, whilst neighbouring **Ville d'Avray** was home to French politicians and artists who lived by the woods surrounding the lakes. All of these are very sought-after areas, as are the exclusive trio of **Garches**, **Vaucresson** and **Marne-la Coquette**. Like their desirable counterparts across the forests leading to Versailles, the appeal of these communes is the small-town feel, abundant greenery and high-quality housing.

On the other side of the Bois de Boulogne lies **Boulogne-Billancourt**, home to the Renault car company and to the second largest population in the Île de France. Once again, the gentle slip from city to suburb makes this a very sought-after area, even if it lacks a lot of charm. There are plenty of apartments, and the presence of the former Renault factories and headquarters has for years made this commune a kind of fiscal paradise in terms of local taxes, with Renault picking up the brunt of the town's budget. The historic heart of the car works is a large island in the Seine, now disused, and the subject of fierce debate as to its redevelopment. One of France's leading entrepreneurs, François Pinault, intends housing his modern art collection there in a new museum, but there are also plans to build luxury apartments.

The south-western corner of the Hauts-de-Seine across the river from Boulogne is home to two other areas of interest. **Issy-les-Moulineaux** at the end of the métro has been traditionally a workers district and communist stronghold for generations. The area is now experiencing the 'Levallois effect', and upward mobility is evident as young executive families move in. This is the spillover in fact from neighbouring **Meudon**. The lower reaches might not seem attractive, but you are only minutes from the Meudon forest which also houses the major British sporting club, the Standard Athletic Club. Neighbouring **Clamart** appears to be the poor relation in comparison, but it is worth taking a look at for its cheaper prices. Nonetheless, prices here have risen by 40% in the last five years.

Chatenay-Malabry is a quiet and comfortable suburb, best known as the former home to Châteaubriand and now as the centre of drugs-testing for French sport. **Sceaux** is one of the favourite escapes of Parisians. The magnificent gardens rolling down to a grand canal, overlooked by a small nineteenth-century château which houses the Museum of the Île de France, are the centre-piece of bourgeois enclave.

The suburban drift is transforming some of the dowdier 'end of the metro line' towns into sought-after addresses, most notably **Malakoff** and **Montrouge**. Both town centres have been renovated, and a new métro station is due to open in Montrouge in 2007. Prices here have risen by 10% and 20% respectively.

Département 78 – Les Yvelines
Whilst the Hauts de Seine seems to cuddle up to Paris, Les Yvelines offers rural living within commuting distance of Paris, a sort of protecting arm around the capital separating 'them' (the rest of France) and 'us' (the Parisians).

The capital of the département is the royal city of **Versailles**. The historic heart of the town around the great château is full of former ministries, embassies and noble mansions built to serve the court. This is the most sought-after quartier of the town and the liveliest. The Chantiers district may be less sought-after but the house prices are also noticeably different. The château de Versailles still has a cultural life of its own, and concerts are regularly held in the Chapelle-Royale whilst in summer the fountains are activated in *sons et lumières* fêtes reminiscent of the golden age of the Sun King, Louis XIV.

	Average price m^2 beginning 2003 (*Le Point*, May 03) €	Average price m^2 end 2003 (*Challenges* and *Nouvel Observateur*, March 04) €
Chatou	2,353	2,600
Mantes-la-Jolie	1,152	1,226
Marly le Roi	2,211	2,315
St Germain en Laye	2,830	3,033
Versailles	2,893	3,038
Le Vesinet	3,106	3,400
Viroflay	2,563	2,657

Figure 10. Yvelines, département 78, average apartment increases.

Versailles was originally a royal hunting lodge, and the forests of the Yvelines department were littered with other former royal hunting lodges. Many of these have now disappeared, but the park at **Marly-le-Roi** which surrounded one such over-grown hunting lodge is still the principal attraction of this sought-after town. At the other end of forest stands **St Germain-en-Laye** where the exiled Stuart court settled at the end of the seventeenth century. The great château in the town centre is the starting point for a terrace overlooking Paris leading down via restored formal gardens and lawns transformed into a public park by the forest. The town is about 30 minutes from Paris on the RER and, like other former royal towns, has its fair share of fine buildings in the centre. It also has the **International Lycée**, one of the most renowned schools in France catering to foreign residents, with English and American sections amongst others.

On either side of the Forêt de Marly lie the two straggling villages of **L'Etang la Ville** and **St Nom la Bréteche** (also known as St Nom le British!). Both are very popular with the English-speaking communities, but you are definitely lost here without a car.

West of Versailles, you will also fall into very rural territory, beginning with **St Cyr l'Ecole**, the élite military academy. To the south lie **Damperre**, **Chevreuse**, and the sought-after but isolated villages of the **Yvette** valley. If you do choose to look for a home in these areas, you should be wary of isolating yourself too much, especially in the early stages of your move to France. **Rambouillet** in the centre of its own forest, is built around one of the official presidential residences occasionally used for international conferences. Discretion and calm are the key words of this part of the world, although between Chevreuse and Versailles you will find a more industrial area stretching from **Trappes** and the new town of **St Quentin en Yvelines** to **Viroflay** and **Vélizy** (with its large shopping centre) on the département borders.

Between Marly-le-Roi and the département border are the more developed but highly sought-after suburbs of **Louveciennes, La Celle St Cloud** and **Bougival**. Across the river lies **Croissy-sur-Seine**, another Anglophone favourite, with the British School of Paris split between the junior school in Bougival and the senior school in Croissy-sur-Seine. The neighbouring towns of **Chatou, Le Vésinet, Le Pecq**, and **Montesson** complete the 'Golden Triangle' formed by St Germain-en-Laye, Marly-le-Roi and Le Vésinet. All have significant American and British presences.

Beyond the A14 autoroute you will find another extremely popular expatriate community base in **Maisons-Lafitte**, originally centred on the racecourse beside the impressive town centre château, and stretching down to **Le Mesnil le Roi**. Maisons-Lafitte was first colonised by British railway workers constructing the first French railways in the mid-nineteenth century, and a second wave of British immigrants arrived with the development of the stables and races. Maisons-Lafitte and Bougival have their own Cubs and Scouts, Brownies and Guide packs in addition to being near to the British schools, and there are thriving Anglican/Episcopalian churches in Maisons-Lafitte and Versailles.

The rest of the département is a mixture of small country villages and less interesting modern towns displaying clear signs of urban problems. Some of the older towns such as **Poissy** (former home to Pisarro) have attractive medieval centres, but others such as **Mantes-la-Jolie** fail to live up to promising first signs.

By the time that you reach Mantes, only 40 minutes by fast train from central Paris, you are on the doorstep of Normandy, and the grand collegiate church and medieval town centre may seem very appealing. But you should be careful here. Not only are the best areas away from the town centre, once again requiring a car to begin your journey, but the town also is home to one of the most troubled collection of cités around Paris, along with Chanteloup-le-Vignes further down the river. Before you choose where to live in Les Yvelines, you do need to check on where your transportation lines run.

THE NORTHERN SUBURBS

Départements 95 – Val d'Oise, 60 – Oise and 93 – Seine St Denis

There is a stark contrast between the western and northern suburbs of Paris, and both the Val d'Oise and the neighbouring Seine St Denis are the infamous 'bad boys' of the suburban Parisian pack. However, the 'Neuf-Trois' and the 'Neuf-Cinq' as they are known represent in microcosm the best, the worst, and the most challenging aspects of Parisian and French contemporary society which cause alarm. The challenge for politicians and urbanists is to produce good out of the bad crop from where urban ugliness was sown.

The best areas

As the rural sounding départemental name might suggest, the Val d'Oise (95) has been subject to some of the worst effects of reckless urbanisation. Moreover, it suffers from the domination of France's major international airport, **Roissy-Charles-de-Gaulle**. The result is a hard-core of problem areas bordering on the Seine St Denis (93), obscuring some extremely desirable regions in the northern wooded areas of **Montmorency, Taverny and L'Isle Adam**.

	Average price m² beginning 2003 (*Le Point,* May, 03) €	Average price m² end 2003 (*Le Point,* November 03) €	Estimated price increase in 2003 for older apartments (*Le Point,* November 03)	Average price m² apartments end 2003 (*Challenges* and *Nouvel Observateur,* March 04) €
Argenteuil	1,319	1,280	11%	1,286
Enghien les Bains	2,041	2,123	12%	2,166
Garges les Gonesse	864	898	19%	NA
Gonesse	1,323	1,383	11%	NA
L'Isle Adam	1,835	1,940	16%	NA
Montmorency	1,780	NA	31% for houses	1,806
Pontoise	1,292	1,524	25%	1,513
Sarcelles	1,115	968	14%	1,004
Taverny	1,440	1,459	11% for apartments 61% for houses	NA

Figure 11. Val d'Oise, département 95, price increases
for apartments and houses.

These three communes represent 'the acceptable face' of the Val d'Oise, a reverse situation to Neuilly Levallois and Boulogne in département 92 where the city and suburbs merge. For, in the further communes of département 95, the suburbs and the countryside merge effortlessly with the bourgeois calm of the equestrian village of **Chantilly** (60) centred on its great château and racecourse in the forest, and the noble and exclusive **Senlis** (60). You can dream of buying a house in Senlis, but do not count on it unless you marry into one of the local families who have lived there for generations. Chantilly, on the other hand, has long British links once again via the racecourse, and boasts a busy Anglican church and community centre, and English lessons for local Anglophone children run by a local association of English-speaking families (APARC, BP 60634, Chantilly Cedex, e-mail address: aparc@aol.com).

Nearer the centre of Paris, the other isolated area of note
is **Enghien-les-Bains**, the sophisticated lakeside playground with its casino and racecourse. Like the other
towns mentioned above, Enghien was a favoured retreat
for Paris businessmen and stars. The result in all of these
towns is an ample selection of fine nineteenth- and early
twentieth-century villas, side by side with more recent
luxury developments.

Pontoise has been completely eclipsed by the new town on
its outskirts, **Cergy-Pontoise**, a tough new town at the end
of the RER line which should be avoided. But beyond to
the north-west lies a large stretch of the Val d'Oise which
really does not associate itself with Paris but is still
nonetheless in striking distance, a land of small calm
country towns and villages pushing down towards the
Norman border.

The fall and rise of northern Paris

When you see the poverty of some of the northern suburbs
which you should definitely avoid (Sarcelles, Gonnesse,
Stains, Aubervilliers, Aulnay-sous-Bois, La Courneuve), it
is difficult to imagine that this Roissy was once a Roman
rural retreat, and that the solitary medieval church in
Gonnesse was the centre of a rural community. These
towns and others around about are now 'the badlands' of
Paris, the tribal homelands of the **racaille** (hoodlums or
yobs), easily identified by the baseball cap and designer
label sportswear 'uniform' they have created for themselves. The prevailing atmosphere is violent, drug-
trafficking is rife, unemployment endemic, and crime is
for many a way of life. Think Bronx or Brixton in the
1980s, and you will start to understand.

At some stage you will be confronted with this reality, even if you do not find yourself living among it. You will not be able to avoid crossing these areas when you take public transport to and from the airport; or a train at the Gare du Nord or de l'Est; or a métro which finishes up at Bobigny or La Courneuve but runs through central Paris and across to the other side. The sense of insecurity you will feel will help you understand why security has become such a dominant issue in France.

The challenge for the politicians is now how to create a sort of pincer movement: both repressing the violence and flagrant disrespect of the law, and successfully changing the mentality of the perpetrators to integrate them into society. The reasons for this situation are many and varied. But among the principal reasons has been the both the disastrous urban constructions in the dormitory towns around the périphérique and the lack of respect shown to the people who live in them. Both are now being addressed, and 'trendologues' tell us it is having the desired effects. You should be wary of false prophets, but it is true that there are definite signs of positive efforts to change the situation.

The cultural revolution

It is hard to understand how the French state could have allowed one of the finest monuments of French Gothic architecture and one of the cradles of French history to become enveloped by a town known for squalor. But this is precisely what has happened to the **Basilique St Denis**, (93) which was France's equivalent of Westminster Abbey. The result is a magnificent and unique display of royal tombs and sculpture and soaring architecture best viewed on a sunny day when light floods the cathedral, home to a renowned annual music festival. Nearby the renowned **Stade de France** built for the last Football World Cup is the new centrepiece to this ancient city under slow renovation. There is also talk of trying to renovate the nearby canal de l'Ourcq which runs down to La Villette on the northern edge of Paris.

Bobigny, the capital of Seine St Denis, has always been known as one of the main trouble spots of deeply-troubled area. For this reason, it was one of the sites chosen for another Mitterrand era theatre, the **MC93**, which hosts major productions and visiting companies, including many in English. The town has also become the centre of the popular annual **Banlieues Blues** jazz festival which is part of a successful cultural renewal. The other component is the local Rap scene, and many of France's leading rappers hail from the high-rise blocks and low-living northern suburbs. Their music not only expresses the source of local tensions, but also employs the local dialect which has grown up mixing Arab and French with American words from favourite sit-coms. In as much as Paris could be said to have any form of local dialect, this is probably now it, although it is far from eloquent.

The cheapness of land and property in this environment has led a number of major companies to relocate to métro-served towns such as **Pantin**, and ironically the headquarters of Hermés can be found in Pantin, and the exclusive tableware store **Christofle** is based in **Montreuil**. At **Aubervilliers**, tempers flared over the arrival of a major hypermarket complex bringing jobs to the area, but also threatening local traders (although the majority of local street traders in this area are not the sort that the local authorities would necessarily approve of ...).

	Average price m² beginning 2003 (*Le Point*, May 03) €	Average price m² end 2003 (*Challenges* and *Nouvel Observateur*, March 04) €	Estimated real price increase in 2003 for good quality apartments (*Nouvel Observateur*, March 03)
Bagnolet	1,630	1,634	9.2%
Les Lilas	2,077	2,194	16.7%
Montreuil	1,594	1,658	10.4%
Pantin	1,488	1,646	16.8%
St Denis	1,190	1,313	10.9%
St Ouen	1,427	1,551	14.8%

Figure 12. Seine St Denis, département 93,
price increases for apartments.

THE UP-AND-COMING EAST

In the east of the Seine St Denis, the push across the périphérique has produced of pockets of urban renewal feeding off the 20th arrondissement, with Bobo colonies in loft apartments and small houses in **Lilas** and the **Pré-St Gervais** at the end of métro lines. But the real success story has been **Montreuil** between the métro stops Croix de Chavaux and Robespierre. The proximity to Vincennes has led many families to wander into Montreuil unknowingly but not unhappily. Running off the lower end of the avenue Président Wilson and along the rue Carnot, you will find a great selection of houses in all shapes and sizes. The area is calm, but the living is good, and you are in close proximity to both central Paris and the Bois de Vincennes. **Rosny-sous-Bois** with its police headquarters is another growing favourite, and the neighbouring town of **Le Raincy** has also caught the Bobo bug. Families will need to bear in mind the problems of schooling in these areas, but also the better living space on offer when deciding whether to move here. You are still definitely in the working-class banlieues in the east of the département, but the contrast between the troublesome volatile central areas and the calmer east is remarkable.

THE EASTERN AND SOUTHERN SUBURBS

Département 94 – Val de Marne

The inner eastern suburbs of Paris are amongst the most sought after for a number of reasons linked to the landscape of the Île de France. The département takes its name from Paris's second major river, the **Marne**, which joins the Seine at **Charenton**, and the towns running along the borders of the **Bois de Vincennes** and within the loop of the river Marne are amongst the most sought after: **Charenton**, **St Maurice**, **Maisons-Alfort**, **St Maur**, **Join-ville-le-Pont** and **Nogent-sur-Marne**. All of these towns have good transport links to Paris, and the métro runs out to **Créteil**, the départemental capital. Créteil itself is another modern mess from the 1960s and 1970s, but it does have a university, shopping centre, and is the basis for a number of festivals and experimental theatre and dance.

North of the Bois de Vincennes are the two gems in the départemental crown, the adjoining towns of **Vincennes** and **St Mandé**. The latter is the chicer of the two, and rolls effortlessly into bourgeois Paris. Vincennes, on the other hand, rolls up and out into neighbouring **Montreuil** and **Fontenay-sous-Bois**. With its fortress and RER and métro

	Average price m² beginning 2003 (*Le Point,* May 03) €	Average price m² end 2003 (*Challenges* and *Nouvel Observateur,* March 04) €	Estimated real price increase in 2003 for good quality apartments (*Nouvel Observateur,* March 03)
Creteil	1,593	1,678	NA
Fontenay-sous-Bois	2,024	2,182	NA
Ivry sur Seine	1,616	1,783	14.1%
Joinville le Pont	2,141	2,252	17.5%
Nogent-sur-Marne	2,490	2,679	13.3%
St Mandé	3,228	3,448	12.3%
St Maur des Fossés	2,388	2,470	14.3%
Vincennes	2,908	3,116	11.9%

Figure 13. Val de Marne, département 94,
price increases for apartments.

stop, Vincennes is in fact the better served of the two.
Both give access to the immediate attractions of the Bois
(the boating lakes, the château, the zoo, and the Parc
Floral children's area), making them a highly desirable
family living space.

The south-western corner of this small département is
dominated by Paris's second major airport **Orly**, the
displaced Paris food market of **Rungis**, and the main Paris
prison at **Fresnes**. All of these closely succeed one another
on the borders with the neighbouring département.
Forming a thin barrier between these areas and the
périphérique are the southern tips of the métro lines at
Villejuif and **Kremlin-Bicêtre**. As might be expected, these
are the problematical areas of the department, although
they have experienced the same change in population in
recent years as other towns such as Pantin, Malakoff and
Montrouge.

Département 77 – Seine-et-Marne

When I first came to Paris in 1991, France was still in culture shock from the arrival of Mickey's Magic Kingdom at **Marne la Vallée**. The reasons for the culture clash have already been elucidated at length elsewhere, but the real reason for the shock and the violence of French reactions is to be found in the local landscape. The French government had sold prime farming land at a rock-bottom price to establish a major theme park and new urban pole to the eastern Paris region, and the impact was staggering.

	Average price m² beginning 2003 (*Le Point*, May 03) €	Average price m² end 2003 (*Le Point*, November 03) €	Estimated price increase in 2003 for older apartments (*Le Point*, November 03)
Fontainebleau	1,777	1,901	13%
Meaux	1,258	1,273	10%
Melun	1,367	1,397	9%
Noisiel	1,313	1,379	18%
Roissy en Brie	1,245	NA	8% 2001–02 apartments 65% 2003 houses
Torcy	1,426	1,460	12%

Figure 14. Seine-et-Marne département 77,
price increases for apartment and houses.

The first time I saw the site was in early 1992 when I was invited to act as an advisor on the care of the anticipated influx of British and English-speaking young workers at the park. I was driven across open fields along country roads, until suddenly the road surfaces became smooth and in the distance the great pink castle soared out of local fields. The impact was stunning. The contrast was further exaggerated by arriving at the village hall to find wood smoke curling out of the chimneys, and to listen to local community leaders expressing their consternation faced with an influx of foreigners who did not speak their language in an area which already had a housing shortage. The result was that apartment prices had rocketed to the same as central Paris! The fraught meeting with an urban planner continued to demonstrate the exclusion of local people from the grand plans that others had taken on their behalf.

More than a decade later, the **EuroDisney** experience has worked for local people, but remains an exceptional site which has had a profound impact on an otherwise rural area. It also represents the willingness and desire of the urban planning authorities to push expansion out into the fields around Paris in order to offer new space for families.

It is perhaps this sudden expansion – and even worse in the Brie country which produces one of France's most famous cheeses! – which really caused the cultural shock, more than work practices or large pink castles. In seeking to offer a better standard of living to those people who have now found homes in the new developments which have finally spun off from the Disney park, part of the traditional local culture was brusquely sacrificed. The arrival of the attraction park had as big an impact on the rural Seine-et-Marne as the arrival of the airport in the rural Val d'Oise in the 1960s. However the effect has definitely been more positive, with the urban damage limitation and many advantageous spin-offs, such as fast-tracks into Paris by road and rail, and TGV and Eurostar links. This is quite a good place to be, especially for young families, even if the local infrastructure is still being developed to support the new arrivals.

Beyond Marne la Vallée lies the beautiful medieval town of **Meaux**, the capital of the Brie country, with its cathedral and walled medieval centre. The hour-long train journey into Paris may be a turn-off for some people, but you will still have a good quality of life here. The rest of the département is pretty much nothing but rural villages, and this is certainly not somewhere you would consider living without a car.

The southern half of the département is dominated by forests. In terms of urban patterns the south resembles the north, except that it is the more sought-after area of the département, especially towns such as **Lesigny**, or **Barbizon,** the artists' village, where the British community in Paris used to send their young and invalided for fresh air. But the dominant forest and town in the south of the département remains the former royal town of **Fontainebleau** in the heart of the forest. The vast château is a popular attraction, but the main pole of foreign resident interest in the area is the internationally-renowned INSEAD business school.

An English-speaking church has been formed at Fontainebleau, and there is an English-speaking section at the Lycée offering education in English for children aged 6–18, with British examinations and preparation offered for American and British universities (tel: 01 64 22 11 77). In the northern half of the département, as might be expected with the proximity to EuroDisney and to Paris, a private state-approved bilingual primary school for children aged 6–11 has been opened between Marne la Vallée and Meaux (tel: 01 60 04 34 70, *www.frINTsch.fr*).

It is possible that further expatriate community infra-structures will develop in this area in years to come, but essentially you must realise that if you do choose to make your home in the Seine-et-Marne, you will be choosing immersion into French lifestyle.

Département 91 – Essone

Like its neighbours, the Essone département sprawls out into deep countryside to the south of Paris where forests, farms, villages and rural pursuits predominate rather than the hurly-burly of Parisian life. With fewer forests than either Les Yvelines or the Seine-et-Marne départe-ments, the area may appear to be less attractive than others. But the **Yvette** valley and the villages which straddle along it, served by the RER line, are very popular areas for Parisians with a taste for country living. **Orsay** with its university population is another preferred spot within easy reach of Paris.

On the eastern edge of the département the **Forêt de Sénart** provides a welcome green lung along the lower banks of the Seine, but the towns on the opposite bank such as **Arpajon, Juivsy** and the départemental capital of **Evry** are modern urban expansions which face the same problems as some of the more well-known suburbs of the north. **Evry** does boast the most recent French cathedral but not much else to recommend it as a town, and the Russian cemetery at **St Genevieve des Bois** is the last resting place of Rudolf Nureyev.

Overall, the north-east of the département is the most industrialised, although factory closures threaten to cause

	Average price m² beginning 2003 (*Le Point*, May 03) €	Average price m² end 2003 (*Le Point*, November 03) €	Estimated price increase in 2003 for older apartments (*Le Point*, November 03)	Average price m² apartments end 2003 (*Challenges* and *Nouvel Observateur*, March 04) €
Arpajon	1,737	1,672	17%	NA
Bretigny sur Orge	1,613	1,589	7% for apartments 38% for houses	NA
Brunoy	1,616	1,526	9% for apartments 47% for houses	NA
Evry	1,017	1,064	12%	1,060
Gif sur Yvette	2,144	2,319	14% for apartments 45% for houses	2,343
Orsay	2,258	NA	30% for houses	2,361
Palaiseau	1,824	1,834	8% for apartments 49% for houses	1,889

Figure 15. Essone département 91,
price increases for apartments and houses.

renewed problems in this sometimes troubled area.
Probably the main attraction of the Essone département
over its neighbours is that the RER cuts deeper into the
southern countryside and forests, to **Dourdan, Etampes**
and **Malesherbes**, than in other comparable areas. If you
can stomach the long rides on branch lines of public
transport this could offer you a chance to really enjoy
country living and combine it with urban professional
practice. However you will be limited in your movements
by public transport, and at the time of writing, the Essone
département does not offer any form of infrastructure
designed to support expatriate families who are not able
and willing to blend into the French social landscape.

Renting Property in Paris

A survey in Paris in November 2000 showed that Paris property is still largely in private hands. In Paris 49.8% of buildings belong to **copropriétés** (collective owner- ships), and 20.2% belong to individuals, many of whom are also owner-occupiers. About 17% of the Paris property market belongs to companies including holding companies of banks and insurance companies.

Your experience of negotiating your way into a lease will depend largely upon whom you are dealing with, a company or an individual. There is increasing alarm at the level of information being demanded of applicant tenants. Even working for a big-name foreign corpora- tion may not necessarily spare you from demands for a near-humiliating range of documents. This seems to be truer of rental agencies acting on behalf of landlords or companies than of the landlords themselves. The only advice that can be given for dealing with these scenarios is that you have to grit your teeth if you really want to break into the property market to rent an apartment in Paris.

There are two points which you should consider when renting property in France. Furnished accommodation is generally more expensive than unfurnished accommodation; and suburbs are generally less expensive than city centres, although this will depend upon location.

FINDING THE ADVERTS

Obviously you can use real estate agencies (**agents immobilier**) when you first arrive, but there will be a charge to pay for their services. Many of the agencies now have websites which may speed up your initial search, eg, *www.century21.fr, www.seloger.com,* or *www.immostreet.com.*

As a foreigner in Paris, you may well find it easier to deal directly with landlords rather than agencies. Magazines, newspapers and notice boards are all indispensable for the new arrival. The best sources are:

1. *Le Figaro* and *Libération* (newspapers) – daily. Mainly agencies, some independent landlords. You will find many same-day appointments (eg, be there at 12h00 today and tomorrow). The problem is of course that the first person who comes with the right profile for the landlord is normally the lucky new tenant. The free weekly paper distributed in the métro, *A nous*

Paris, also includes housing offers, mainly from agencies.

2. *Particulier à Particulier* (*www.pap.fr*). Comes out every Thursday, available at all major newsagents and kiosks. The major way to find an apartment, although some agencies once again do masquerade behind the ads from the vast majority of independent landlords. Be prepared for an early start every Thursday – you need to get the *PAP* around 07h30, mark up the ads which interest you, and call as soon as possible. Some are let before the paper even comes out, and landlords receive hundreds of calls about these advertisements. Long-running advertisements should make you wonder what exactly is being offered and what the snags are.

3. *France-USA Contacts (FUSCAC)* 26 rue Bénard, 75014 Paris. Tel: 01 56 53 55 54, fax: 01 56 53 54 55, *www.fusac.fr*; US office: France Contacts, PO Box 115, Cooper Station, New York NY10276. Tel: 212 777 5553, fax: 212 777 5554. This bi-weekly free and extremely useful magazine is available in English-speaking churches, bars, and shops in Paris. You should be slightly wary over the rents advertised, as many are inflated for higher foreign budgets.

4. *The Paris Voice*, 7 rue Papillon, 75009 Paris. Tel: 01 47 70 45 05, *www.parisvoice.com*. Another very useful free English-language magazine, available in roughly the same places as FUSAC, but including arts reviews, etc, as well as housing advertisements. You should check another free occasional magazine, *Irish Eyes*.

English-language community notice-boards are also a useful source of adverts, and this is especially so in Paris. Keep a pen and paper handy with you, and call as soon as you can for the offers. The main contact points are:

- **The American Church in Paris**, 65 quai d'Orsay, 75007 Paris. M°Invalides or Alma-Marceau. A major housing, employment and community centre for expatriates. New advertisements go up every day about 14h00. Some landlords literally hang around looking for tenants. This is also a good contact point for those seeking flatmates for apartment shares. You can also place an advertisement seeking accommodation, but you must pay for this.

- **The American Cathedral in Paris,** 23 avenue George V, 75008 Paris. M° George V or Alma-Marceau; **St George's Anglican Church**, 7 rue Auguste-Vacquerie, 75116 Paris. M° George V or Kléber; **St Michael's Anglican Church**, 5 rue d'Aguesseau, 75008 Paris. M°Concorde.

You should also keep an eye out in **local neighbourhood stores** such as groceries, pharmacies, bakers and newsagents, where you will often find small advertisements from independent landlords.

UNDERSTANDING THE ADVERTS
Once you locate the housing advertisements you need to understand the terms and shorthand used in property advertisements so that you can concentrate on looking for the style of home which suits you and your budget. The examples given below will help you understand the jargon, and save you much valuable time.

14ᵉ *Studio meublé, salle d'eau. Prés Montparnasse. 385 euros/mois + charges. Tél. après 20h00.*

Furnished studio in the 14th arrondissement of Paris. Includes a 'bathroom' (probably) consisting of shower, wash-basin and WC. Near to Montparnasse station. 385 euros per month plus building charges. Telephone the following number after 8pm.

Comment: This is probably a very small studio flat of about 18-20m². Much important information is missing. When you telephone to enquire about such studios ask: the size of the flat; on which floor it is situated; if there is a lift; what are the kitchen facilities; what furnishings are provided; how much are the building charges (ie, how much is the total rent). If there is no mention that it is furnished (**meublé**), then you must assume that there is no furniture at all. This may also be one or possibly two **chambres de bonne** (maid's rooms) knocked into one flat. These are small rooms in the attics of large residential buildings. Single chambre de bonne are often let to students, but you sometimes have to share a WC and shower with other residents on the corridor.

3ᵉ Beaubourg. Immeuble ancien renové. Digicode, interphone. Studio 35m²; neuf, aménagement standing. Séjour avec 2 fenêtres, poutres apparentes, cuisine équipée, salle de bains, WC, rangements. Libre 31/12 625 euros/mois charges comprises.

(Unfurnished) studio 35 m² in the 3rd arrondissement of Paris, in the Beaubourg quartier, in an old building which has been restored with both door code and inter-phone. Newly redecorated to a good level. (Principal) living room with two windows, exposed beams, equipped kitchen, bathroom, WC, and built-in cupboards. Available from 31 December. 625 euros per month including building charges.

Comment: This is a much clearer advertisement. You still need to check about which floor the studio is on as it could well be 6th floor without a lift. Space is at a premium in French flats, and so it is important to know that there are built-in cupboards. Other terms for these are **placards** and **penderies** (normally referring to small built-in wardrobes). Check what is included in the kitchen area.

> *15e Convention. Immeuble pierre de taille, 2 pièces, 41m^2, clair, exposé sud. Fenêtre dans chaque pièce. Calme. Au 4e sans ascenseur. Digicode. Entrée, salle de bains (baignoire), WC, branchement lave-linge, séjour, coin-cuisine, chambre.*

(Unfurnished) two-room flat in the 15th arrondissement of Paris near Convention métro. Two rooms totalling 31m^2. South facing with a window in each room. Quiet, situated on the 4th floor without a lift. Door code. Entrance hall/passage, bathroom (with bath), WC, outlet for a washing machine, sitting room with 'kitchen corner', and bedroom.

Comment: This is a classic one bedroom flat. The digicode refers to the means of access to the building from the street. There may also be an inter-phone system as in the example above. The 'kitchen corner' is a classic feature of smaller flats. You will also see references to a **cuisine americaine**. This is kitchen with a bar to separate it from the main room. **Pierre de taille** indicates that this is a good-quality stone building, probably well-maintained.

> **CLAMART (92)** *Maison 4 pièces, 80m², sur terrain 272m². Cuisine aménagée, salle de douche, WC séparées. Près commerces, écoles et transports. Dans quartier résidentiel calme. Chauffage gaz.*

A four-roomed house in Clamart in the département 92, 80m² of a total property site of 272m². Fitted kitchen, shower room, separate WC. Near to shops, schools and transport. In a quite residential area. Gas heating.

Comment: The number of rooms (two or more) does not normally include the entrance hall, WC, or bathroom. In this case, there will be a sitting room, at least two bedrooms, and either a significant kitchen, or a dining room, or a third bedroom. The total property site probably includes a garden and parking space. It is a small house, but the advertiser is obviously seeking to attract a young couple with a small family. Note the facilities on offer.

Heating (**chauffage**) is either **individuel**, ie, you control and pay for this yourself, or **collective** in which it case it is included in the building charges. However, in this case it is switched on and off at a defined date which may not always suit you. Air-conditioned residential property is almost unheard of.

Houses may have attics, but few if any flats will. However, certain flats will include the use of an individual cellar (**cave**). You should check the security and state of the cellar before deciding whether to use it to store your belongings. Large flats may have a **chambre de bonne** attached several floors above, although many chambres are now rented out separately.

Some flats may also have a parking space attached to them. This will instantly increase the price of the flat, certainly in cities and large towns. Check whether the **parking** is in an attached car park, or a garage complex under the building. Parking (also known as a **box**) can also be separately rented if needed.

VIEWING PROPERTY

Select the properties which interest you, and call the numbers quickly to arrange to view them. If you are careful, you should be able to view several in one day, and so compare the properties more easily. In some cases the advertisements will simply announce a date, time and address to which you should come in order to visit. Expect to queue, and get there early.

Remember that when you go to view a property, you yourself are being viewed by the landlord as a prospective tenant. Competition is sharp for good homes, so you must be prepared.

- **Appear friendly and professional**. Smile and dress

smartly. Nobody wants a difficult tenant, and a landlord will want to feel sure that you can pay the rent.

◆ **Take proof of your spending power**. Money talks loudly. Take along as many recent wage slips as you can, and also bank statements. They will almost certainly be asked for by the landlord. If you refuse to show them, it is very unlikely you will be accepted as a tenant. If you have just arrived, take along your engagement letter if you already have employment (**lettre d'embauche**) stating your salary.

◆ **Have your cheque book ready** to make a down payment on a rental if you and the landlord agree terms. However, **be careful** to ask for a receipt from the landlord, and preferably your signed rental contract.

Questions the landlord will ask you

Expect to be asked at least one of the following questions by a prospective landlord:

1. If you are employed, **'Do you have a permanent contract?'** If you have just arrived, take along past pay slips, and an **attestation d'emploi** from your employer, stating that you have an indefinite contract, and your annual or monthly salary before tax.

2. If you are a student, **'Do you have a carte d'étudiant?'** Renting to students is advantageous in one sense as there are tax benefits for landlords.

3. '**Are you sure that you can afford the rent?**' Officially your monthly salary after tax and social security deductions must be three times the total rent on your home. In practice, this is rarely the case. However it can be a sticking point, and with good reason. **Do not over-stretch yourself financially.**

4. '**What guarantees can you offer for the payment of the rent?**' Very frequently landlords will ask for **références serieuses** and **garanties parentales**. This is a written undertaking either by your parents, or your firm in some cases, that if you default on the rent, they will settle any outstanding debts. It is not an undertaking to be made lightly, as the standard notice period for a rental arrangement is three months.

RENT GUARANTEES

Students will almost certainly be asked for references and guarantors, but so too will young people who are in full-time employment (single or married). According to one newspaper article (*Libération*, 13 September 2000), rental agencies are now insisting on social security details, access to the previous three months bank statements, and even court rulings regarding divorce settlements and loan repayment plans, in order to assess your financial capabilities to pay the rent. Foreigners have been traditionally singled out in the recent past for this kind of treatment on the grounds you may flee owing months of rent. Gentle negotiation and reassurance with an individual landlord can often resolve the problem however.

TAKING OUT A LEASE

Once you have chosen the property which interests you and been accepted for the tenancy, you will have to sign the lease (**contrat de location** or more properly the **bail**, pronounced 'bye'). Usually this is a standard grey and green form, including mentions of the laws governing rental agreements. They can be obtained from Tissot, 19 rue Lagrange, 75005 Paris. The front and back will be filled in and signed by your landlord and yourself, and the inside pages will include the general terms of the agreement. Two identical copies of the contract are signed and completed, one for you and one for the landlord.

Beware of 'home-made' contracts which could lead to difficult situations should a problem arise. They will certainly not offer you the same legal protection and security of residence as the formal contracts. Some landlords may have had a separate contract prepared by a lawyer for larger properties. Read contracts carefully before signing them, and if necessary seek professional advice. **Do not panic and do not 'lease' cash-in-hand and do not hand over your money without a contract in return.**

To conclude the contract, take along copies of your carte de séjour or passport, and your deposit (**caution**) for the flat. This sum is normally equivalent to two months' rent, but must be defined and mentioned in the contract. Normally the first month's rent is also paid in advance, making a total of three months' rent in advance.

The contract should include the name of the landlord; your name; the full address of your flat including the staircase, etc; a description of the property; the length of the contract; the rent you are to pay, including building charges; when you are to pay it; and the amount of the caution you have paid for the property.

État des lieux

The contract is not completed until one final process has taken place known as the **état des lieux**. This should happen **before** you move in, and is undertaken with the landlord (or their representative), to establish the exact state of the property (eg, cracks in the wall, broken windows, etc).

Both of you keep a signed copy. Keep this safely in case your landlord later tries to make you pay for repairs which are not your fault. For furnished lets, you should also have an itemised inventory of the furnishings provided.

The état des lieux is the moment to try to negotiate minor changes in the presentation of the apartment before you move in. No landlord is going to agree to redecorate completely and re-equip an entire kitchen. Some will, however, agree that you need a cooker and that the damp patch in the bathroom must be dealt with before you can safely be said to be 'enjoying' the property. You are not obliged to forever hold your peace once you move in, but you can hopefully save yourself a lot of hassle by correct anticipation.

Additional costs when renting property

In addition to the caution and first month's rent, you may

also find yourself presented with a bill for the **frais** or **honoraires** as they are sometimes called. These will be the costs involved in preparing a contract, and undertaking the état des lieux. A landlord is within their rights to use a bailiff (**huissier**) to undertake the état des lieux. All of these charges will be at the tenant's expense.

The other additional cost you may face will be the estate agent's fee if you have used their services. This is also normally equivalent to one month's rent. Remember to check this before you take advantage of their services and include it in your budget.

Rent increases normally take place once a year on the anniversary date of the signature of the rental agreement. They are limited by law to an average figure indexed to national building trade costs. Generally, the maximum increases are about 4% per year, if they are applied by landlords. The decision to apply an increase or not is at the discretion of a landlord. If your lease runs out, and you start a new lease, currently rent increases are in the order of 10% in Paris.

Your responsibilities as tenant
The general conditions of the standard contract list 16 responsibilities, the first of which is to pay the rent on time! The other most important responsibilities are:

1. Using the premises in a calm and reasonable manner for the purposes for which they were intended. Also not to transform them for another 'purpose', eg offices.

2. Taking out a standard insurance policy against fire, water damage, etc.

3. Obeying the regulations governing the day-to-day running of the building and concerning the **parties communes** (eg, lifts, corridors, etc). These rules are agreed by the all the owners (**copropriété**).

4. Do not sublet your property without prior written approval from your landlord.

5. Day-to-day minor repairs are the responsibility of the tenant. Be careful to note that certain preventative maintenance, eg, an annual check-up for the boiler, is also the tenant's responsibility. This can prove to be important should you need to change the boiler (one of the landlord's responsibilities) later on.

6. If you rent a furnished property (**meublé**) then you are obliged to ensure that either the furnishing stay in the apartment when you are living there, or they are correctly and safely stored for return to the apartment when you leave. If you do decide to discreetly move one or two items of dubious taste out of your view and into your cellar, make sure the cellar is clean and safe and the items are well protected against pests such as wood lice or rodents. Otherwise, talk nicely to your landlord.

The landlord's responsibilities

1. Ensure that the property is clean, that all repairs have taken place, and that all appliances included under the contract are in working order when the tenant enters the property. The landlord is responsible for ensuring that the wiring is in order and that all plumbing is in full working order.

2. Ensure that the tenant can 'peacefully enjoy' the use of the property. Should you find yourself with noisy neighbours or a problem elsewhere in the building, this will be important.

3. Undertake major repairs which are not the responsibility of the tenant.

4. Not to oppose improvements to the property which will not change the basic use and structure of the property. This means a tenant can redecorate an apartment, even against the wishes of the landlord. However, it is best to obtain agreement from the landlord otherwise you are obliged to restore the original decorations etc when you leave the apartment. A tenant is responsible for giving back exactly what she or he receives.

SHARING PROPERTY

Flat-sharing on the Anglo-Saxon model (ie a large apartment or house shared by a number of roughly financially-equivalent people looking to benefit from combined spending power and personal companionship) is becoming increasingly popular in France, especially in the 'Twentysomething' fledgling executive group.

In the case of a formal property share, for example two or more friends or an unmarried couple, it is best to arrange a separate formal lease between the landlord and each tenant in their own name dividing the rent between the tenants. Should one party then leave, the others will not be responsible for the rent of the person who has left. For unmarried couples who have signed a PACS (civil contract for both heterosexual and homosexual couples which requires cohabitation as a prerequisite), in the case of an untimely event the surviving partner is protected from eviction as was often previously the case.

It is also a good idea to put the electricity bill in the name of one tenant, and the telephone bill in the name of another. This provides each person with another proof of residence (**justificatif de domicile**), and helps to ensure each person's rights should a problem arise. In the case of an informal flat share (ie, subletting a room in a flat or house without a written contract, which is strictly illegal), you may be asked to pay a smaller caution (eg, one month instead of two). But you should still **be sure to ask for a receipt from the person to whom you pay the caution**. Your rights in this situation are much less well-defined, so do be careful.

The French often say they do not like sharing with other French people as they are not good flat-mates! If you share a flat with a French person because you want to improve your French, remember the 'other side' may also wish to improve their English. Think carefully before entering into a flat-share and try to protect yourself as much as possible.

FINDING OUT MORE

In addition to the sites mentioned above, you should also check out the following sites:

♦ **L'Agence National de l'Information sur le Logement (ANIL)** *www.anil.org*. The National Housing Board.

This is an essential site for anybody buying or renting property in France. An important part of the site is multi-lingual – just click on the button to switch into English. Other parts of the site, including the 'spotlights on ...' are only in French.

◆ Some of the suggested sites in this chapter also have advice columns (in French), such as the site for *Particulier à Particulier, www.pap.fr*. These are good sources of extra, detailed information, such as the formula used for rent increases (which allows you to check your landlord's requirements).

Buying and Renovating Property in France

Property prices in Paris in 2004 have now returned to the market highpoint of 1991. One of the driving factors in French property markets now is the mass influx of British buyers. Paris has not been left out of this phenomenon, and property agents have noticed clear British interest in certain of the most expensive areas of Paris, notably on the Left Bank. Other specialists have also noticed a marked increase in Irish-based buyers, and American purchasers are also continuing their love affair with the 'city of light'.

FINDING THE ADVERTS

As with the rental of property, using professional real estate agencies implies a certain cost for the transaction.

However, this can be weighed up against the protection of a professional contract with the agent acting on your behalf, should anything go wrong.

About half of all property transactions in France are dealt with by estate agents (**agents immobilier**). An estate agent cannot enter into negotiations unless she or he holds a **Mandat de Vente** (written power of attorney for sale) from the seller, or a **Mandat de Recherche** (written power of attorney to make a search) from you as the purchaser.

The seller usually has to pay the estate agent's commission, fixed by power of attorney, upon written completion of the transaction. Anything not referred to in the power of attorney cannot be charged by estate agents. They may fix the amount of commission they receive, but their scale of charges must be on open display. The commission must also represent a percentage of the purchase price. The price displayed for a property must include the commission.

If an agent is the sole agent for a property, they will have the **exclusivité** mentioned in the advertisement. However, both buyers and sellers eager to maximise their profit and minimise their costs can and do organise their own property sales. You are most likely to find direct advertisements from private home-owners in the *Le Figaro (www.explorimmo. com)*, *Libération (www.libération.fr)*, and *Particuliers à Particuliers* (*www.pap.fr*) on Thursdays.

UNDERSTANDING THE ADVERTS

Advertisements for properties for sale use much of the same jargon and shorthand as those for rented property, already decrypted in the previous chapter. However, important extra information will also be included in sale advertisements, and you also need to understand this before deciding if the property corresponds to your search. The real examples given below will help you understand some of the most important extra points:

CLAMART – Secteur pavillonaire. Petit Résidence. Studio 30m² – 50.308E.

In Clamart (92). In the part of the town which contains small individual houses (**pavillons**). In a small modern apartment block (**résidence**). A studio of 30 square metres.

Comment: A pretty minimalist advertisement from an agency (often indicated simply by reference letters such as GEI, LF etc followed by a telephone number). The term résidence in this context normally applies to a modern apartment block without a **concierge**, but with a **digicode** at the front door and/or a second **interphone**. There will probably be no more than ten apartments in this building, which may have a small garden in front or behind the building. A **pavillon** is a term used to describe small detached suburban houses.

Nation (5mn) 2P 34,5m² (loi Carrez) – 2é étg.Cuis.éqp., séjour, chambre, SdB, WC sép. Très clair. Parquet. Refait neuf. 105.190E.

Five minutes from Place de la Nation (in Paris), a two-roomed apartment of 34.5 square metres (certified in accordance with the loi Carrez). Second floor. Fitted kitchen, sitting room, bedroom, bathroom, separate WC. Very light. Parquet flooring. Completely redecorated.

Comment: Much clearer but still ambiguous on one important point; what does the five minutes refer to? A car drive, a métro ride, an RER ride, or walking distance – and in which direction? This is a major consideration. The **loi Carrez** is the recent French law which requires certification of the square meterage of apartments (but not houses) as a basis for sale. If you buy a property and find that you have more than 5% square metres less than what was stated, you are entitled to renegotiate the price. This vendor has already undertaken the necessary official verification and certification process. The fact that it is **refait neuf** might explain a slightly elevated asking price per square metre, depending on where it is situated. In theory, you will have no extra burden to bear in terms of renovation costs. However, this should be checked carefully. (See also the decision checklist below.)

> *Buttes-Chaumont 3P 2 ch 52m^2 Parquet, moulures, à rafraichir. 114.337E.*

In the Buttes-Chaumont area of the 19th arrondissement of Paris. A three-room apartment including two bedrooms, of 52 square metres. Parquet and mouldings/ cornices. Needs to be 'refreshed'.

Comment: You need to check on the layout of this apartment. Many Parisien apartments have bedrooms leading one off each other, so that to get to the bathroom, for instance, you are obliged to cross somebody else's bedroom. It is obviously an older building in co-ownership with the presence of both mouldings and parquet. But the most important point is that it needs to be redecorated. You need to find out just what is involved and then add an estimate figure to the cost of your purchase to get the real total cost.

OWNING PROPERTY IN FRANCE

If you decide to buy property in France, either as your principal home, or as a second home, the basic process is the same as regards the contracts you will have to sign and the charges you will have to pay.

The distinction between 'freehold' and 'leasehold' does not exist in French property law. Instead, a distinction is drawn between co-ownership and free-standing property.

◆ Co-ownership means that the property (normally an apartment block) is divided into units (**lots**). Each unit has a private area and a proportion of the communal area. The co-ownership regulations are known as **Le Règlement de Copropriété**. These regulations govern boundaries between private and communal areas, conditions for use of the building, etc. An assembly of the co-owners decides on changes to the regulations, and any major building works. The costs of works are divided amongst the co-owners.

◆ If you are buying your property independently, eg, you are buying a house with a garden, you will have all the rights of ownership.

♦ In either case, your purchase will be subject to the complicated French inheritance laws (see pages 235–236), and you should discuss these with your French legal advisors when you are planning your purchase.

DECISION-MAKING CHECKLIST

As you will have seen from the comments on the sample advertisements above, there are a large number of considerations to be made before making an offer on a property and signing any binding documents. These are mainly in addition to the basic questions you need to ask yourself outlined in Chapter 6: size, facilities, transport and security.

Obviously you need to weigh up the risks quickly, especially in the cases of sought-after areas and types of apartments. But do not allow yourself to be rushed into a wrong and potentially expensive and disturbing choice.

1. **Check on the surface area**. The price of an apartment is estimated on the basis of a price per square metre. The loi Carrez introduced in June 1997 obliges all vendors in **copropriétés** – but not individual house-owners – to detail the exact surface area of the apartment offered within a maximum error margin of 5%. All surface areas with a **HSP** (**hauteur sous plafond** – floor-to-ceiling height) of at least 1m80 (about 6 ft) must be included in this estimate. **Mezzanines** (split-levels artificially introduced into a room to create a double-surface area such as bedrooms), attics and staircases are not therefore included. However cellars (**caves**) may be, depending

on the age and style of the building. Garages, balconies, and terraces are not included in the surface area estimation, although they may well influence the price. Terrace square areas tend to be noted separately in the advertisements (eg ' + **terrasse** de 5m^2'). If the surface area advertised is less in reality than 5% of the figure advertised, you are entitled to have the price reduced by legal ruling if necessary.

2. **Check on the communal charges**. The communal charges of a copropriété (eg, lifts, concierges, renovation, etc) are shared out by the owners according to the size of their lot and is estimated in **millièmes** and **tantièmes**. This will have a direct effect on your annual bills. Every year the owners meet to vote new works on the building and the budget for the year. You should make every effort to determine what has already been spent (which will also indicate if you are entering a spend-thrift environment), what has been voted but not yet paid for (which will be **your cost** if you buy the apartment before the work is actually carried out **even if you did not vote for it**), and what is planned for the near future. In the worst case scenario, the copropriété could have voted for a facade-renovation (**ravalement**) which has not yet been executed but which will then take place, and could be planning to change the lift(s) in the building the following year. Both of these are very costly exercises. You can demand copies from the vendor of recent minutes (**procès-verbaux**) of the general meetings (**assemblées générales**) of the copropriété, and also enquire if a technical survey has been undertaken of the building. If you receive a negative response, there is nothing to stop you organising your

survey (**diagnostic technique** or **expertise**) of the building. If, in addition to the cost of the facade and the lifts and any personal renovations you need or want to undertake, there is also a problem of subsidence requiring underpinning, etc – think again.

3. **Check the property is correctly valued**. Detailed studies appear regularly each year in the general press. These will allow you to check the price per square metre of the property, which is the basic cost element. Compare prices with comparative size properties in different agencies. Many factors come into play when pricing property, but you need to get a feel of the basic value of your purchase.

4. **Check on the hidden costs**. Ask the vendors to tell you how much the building **charges** have been over the last two years. Ask also how much they have been paying in **impôts locaux** (local housing tax). The cost varies from area to area, according to the size of your apartment, the state of the building, and an official estimation of its market value (which may be out of date). You should also ask the vendor for copies of the bills for major works to the property which in his or her eyes justifies an elevated price; find out just how much it really cost, and what precisely was done.

5. **Check on precisely what the building is used for**. Are all your neighbours in a co-owned building simply living there and working elsewhere, or are they doing the opposite? If one or more is, who has the code to the building? Is it a small one-person independent outfit, or will you be regularly kept waiting for the lift because of clients or because a delivery put it out of

action? The more people who use your building and its facilities, the more wear and tear there is. How safe are you in your own building?

6. **Check on environmental issues**. If you are buying a house in one of the outer rural areas near to a river, what is the likelihood of **flooding** in the area? This has been a real problem in recent years throughout France. A rural idyll could turn into a soggy nightmare in a wet winter. Think also about **transport issues**. You may be tempted to buy in an area because of a new high-speed transport link but make sure it is not going to run under your ground and your foundations, or that you have closer access and greater noise pollution than you had bargained on. The local mairie will have plans for any such developments, and also will be the place to find out about planned building projects which may change your gracious view into *vis-à-vis* with new neighbours. Local **schools** normally lead to higher prices as families seek proximity, but they also mean noise and congestion.

7. **Check on asbestos, lead and pests**. For buildings in collective ownership, **asbestos (amiante)** checks on all common areas and private residential lots are obligatory, and a copy of the statement concerning your chosen building must be given to you no later than the day you are due to sign the **promesse de vente**. You should be able to obtain a copy well in advance in most buildings. For buildings dating from before 1948, a similar document is also obligatory in Paris concerning the risks of **lead** poisoning from paintwork

or pipes. **Pests** such as cockroaches and notably **termites** are munching their way across some of the smartest parts of Paris. Annual rodent and pest control exercises are the responsibility of the copropriété, and you will find references to money voted for these works in the minutes of general meetings. For termites, the vendor should attach an **état parasitaire** to the sale contract stating the level of infection, dating from within three months of the contract date. Once again, you should be able to obtain this in advance of the signature date. If the building or property is at risk from any of these three dangers, then you will need to know the costs involved for dealing with the problems, and what if anything has already been voted but not yet paid by the copropriété. Information regarding these problems amongst others and contact details for professionals qualified to deal with these problems can be found on the websites of both the housing ministry (*www.equipement.gouv.fr*) and the ministry of health (*www.sante.gouv.fr*).

SIGNING THE CONTRACTS

When you and the seller have reached an agreement, there is a choice of two kinds of pre-contractual agreements which are possible:

1. **Promesse de vente**. This is a unilateral agreement to sell, signed by both the seller and buyer. The seller agrees to sell you the property by a certain time, for a set price, and according to set conditions. The buyer is allowed time to reflect on his decision, but must

nonetheless pay a deposit, normally about 10% of the full price. The advantage of this kind of agreement, is that the seller cannot withdraw his or her acceptance of your offer if all the conditions of the agreement are met. The disadvantage is that if you as the buyer withdraw from the agreement, you lose your deposit.

2. **Compromis de vente**. Both sides commit themselves to the transaction. However, certain 'way out' clauses can be included in the agreement, known as **conditions suspensives**. These might include the granting of a mortgage (for which you normally have 40 days), or a town planning report (**certificat d'urbanisme**) etc. All of these clauses must be adhered to, or you are entitled to cancel the agreement and reclaim your 10% deposit.

Once the **notaire** (see below) has all the necessary information, a **projet de l'acte** (draft contract) can be produced. Copies are sent to the buyer and the seller for approval before the final contract is drawn up.

The **Acte Authentique de Vente** is the conveyance agreement between the two parties. It will reiterate clauses from the pre-contractual arrangement, and will also clarify any further details. The following information must appear in the acte:

♦ Identification of both parties.

♦ Identification of the property in precise terms and the title to the property (**origine de propriété**).

♦ The date when you will take possession of the property and be entitled to use it (**propriété de jouissance**).

♦ A **certificat d'urbanisme** which restates any town planning regulations affecting the property, discovered by the notaire. Bear in mind that rural sites are not guaranteed against industrial developments.

♦ Any guarantees and estimates.

The notaire retains the original contract, and copies are given to the buyer and seller, known as **l'expéditions**. Once the sale has been registered at the **Bureau des Hypothèques**, no one else has any claim over the building. Finally the relevant section of the title deed is sent to the Land Registry.

SURVEYING YOUR PROPERTY

Structural surveys are not common practice in France. Stringent building and construction regulations mean that there is usually no need. The seller, or in the case of a new house being built the construction company, are obliged to issue guarantees on the property. Builders must also be insured for work undertaken for 10 years thereafter, and even in case of bankruptcy. The 10-year guarantee also applies to older buildings which have been bought and renovated by a developer.

The notaire can include details guarantees on the property and a list of builders involved in your final agreement. A notaire or estate agent can carry out a simple survey if required. Otherwise, an **expert géometre** can check the total surface area of your new property, or you can arrange for a survey by an architect. If you are buying an apartment in a renovated building, be sure to check on precisely what the builder is charging you for, and check the efficiency of sound-proofing and how well windows actually fit.

LOOKING AT THE LEGAL ISSUES

The role of le notaire

Under French law, every property transaction in France must be overseen by a **notaire**. The distinction in the French legal profession is between **avocats** who can appear in the courts, like barristers in the UK, and notaires who undertake contractual work rather like solicitors in the UK.

Notaires must be impartial between the two parties of a property sale and are responsible for legally validating the deeds involved, advising clients, and drawing up the necessary contracts. He or she can and does also sometimes act as a tax consultant, and also as an estate agent in certain cases.

The notaire is entitled to a legally determined sum as commission when acting as a sale negotiator. Normally this is around 8% of the purchase price. If the building is a new property the notaire's fee is reduced to no more than 3%. A building less than five years old which has never been occupied since construction also qualifies for this reduction.

Notaire's fees (**frais**) will include money paid on your behalf, taxes, dues and contingency duties. Overall costs are high but vary from region to region within a set scale, and depending on the type and value of the property.

The notaire's responsibilities when acting as intermediary for a sale are:

1. Verification of the seller including his/her right to sell the property.

2. Obtaining the relevant Land Registry papers, showing any planning objections to the property.

3. Contacting anyone with pre-emption rights to the property, and determining whether they plan to exercise these rights.

4. Contacting the **Conservation des Hypothèques** (mortgage/Land Registry) which must issue an **état hors formalité**. This shows any mortgages, securities etc on the property. Such debts must be payable and lower than the sale price to avoid redemption proceedings.

If you pay for the property through the notaire, she or he can withhold payment if it is discovered that the seller has used the property as collateral on a loan, until a **negative état sur formalité** has been issued.

Inheritance issues
It is extremely important that you take good professional advice when buying your property in France, as regards questions of ownership and inheritance. You must do this before you sign the contracts; afterwards, it will be too late. You should also bear in mind that the legal system is both very slow and very expensive in France.

The main thing to watch out for is that the notaire does not draw up a contract whereby you buy the property **en**

division. The much more preferable option is to buy **en tontine**. There are other possibilities (eg, an **acte de donation**); but you will need to discuss these with your legal advisors.

If you and your spouse buy a property en division, you will each own half of the property. When one of you dies, the 'half' which belongs to the deceased person will pass automatically to his or her heirs. The surviving spouse will then own half a house or apartment, with the right of abode for the remainder of their life.

If you have children, you cannot leave your half of your property to your spouse. You can leave part of it to your spouse, but he or she will be liable for Succession Tax on the part they have inherited. If there are more than three children, they automatically inherit three quarters of the deceased person's estate. Inheritance Tax is then payable immediately, even if the surviving spouse continues living in the house. The property cannot be sold to pay the Inheritance Tax without the consent of the surviving spouse, nor if one of the children is under 18 years old.

FINANCIAL CONSIDERATIONS

Financing your purchase
In France, the most common method of obtaining a mortgage is to apply to a high street bank. A French bank will calculate the amount of money available for your mortgage according to your cash flow. A mortgage should be granted as long as your outgoings plus your mortgage repayments equal less than 30% of your pre-tax income.

Successive French governments in recent years have tried to boost the property market by permitting loans at very low rates. It is worth enquiring widely about the possibilities before taking a decision. Banks and financial institutions vary from inflexible with anybody but the known and trusted clients, to more flexible and competitive in the face of opposition from high street competitors.

Paying tax on your property

Your purchase will make you liable for the following French taxes:

◆ **Government registration tax**. This tax is payable when you are completing your purchase, and when added to the fees of the notaire amounts to about 11% of the property's purchase price.

   You will also be required to pay the equivalent of UK Land Registry fees and Stamp Duty. The rates depend upon the size of the property and any grounds and annexes, and the age of the property. Once you have bought property in France, it must be registered with the tax authorities. If it is a secondary residence, contact the **Centre des Impôts des Non-résidents**, before 30 April.

◆ **Taxe foncière**. This is a local municipal tax levied on you as the owner. Your name will be added to a register at the local mairie. The register comprises lists of owners, tax rates paid, and notional letting values of the property concerned. In some cases you will be exonerated from the taxe foncière (see below).

◆ **Taxe d'habitation**. Unlike the two taxes above, this local tax is not necessarily payable by the owner of the property, but by the occupant. If you rent a property you will be liable for this tax. The rate of tax payable is determined by the building's amenities and size. The basic rate is calculated according to the nominal letting value of property in the local area.

Insuring your property

You are required by French law to take out third-party insurance as soon as you move into your accommodation, or as soon as work has begun on your future home if it is still being built. This is known as **Civil Propriétaire**.

It is also highly advisable to take out insurance against fire, theft, etc. Comprehensive policies known as **assurances multirisques** are available, as are specific policies. The sum insured should reflect your insurable interest or potential loss according to the contract arranged. Co-owners should already be insured for the building itself and all communal areas. In addition you need to take out insurance on your own belongings.

RENOVATING YOUR PROPERTY

Owner-occupiers intending to in some way add to, transform, or renovate their properties should take careful note before unadvisedly beginning starting to knock down walls, which may lead to situations which only gluttons for punishment would relish, faced with the slow and expensive French legal system.

Basic rules regarding planning permission include a limit on the number of habitable or serviceable square metres which can be added, as well as all changes in use of the property or exterior appearance require official approval from the local mairie.

What you can do without planning permission

◆ If you are planning to change the interior of your apartment, you can do so as long as it does not change the exterior of the building, or its volume or surface area. For example, adding another shower room in the existing floor plan is not a problem, and there is no need for planning permission.

◆ If you have a garden and you want to install a patio or terrace, you can do so as long as it is not more than 60cm (2ft) above ground level. The same goes for a greenhouse, potting shed or a garden house, as long as it does not cover more than two square metres and is not more than 1m50 high. Anything over these limits requires planning permission.

◆ You can build a wall in your garden up to 2m high, as long as it is not a dividing wall from a neighbouring property.

What you can do with only a preliminary notification (*déclaration préalable*) at the mairie

◆ You can add less than 20 square metres to your surface living area (eg, you convert an attic or a garage into living areas).

◆ You can build a garage of up to 20 square metres.

◆ You can build a swimming pool in your garden as long as it does not exceed 20 square metres.

What you cannot do without planning permission
All other building work over these limits, including the construction of a large pool or shed, or adding another floor to your property or a roof garden or terrace, all require planning permission from the local mairie. This also applies if you purchase a larger property and convert all or part of it into commercial offices, as you have transformed the nature of the property.

In copropriétés, your plans also have to be approved by the other co-owners at the annual general meeting. The rules of the copropriété will expressly allow certain building works, but other changes (eg, a roof terrace or attic conversion) will have implications for the whole building which everyone has to agree to.

Financial assistance for renovation
There are a number of possibilities which exist for obtaining state aid to renovate your property. Most aids are means-tested and will depend on how long you have lived in France and contributed to 'the system'. However providing that you are a full resident and paying your social contributions and tax here, then there is no reason why you cannot successfully apply for these aids if you meet the criteria.

Information regarding all the benefits on offer for those who undertake major structural work can be obtained from the agences départmentales d'informations logement (ADIL) *www.anil.org*. Some of these are cumulative.

One aid of note is the **prime à l'amélioration de l'habitat**, a means-tested 'bonus' available to owner-occupiers which varies from region to region. **This benefit is of particular interest to those adapting homes for people with handicaps or disabilities**, amongst other more common measures regarding health and hygiene. The total amount of the bonus cannot exceed 20% of the real costs of the works, within a limit of just over €10,000. However, this bonus can also be added to another bonus worth 50% of the works necessary to allow access for, or conversion for use by, handicapped people. The limit on this second bonus is €3,050. Applications for this benefit should be made to the **section habitat of the direction départementale de l'équipement** (except in Paris where applications should be made to the préfecture).

Looking at tax advantages
In September 1999, the French government decided to kick-start the economy via the building and construction industry by reducing VAT on work by professional builders from 19.6% to 5.5%. This applies to all home improvements, maintenance and renovation undertaken by professionals. The drop in tax rate also applies to the materials they use but this is a concession made only to professionals.

If the property you purchase is an old building which has been renovated by a developer and then sold off as apartments, the lower rate of VAT also applies to all works and purchases for those works undertaken within the habitable areas of the building. Certain **parties communes** such as a boiler for the building or a lift are obviously not covered in the lower rate of tax, but tax breaks are offered of up to 15% against the purchase of this kind of equipment for which VAT is 20.6%.

Do-it-yourself fans should note that they will still be charged VAT at 19.6% for any purchases they make to deal with household renovations themselves.

Finally, if you have purchased a new property but still decide to undertake some form of reorganisation etc, then you will be exempted from the taxe foncière for two years after completion of the works.

FINDING OUT MORE

If you want to start your property search before even arriving in France, the development of websites now gives you easy access to visit the properties on offer at your leisure. The French magazine *Challenges* produced an excellent guide to the French property market in March 2001 which shortlisted the following websites as presenting the best value and interest for home-hunters:

www.123immo.com   *www.immo-by-tel.com*
www.pro-a-part.com   *www.century21.fr*
www.immostreet.com   *www.se loger.com*
www.explorimmo.com   *www.minitelorama.com*
www.smartimmo.com   *www.fnaim.fr*
www.nexdom.com   *www.homevillage.com*
www.pap.fr

- L'Agence National de l'Information sur le Logement (ANIL) *www.anil.org*. The National Housing Board. **This is an essential site for anybody buying or renting property in France**. An important part of the site is multi-lingual – just click on the button to switch into English. Other parts of the site, including the 'spot-lights on ...' are only in French. You can find contact details for your local agence (**agence départemental = ADIL**) by clicking on the map.

- *www.directgestion.com* is a useful website for those people considering buying and renting out a property in France, and offers free advice from property business experts such as lawyers and architects; *www.batiweb.com* is a website regrouping building industry contact and information for those considering building or renovating a new property.

$$\left(12\right)$$

Settling Into Your Home

Setting up home in France can feel a bit like being both 'the chicken and the egg'. Without an address you cannot formally open up your own bank account, but without a bank account you cannot make an official down-payment for an address. This in turn means that you cannot have a proof of residence (**justificatif de domicile**) because you will not even be able to open an electricity account.

Somewhere along the line, you *will* manage to square the circle. This is often at the moment that you find an apartment and a landlord willing to accept a cash payment or perhaps a cheque drawn on a foreign account. Once you have secured your new home, you need to move swiftly to put into place the other essential elements of your new home life.

MANAGING YOUR MONEY

There are four principal French banks: BNP-Paribas, Crédit Agricole, Crédit Lyonnais (owned by Crédit Agricole), and Société Générale. Of the major Anglo-Saxon banks, Barclays is the best represented in France with about 100 branches in Paris and across France. In Paris Citibank has a number of branches, and Société Générale on the boulevard Haussman has an English-speaking international client service. HSBC owns the French bank Crédit Commercial de France (CCF).

To gain access to banks in France, press the bell outside the street door. When the green light flashes enter and wait until the door closes. Then press the second bell, and open the door when the second green light flashes. Follow the system in reverse to get out again.

Opening times

French banks are generally open from 09h00 to 16h30 Monday to Friday. Many French banks in cities and large towns are now also open on Saturdays. Lunch hours generally run from 12h30 until 14h00. They are closed on all public holidays, and may close for **le pont** (see page 417).

Opening a French bank account

You will become accustomed to red tape and paperwork in France. However, opening a bank account is one of the easiest steps to take. There are two options:

♦ A non-resident account (**compte non-résident**). With this account, you can negotiate loans, but you cannot have an overdraft facility (**découverts**). This facility would be appropriate if you buy a second home in France.

♦ An ordinary current account. If you are resident in France, or are working principally in France, then you will normally be able to open a current account entitling you to a cheque book and a **carte bleue**, the standard French credit card.

To open your account, take the following original items, plus copies of each:

♦ Passport, or carte de séjour (for resident accounts).

♦ Proof of address (**justificatif de domicile**), either a copy of your rental agreement, or a telephone or electricity bill with your name and address on it.

You will sign customary account-opening forms and give a specimen signature to permit the payment of cheques written by you.

How the system operates

♦ Some banks may make you wait to receive your carte bleue. However, they will give you a cash card which will allow you to use the bank's automatic distributors. You can use your card not only to withdraw cash, but also to give you a statement of the balance of your account (**solde**), and also a statement of the most recent transactions on your account (**relevé**). Some banks also offer other services such as ordering cheque books, paying in cheques, etc.

◆ Cheques normally take about three days to clear once they have been paid into an account. This can take longer if they are drawn on an account (**compensable**) in a more distant town or city, or from another bank. Nonetheless, the date that will appear on your monthly statement (**relevé de compte**) is the date on which the cheque was deposited into your account.

◆ Cheques are used almost as frequently as cash in France for payment. To fill out a French cheque, write the amount in figures in the box or line provided, and then in words on the first (and second if necessary) lines of the cheque. Then fill out the name of the person or company to whom you wish to pay the cheque. Remember to sign the cheque in the space provided on the bottom right-hand corner, and to fill in the date and town where you wrote the cheque. Many shops now have machines which automatically fill out the amount of the cheque, date, place and to whom it is payable. You can cash a cheque at any branch of your own bank. Simply make it payable to yourself. **A piece of official ID is normally required to endorse cheques, and is always required when cashing a cheque in the bank**. There are no cheque cards in France.

◆ Cheques can only be stopped in France in the case of loss or theft of your cheque book. They cannot be stopped because of unsatisfactory goods or services.

◆ A cash deposit to your account (**versement d'espèces**) will normally be registered much more rapidly than a cheque deposit.

- Direct debits (**prélèvements**) can be used to pay for many services in France, including taxes, electricity bills, telephone bills, and rent.

- **It is illegal to be over-drawn in France without a prior agreement with the bank, or to exceed your overdraft limit. <u>There can be serious consequences if you break this rule</u>.**

- There is no reason at all why you should close your bank account in your home country. It is probably a good idea to keep a reserve sum of money in your national currency in order to avoid conversion rates when you return home.

- You should also consider opening a deposit account in order to save for tax bills (which for the first year are a large lump sum) or to provide yourself with some form of security in time of trouble. The main accounts are the **Codevi** (limited to a maximum of €4,600) with instant access; and the **Plan d'Epargne Logement (PEL),** with minimum savings periods of 18 months or five years.

- Changing banks can be a very expensive process if you decide to transfer your accounts to another bank. Unless you are wealthy, French banks will react coolly to threats of a change of bank.

Credit cards

The principal French debit card is the **Carte Bleue Visa**, issued by all major French banks. This will give you the right to draw money from all cash distributors in France, and is the most widely recognised and used of all cards.

You will have your own PIN number, which not only gives access to cash distributors, but also is essential for paying for goods in shops and restaurants. When you use the Carte Bleue the money is debited from your account (it is not a credit card).

Standard credit cards are generally accepted, with Visa being the most widely accepted. If the sign of your own credit card is not displayed at the entrance to a restaurant, you may wish to check it is accepted *before* spending any money. Many stores and commercial groups have account credit cards.

Some British credit cards without microchips are refused in France, although they *are* valid. If your card is refused, you should politely insist.

> **If you lose your card or it is stolen: Telephone 08 36 69 08 80. Other emergency numbers can now be found on most cash distributors if the card is stolen while you are out. You must cancel the card immediately, and report the loss or theft to the police, and to your bank. All of this should be done as quickly as possible to avoid fraudulent use of your card. French banks will arrange replacement Cartes Bleues fairly rapidly.**

Tipping

There are no definite tipping rules, but generally the following people are tipped: porters, taxi drivers, door-men, room service, waiters, cloakroom attendants, hairdressers, and lavatory attendants. Taxi drivers are usually given 10–15% and hairdressers 10%. In restaurants the service is usually included, in which case the bill will read 'TTC' (**toutes taxes comprises**).

If you have received good service, it is customary to leave a tip nonetheless for the waiter. Never leave cents as a tip. This is considered very insulting, and it would be better to leave no tip at all.

You should tip the concierge of your apartment building at Christmas, depending on the level of service you have received from them. Should you live in a small garret at the top of the building, a smaller gift will be equally appreciated. Around Christmas, others will call on you for their 'Christmas Box' – postmen, refuse collectors, and the local firemen. You are not obliged to give money to these people, and such collections are, strictly speaking, illegal.

LOOKING AT HOUSING ASSISTANCE
The **caisse d'allocations familiales** (**CAF** – *www.caf.fr*) administers various housing benefits for those with limited resources. You cannot receive more than one of these benefits at any given time, and your right to access any of the benefits will almost certainly depend upon the length of time you have lived and worked in France. All the benefits are means-tested. These benefits include:

1. **L'aide personnalisée au logement (APL)**. This never covers the total amount of your housing expenses but only one part. It is available to owner-occupiers who have undertaken to improve their property under certain conditions, and also to tenants.

2. **L'allocation de logement familiale** and **L'allocation de logement sociale**. These benefits are available to tenants in a wide range of situations:
   - if you are already receiving another family benefit; or
   - you have a child under 20 years old living at home; or
   - you have been married for less than five years and have no children; or
   - you are looking after a relative over 65 years of age or are unable to work;

   then you may be eligible for this benefit, depending upon your resources. A moving allowance is also available for those with limited resources. Applications should be made for this at your caisse d'allocations familiales when you move in.

MAKING CONNECTIONS

Electricity and gas

Probably the easiest way to deal with gas and electricity contracts administered by the state run EDF-GDF company (*www.edf.fr* and *www.gazdefrance.fr*) is to take over the contracts of the previous residents of your property, whether rented or purchased. Contact your local EDF agency to arrange to have the meter read before you take possession of the property and take over the contract. Otherwise, go the local EDF store with a copy of your rental agreement or your **acte de vente** if you are an owner, and a piece of official identity (eg, passport or carte de séjour), and you can open your new account. If you do take this option, you will have to pay the rental fee, and arrange to be present on the date that the EDF set.

Bills normally arrive quarterly, and can be paid at the post office using a **mandat** (postal order), or by cheque sent by post. Notices regarding meter readings will be sent to you or posted in your building. You must ensure access on the day of the reading. Normally concierges are willing to help if you live in an apartment and cannot be present. Collective heating is controlled by the date not the temperature. Normally it is turned on in October and turned off in April. In smaller and older properties, you may need extra electric heaters.

Water
As with electricity and gas, it is probably easiest to take over existing contracts when you purchase a new property. Tenants normally have their water charges included in the general charges they pay with their rent. Water is supplied by private companies. Arrange for a reading of the water meter when taking over a contract. Bills arrive about every three months.

Telephone
In 1998, France Telecom lost its national monopoly in France. In 2004 it is no longer obligatory to open a France Telecom line, if you subscribe to a high-speed Internet access service via Free.fr or Neuf Telecom. However you should consider carefully whether to take this option, as certain after-sales service options are not included in the Free and Neuf subscriptions. You are also vulnerable to power cuts which could lead to temporary line closure.

In reality you probably still need to take out a France Telecom contract for line rental. Competitors (eg, Cegetel and Neuf Telecom), offer very attractive rates for long-distance calls to the UK and the USA. You will need to contact each operator to discuss the offers available. If you take out a Cegetel of a Le 9 line subscription (**abonnement**), you simply dial 7 or 9 before dialling the standard number.

France Telecom now offer a **toll-free helpline in English on 0800 364 775** Monday–Friday 09h00–17h30 (*www.paris. rancetelecom.fr/anglo*). Phones can be rented or bought from France Telecom shops but can also be purchased from major stores such as FNAC or small phone shops. Phone directories (***Pages Blanches*** for individuals *www.pagesblanches.fr*, ***Pages Jaunes*** for businesses and services *www.pagesjaunes.fr*) can also be found free of charge at your local France Telecom shop. The websites offer a guide in English to help you find your way around the services on offer, a street plan and even photos of many addresses.

France Telecom offer a number of cost-saving plans for overseas calls, the numbers most frequently dialled, etc (**Primalistes**) which you can find out about from France Telecom. There is also an Internet Primaliste with 50% off Internet calls at weekends and week-day evenings. Cheap rates for France Telecom phone calls are at weekends, French national holidays, and between 7pm and 8am (until 1pm for North America) on weekdays.

France is divided into five area codes, numbered from 01 (for Paris) to 05 (for the south-west). Dial the area code plus the eight figure number to reach your correspondent. For international calls dial 00 plus country code plus city code plus telephone number.

Call-back systems are readily available in France. Details of subscription rates and services can be found in 'international' magazines. Savings on international rates are often at least 30%.

Television

When you buy or rent a television in France, the shop from which you purchase or rent the machine will automatically send your name and address to the TV licence office (**Centre de Redevance Audiovisuel**). You will then be liable for an annual licence fee. You only have to pay a licence fee for one TV per household, so if you buy a second TV for the bedroom or the kitchen, it will be covered under the first licence. A new law voted in 2004 intends linking the licence fee directly to the **taxe d'habitation**. Licence fees for TVs in a second home may be reduced by half under the new plans.

DEALING WITH PROBLEMS

Structural problems

If you are the cause of a problem, such as a short-circuit or leak, you are obviously responsible for repairing the damage or the problem. Contact your insurance company rapidly in order to establish what help they can offer you in the case of a major problem.

Tenants who are the victims of such problems should inform their landlords immediately. Landlords often have their own plumbers and electricians who deal with such problems for them, and send the bills directly to them. If you cannot contact your landlord, and the situation is an emergency, you will have to arrange and pay for action yourself. Keep copies of the bill, and send the original bills to your landlord for reimbursement once you have explained the situation to him or her. The **Syndic** of your building will have the names of companies they use in such situations, and whom they can recommend to you. But it is a good idea to try to arrange at least one other estimate in order to keep the costs involved at a minimum. You should note that calling out an electrician or plumber for an immediate visit or at the weekend will normally prove expensive.

Insects, pests and vermin

Your local mairie very often will have a department which deals with insect problems such as wasp nests or cockroaches. Call to find out about this service, and check how much it costs. It is not too expensive, and can save a great deal of unpleasant trouble.

Cockroaches (**cafards**) unfortunately tend to appear in clean homes as well as dirty ones. There are plenty of sprays and traps available for ridding yourself of this problem. Major infestations should be dealt with by professionals. Vermin can also be dealt with traps and poison but you obviously need to be careful about using these methods. Regular disinfections should take place of your entire building organised by the Syndic. Be careful to note when these are to happen, and arrange for access to your flat even if you do not have a problem. All flats in a building need to be disinfected for the process to be really effective. If you have a problem with vermin, warn your landlord and the Syndic so that they can take precautions.

Problem neighbours

Dealing with problem neighbours is often difficult and unpleasant. In the first instance, you need to try to speak to them about whatever is the source of the problem, whether it is noise or a leak. Try to remain calm and reasonable, even if your neighbours appear to be the opposite.

If the problems persist, you will obviously need to speak to them once again. Keep a careful note of when you spoke to them, and a brief record of your conversations. Tenants with persistent problems are fully entitled to contact your landlord for help. Eventually putting your complaints in writing is a useful way of proving you have tried to resolve the situation. The final resort for dealing with neighbours depends on whether they are tenants or owners.

♦ **Tenants**. Speak to the concierge and find out the name of their landlord. You may need to ask your own landlord to help you. If a landlord receives repeated complaints, problem tenants may be forced to leave.

♦ **Owner-occupiers**. This is a more difficult situation. Ultimately you would need to have a petition signed by the other residents of the building (many of whom will probably refuse even if they are sympathetic) before any definite action could be taken.

In both cases, the police can be asked to intervene. By law, excessive noise before 08h00 and after 22h00 is not permitted. If you own your property in an apartment block, you can also contact the Syndic of the building for advice and help.

Avoiding problems with neighbours

If all of the above sounds rather drastic and worrying, then remember that there are certain basic courtesies which will at least mark you out as '**correct**' in French eyes and help you avoid problems.

Always remember to say good morning/evening, and generally mind your manners in courtesy-conscious France. The French do not have the same Anglo-Saxon notion of popping in to see the neighbours. You might consider a Christmas drink, but do not expect to establish a Saturday morning coffee-and-chat.

If you have building works in your apartment, apart from the common courtesy of warning your neighbours, make sure that your workmen clean up after themselves in the corridors and lifts. If you like throwing parties place a little explanatory notice in the lift or entrance hall asking your neighbours to excuse the disturbance in advance. There is not normally a problem if you are polite. Avoid holding too many parties, and remember to keep the noise down, including when your guests leave.

KEEPING IN TOUCH

Using public telephones

Coin-operated telephones are now only found in cafés, hotels, restaurants, and some cinemas. Otherwise, all public telephones are generally operated by phone-card (**télécartes**), sold in post offices and tobacconists (**tabacs**). Rates are cheaper after 21h30, on official holidays and Sundays. Long-distance rates vary according to distance.

Mobile phones

The three French providers are Bouygues, Orange and SFR. If you bring a foreign-based mobile phone to France, remember that your calls will be routed via your home-server, which means that you are effectively making an international call. Calls made to other foreign-based mobile phones must also be made using the international dialling codes, even if your correspondent is also in France. For instance, if you are in Nice, and you want to call your friend in Paris who has a British-based mobile phone, dial 00 44, then your friend's normal mobile phone number but without the 0 at the beginning of the number. **If you use this system you will be faced with very high phone bills as a result.**

The postal system

As in the UK, post offices offer many more services than simply the post. Main post offices are normally open 08h00–19h00 Monday–Friday, and from 08h00–noon on Saturdays. In Paris, the main post office in the rue du Louvre is open 24 hours. Stamps can also be purchased at tobacconist's shops.

Automatic franking machines inside post offices, including scales for weighing letters and small packages, dispense labels (**etiquettes**) for the appropriate value. Using these can help you to avoid the often considerable queues for assistance at the counter. Postage rates differ with destination and weight. In Paris, these machines have a multilingual built-in option, including English.

If you wish to send a registered letter (**lettre recommandée**), there are a number of options:

♦ **with no proof of delivery and no declared value, but with a proof of despatch** – sans avis de réception

♦ **with proof of delivery (which will be sent back to you signed and dated), a proof of despatch, but no declared value** – avec accusé de réception

♦ **with declared value** – avec valeur declarée.

Chronopost is the French equivalent of Datapost in the UK, and next-day delivery is normally guaranteed throughout France.

France uses a five-digit code system, with the code written before the name of the town or city. The first two digits indicate the department, and the last three indicate the city. For instance: the eighth arrondissement of Paris is 75008 (75 for Paris, 008 for the eighth arrondissement).

Internet
France participated fully in the Internet boom of the 1990s. This is both through home-grown sites (eg, *Voilà.fr*

or *Free.fr*), and a strong American presence (eg, AOL) in the French market. You should have no problem connecting your existing equipment to French outlets. The France Telecom Internet service is *Wanadoo.fr*. 'Cyber cafés' can be found across France in towns and cities, allowing consumers to surf the net over lunch or a coffee. La Poste also offers free e-mail addresses. For more details ask at any post office.

LEARNING THE LANGUAGE

In order to get the most out of your time in France, you simply **must** study French and learn to speak it as well as you possibly can. If you do not, you will almost certainly find yourself considerably restricted and you will definitely feel left out. The French place a very high priority on their language, and their opinion of you as a foreigner will depend to a significant degree on whether you speak their language. Although they may criticise your less-than-perfect attempts to speak French, they will respect you far more for having tried than if you insist on speaking English.

There is no easy formula that allows you to become fluent in French. Certain people have a gift for languages. Others tend to be natural mimics, and they have an advantage as they will soon catch on to key vocabulary and pronunciation. The only difficulty with the latter is that you may also pick up a local accent, but the French will find that all the more charming.

No matter which category you fall into – gifted linguist, mimic, somebody with long-lost school French, or an absolute beginner – there are still a number of basic actions which can help you:

1. Try hard to find time to study basic grammar, phrases and vocabulary before you come to France. If you have the opportunity, an evening class would be a very good idea.

2. Bring a good dictionary with you (not necessarily the most expensive), and also a good phrase book.

3. Sign up for lessons when you arrive. There are now hundreds of language schools across the Île de France. They provide tuition at all levels, from basic to advanced, and many offer courses in Business French. Try looking in the *Yellow Pages* (*Pages Jaunes*) or the local phone book, or local expatriate community guides. Welcome offices, consulates, churches and clubs often have details or advertisements from schools and private tutors.

4. Put aside your inhibitions. Nobody, least of all the French, likes making mistakes in public. This is often what holds you back when you understand what is being said, and know how to reply but you still cannot manage to actually formulate and say the phrase. When you let go of your inhibitions, you will often surprise yourself by what you actually do know. You may prefer to use a private tutor at first if you are shy of speaking French in public. This can be helpful by allowing you to build up your confidence with a sympathetic French ear.

5. You may also see offers of 'conversation exchange', whereby you trade-off an hour of English for an hour of French conversation. This could also be a good way to meet people, and you could try joining a conversation group. A relaxed approach will help you gain confidence and will help you to eliminate a mental block on the language, with French only being used for unpleasant or stressful situations, from administration to problems in the home.

6. Use the French press. Try to listen to as much French TV and radio as possible, so that you start to become used to the sound of the language, and the way in which it is used. Listening to news bulletins in French can be helpful, as the same phrases are used over and over again each hour. Also, try reading one of the more accessible French newspapers such as *Libération*, *France-Soir*, or the free papers in the Paris métro in order to develop your vocabulary. Choose small articles with headlines about topics you know something about, and try to really understand two or three articles a day. This will build up both your vocabulary and your confidence.

7. Use bilingual websites. Throughout this book, you will find recommendations for websites with information in English as well as French. Use the information in English to help you tackle the situation you are confronting, but then go back to the websites and look at the same information in French. Once again, you will become familiar with vocabulary, phrases, and style.

8. When you go shopping, read everything, paying particular attention to labels. Make an effort to go to some small local shops, and learn how to pay for the items you buy. After a while you will be able to carry on a simple conversation with the shopkeepers, who are often happy to advise their loyal customers.

Finally, do not be afraid to make mistakes (**faux pas**). Use French whenever you can, and try to forget the natural dread of saying the wrong thing. A sense of humour is essential, and the ability to laugh at your own mistakes. Mastering the French language is a question of confidence, no matter what level you are starting from. Learning the language is like learning to walk – you stumble every now and then. You must not be too upset by unintentional errors. By and large, your efforts will earn respect, an understanding smile, maybe a giggle which you should share in, and a little patient help.

Learning to tell French time
In France, the 24 hour clock is used: for example, 1.20pm is written as 13h20, 8.00am is 08h00, and 5.30pm is 17h30. The French working day usually begins at 9h00 and finishes at 18h00. The long French lunch hour is still observed in French public sector offices. Even if only a shorter period is actually taken for lunch, many private offices will be closed to the public during this whole period.

Early mornings are generally busy with the rush to the office or school, but less so in the school holidays. Buy yourself a French diary which lists the school holidays and

French bank holidays, which considerably affect work patterns.

Listening to French radio
Under French law, at least 40% of airtime every day must be devoted to French music on commercial music radio stations. There are a wide variety of stations available throughout France. The leading 'classic' radio stations are **France-Info** and **France-Inter** (current events, music and discussions), **France-Culture** (arts and literature), **France-Musique** (classical music and jazz) and **Radio Classique**.

The Parisian radio stations are, not surprisingly, the most trendy. The most popular stations for the eighteen- to thirty-somethings are **Europe2**, **Nova**, **Voltage**, and the gay radio station **FG** (only available in Paris) which is highly popular for young people of all persuasions. **Nostalgie** and **Chérie FM** churn out 'golden oldies', including French disco and ballads, a good preparation for your first invitations to French parties. **RTL2** and **OuiFM** will appeal to rock fans and easy listening lovers.

The BBC World Service and Radio 4 are available throughout France. They are also available on the Internet, as are the vast majority of radio stations.

Watching French television
Foreign TV sets do not work in France, so you will need to buy or rent when you arrive. There are six TV channels available throughout France:

- **TF1** is privately-owned. It generally has the 'big name' news presenters and TV journalists. Otherwise, the quality of programmes is variable, with many poor-quality game shows, '**réalité**' shows (eg, tracing missing relatives), and talent shows.

- **France 2** is still under state control. This is the main heavyweight rival to TF1. There is a generally higher standard of varied programmes. **FR3** is also under state control, with regional news-broadcasts.

- **Canal +** is a private pay channel. For part of the day everybody is able to receive their programmes, and part of the day (normally the most interesting part) you must take out a private subscription for a receiver. Many good quality films and the popular satirical but caustic puppet show *Les Guignols*.

- **La Cinque/Arte**. These two stations share a frequency, Arte taking over at 19h00. The latter is a Franco-German company. An intellectual channel, with good documentaries, no game shows, and films in original languages (**version originale** or **v.o.**) including English.

- **M6** is considered a 'lightweight' channel in comparison with the others. Nonetheless there is a good selection of films and reports (especially Sunday evenings), and a much younger dynamic feel to the presentation. Foreign films are always dubbed in French.

On French TV there is a coding system with different symbols on the screen indicating the level of parental consent advisable for various films and programmes. The main programme for the evening normally begins about 20h45, after the news and weather broadcast.

Satellite television, offering a wide variety of channels from sport to history, and including the BBC and leading American channels, is now widely available throughout France. Check to find out if your building is cabled (**cablé**), and ask neighbours about how and where to subscribe. The cable TV stations available include American and 'packaged' BBC programmes including many popular soap operas broadcast both subtitled and dubbed. Amongst the best cable TV channels are **Paris Première** (general arts, lots of v.o. English/American films, and Fashion Week specials), **Téva** (for v.o. American sitcoms), and channels such as **Odyssey** for general interest programmes. The French continuous news channel is **LCI**. MTV is available also, and the French equivalent is **MCM**.

Reading French newspapers and magazines

The principal national French newspapers are:

◆ *Le Figaro* – right-wing, conservative, but a good general read.

◆ *Le Monde* – independent, centre-left, regarded as 'the intellectual's newspaper' for both the right-wing and the left-wing. Takes some getting used to, but worth the effort.

◆ *Libération* – young, centre-left and trendy. Good arts coverage.

- *Le Parisien* and *France-Soir* – sensational headlines, most akin to the English tabloids but much softer.

- *Le Canard Enchaîné* – the scourge of the political establishment, satirical but serious. A bit heavy going until you get into French politics.

Les Echoes and *La Tribune* are the business newspapers (equivalent to *The Financial Times*); *L'Equipe* is the popular sports newspaper; *La Croix* is run by the French Catholic church. Magazines such as *L'Evenement, Marianne, Le Point, L'Express*, and *Le Nouvel Observateur* offer good broad-ranging weekly news coverage from a variety of political perspectives.

The foreign press is widely available each and every day in France, but at a more elevated cost. One way to save money is to take out a subscription to your favourite newspaper, which often leads to considerable savings. All major newspapers are available on the web.

CHANGING YOUR ADDRESS

Moving homes in France is not simply a case of finding and securing your new address, and then informing your family and friends where to find you. A great many other people and organisations, listed below, must also be informed. This information applies to both home-owners and tenants.

Moving home action plan

1. **Landlords.** Be careful to respect the notice periods stipulated in your rental agreements.

2. **Electricity, gas and water**. Contact your current agencies 10 days before you move to have your meter read. The cost of terminating your current contract will be sent to your new address. At the same time, contact your new agencies to establish the new contract or arrange to take over the existing contract.

3. **Telephone**. Contact your current and future France Telecom agencies. Arrange termination of your existing contract about eight days before the move. In certain cases if you are staying within the same exchange area, you can keep the same number if you wish. A recorded message can also be arranged on the old number for three months informing callers of your new number.

4. **Post**. Organise a **faire-suivre** at the post office for all your post. This should be done no later than five days before the move. Generally it works well. However, you might wish to consider tipping your current concierge to check that any post does actually reach the new address.

5. **Carte de séjour and passport**. The new address must appear on your official documents.

6. **Driving licence, carte grise and car registration**. You have one month in which to accomplish the change of address on your carte grise. If you change départements, your car must also be re-registered.

7. **Insurance policies**. You will need to inform your insurance companies of a change of address. You can either terminate your existing house insurance, or transfer it to your new residence. This may cost more

or less depending on whether your new home is smaller or larger than before.

8. **Social security**. Fifteen working days before you move, contact your current and future caisse d'assurance maladie to arrange for your new card(s), and the transfer of your files. This is not the most efficient or speedy of services, so allow plenty of time.

9. **ANPE**. If you are registered at the local job centre, inform your old centre of your forthcoming change of address. Visit your new centre as soon as possible after moving in.

10. **Family benefits**. Inform your local caisse d'allocations familiales of your intended move 15 working days before the date. They should contact your new caisse for you.

11. **Bank**. Inform the bank of your change of address as soon as possible. This will allow them to not only send correspondence to the correct address, but also to print new cheque books for you. You may also wish to change branches.

12. **Tax offices**. Inform your current tax office before you move of your change of address. The following year, you will send your tax declaration to your old tax office, but marked with your new address on the first page. You must also inform the TV licence centre of your change of address. **Correspondence from tax offices is <u>not</u> forwarded by the post office, but sent back to the senders. This can have serious consequences**.

13. **Municipal crèches**. You must enrol your children at your future mairie as soon as possible. You must also

respect the one month notice period for withdrawing your children from their current crèche.

14. **Primary schools**. Before moving, ask the school for a **certificat de radiation**. (This does not mean that your child glows in the dark, but that she or he has been struck off the school register.) At the same time, contact the schools office of your new mairie to arrange an appointment. They will inform you which school catchment area you now fall under.

15. **Collège or lycée**. Before moving ask the school director for a **certificat de sortie** for your children. The appropriate files should then be transferred directly to the new school.

FINDING OUT MORE

♦ **Barclays** is the only British high street bank in France, with over 100 branches (**agences**). Either enquire in the UK for your nearest French branch, or contact the international branch at 6 rondpoint des Champs-Elysées, 75008 Paris. Tel: 01 44 95 13 80, fax: 01 42 25 73 60.

♦ **Britline,** *www.britline.com* is the on-line English-language banking service offered by Crédit Agricole. Originally this was intended just to serve Normandy. **Their website offers a great English-French glossary of banking vocabulary.**

♦ **CIC Banque Transatlantique** is part of the nationwide banking chain. They provide free brochures in English. Main branches are at: 17 boulevard Haussman, 75009 Paris. Tel: 01 40 22 80 00, fax: 01 48 24 01 75; 36 St

James' Street, London SW1A 1JD. Tel: (020) 7493
6717, fax: (020) 7495 1018; 1819 H Street, NW, Suite
620, Washington DC 20006. Tel: 202 429 1909, fax: 202
296 7294.

♦ **Citibank** has a number of branches across France, with
services in English. Tel: 01 49 05 49 05.

♦ **Société Générale International Private Clients branch** –
English-speaking branch. 29 boulevard Haussman,
75009 Paris. Tel: 01 53 30 87 10, fax: 01 53 30 87 30.

Enrolling for Education

The French state educational system is in an on-going period of reflection and potential change at the time of writing. Generally academic levels are very high, and teachers and pupils alike are expected to show a serious commitment to their work. The popular Socialist Education Minister, Jack Lang, put more emphasis on arts and modern languages rather than the traditional French school subjects. His right-wing successors are now emphasising vocational training and education.

Education was one of the major priorities to emerge from the Paris mayoral campaign in 2000–2001, and the city council is spearheading a renovation plan for the more dilapidated schools, as well as seeking to open new schools to meet Parisian needs. Among younger pupils, the principal concern is to teach increased respect, and to diminish the rather spectacular, but isolated, displays of violence which have occurred in recent years. Change is not something which comes easily in France, and while the younger generation of **professeurs** or **profs** (high school teachers) and **instituteurs** or **instits** (junior school teachers) are open to new ideas, the older generation tend to hold the 'eternal' view of French education; 'Learn what we taught in the beginning, teach now and ever shall do'.

THE ACADEMIC YEAR

France very much beats to the rhythm of the academic year. This begins in mid-September with **la rentrée scolaire,** and ends in late June. A mid-term break occurs around All Saints Day (**Toussaint**) at the beginning of November, followed by a two-week break for Christmas and New Year. There is another mid-term break in February, and two weeks for Easter holidays (not necessarily linked to the date of Easter itself). Holiday dates vary from region to region, so check on Paris regional dates.

THE SCHOOL DAY

In state schools, children attend school from 08h30–11h30, and then from 13h30–16h30 from Monday to Saturday, with Wednesday and Saturday afternoons free. Variations occur according the level of education of your child; Wednesdays are completely free for smaller children, whilst Saturday mornings and Wednesdays are obligatory for old children at **lycée**. Some private schools have adopted the simpler five-day week, as have some experimental **collèges**. An attempt to restructure the school day in Paris to a full five-day week and weekends free was rejected by parents and teachers in 2001.

ELEMENTARY EDUCATION (AGE 2–6)

School is not compulsory in France for children until they are six years old. Nonetheless, 93% of three-year-old children in France are enrolled in the voluntary **écoles maternelles**.

Enrolling your child

Enrolment takes place at your local mairie, at the published dates (normally around March), and can be performed as soon as the child reaches the age of two years. At enrolment, you will be informed of the school catchment area you fall into. It is possible to choose another school if you wish by following a long procedure. Documents needed to enrol your child are:

- The **livret de famille** (if you were married in France) or a **fiche d'état civile** of the child.

- A proof of residence (justificatif de domicile) eg, electricity bill with your name on.

- The **carnet de santé** of your child, proving she or he has received all necessary relevant vaccinations.

Once you have received the enrolment certificate (**certificat d'inscription**) from the mairie, you need to make an appointment straight away with your school director. Children are accepted on a 'first come, first served' basis, with priority for older children. Schooling for children under three years old depends on the availability of places.

The classes offered in the école maternelle are roughly equivalent to Early Learning in the UK for French Year 1; the UK Reception Class in Year 2; and the UK Year 1 in the French Year 3 (for five- to six-year-old children). For US children classes equate to nursery schools for French Years 1 and 2, and Kindergarten for French Year 3.

PRIMARY EDUCATION (AGE 6–11)

When your child begins their compulsory education at the age of six, they will enter into the **11ème classe**. The natural progression from now on is to arrive in the **Première** classe and then **Terminale** (equivalent to Upper 6th in the UK and 12th Grade in the USA) at the age of 18 when they will normally take the **baccalauréat (BAC)** examination equivalent to A-levels.

If your child is already enrolled at an école maternelle, she or he will automatically be enrolled at your local school. Enrolments must take place no later than the month of June preceding your child's entry into the school at the **école élémentaire**. For popular schools, the sooner you apply the better your chances are of enrolling your child at the school of your choice. The same processes must be gone through if you wish to choose a school in a different sector. If your child is not already enrolled, you must follow the process outlined above.

In the écoles elementaires, (for 6–11-year-olds) the course of study may change according to the area you live in. Basically a child is taught to read and write, along with basic maths and a few less academic subjects. As the child grows older, she or he is rigorously taught the grammatical rules of the French language, including spelling and the use of tenses.

A great deal of time is spent learning poetry, which is considered good practice for the child's memory. Sciences of observation will take up about an hour a week depending on the teacher. Most schools now spend a few hours a week on English, arts and crafts, an extra sport, and a computer class. A lot depends on the human and other resources available in a school as to what is offered. The use of the Internet in schools and teaching is strongly encouraged, but depends on school resources.

Physical education usually includes two hours per week of general fitness classes, and at some time or other all schoolchildren learn how to swim.

SECONDARY EDUCATION (AGE 11–15)

From the 6ème to the 3ème (11–15 years old), your children will enter a **collège**. Similar procedures exist for enrolling your child in a collège as for other state schools. If you choose a collège outside of your district, your choice requires further justification than at earlier stages. Acceptance depends upon, amongst other factors, the availability of places in the collège chosen.

At collège, pupils have a different teacher for each subject, and classes generally last about fifty minutes. Maths and French are still the most important subjects, and are really still considered as the keys to a child's success. History and geography are taught as one subject, and physics and natural sciences are each attributed equal importance.

When a pupil enters the collège in 6ème, she or he chooses a foreign language to study, usually English or German. In 4ème there is the choice of an optional course, usually one of the classical languages of Latin or Greek.

Repeating a year

When a pupil changes from one cycle to another – at the end of the 6ème, 4ème, or 3ème – the **conseil de classe** composed of the teachers concerned decides if the pupil is ready to move on. If they think not, they can recommend that the pupil repeats a year (known as **redoublement**).

If you disagree with the decision, you must act swiftly to lodge your complaint (within three days). You will need to see the school director to request an explanation for the decision. However, if you still disagree with the decision, you can force the issue to another 'commission' including other parents, and at which you will be allowed to speak briefly. However, the decision here is final once it is taken.

Planning for the future

In February of the 3ème, families fill in a form indicating the proposed career orientation they wish their child to take. Final applications and decisions are taken in May of the 3ème, with input from the school. At the end of the 3ème (aged 14–15), pupils take a 'global' examination known as the **brevet**.

The results of this examination, together with the annual report, are used to decide upon the future education of the pupil. However, it is not an entry examination to lycée, but simply a knowledge test for the end of this section of the child's education. The choices made at this stage affect the type of lycée to which your child will next progress, and the sort of qualifications they will leave school with. The choice of lycées is either **générale et technologique,** or **professionnelle.**

The final decision is taken by a small commission, which informs parents at about the end of June which kind of lycée their child has been recommended for. More than 25% of pupils currently choose to orientate themselves towards professional life by opting to prepare either a **brevet d'études professionnelles (BEP)** or a **certificat d'aptitude professionnelle (CAP),** both of which are two year courses at **lycées professionnelles**. Normally this will lead to an entry into working life almost immediately after leaving school. The current government is encouraging more pupils to choose the offered vocational training at lycées professionnelles.

THE FINAL SCHOOL YEARS (AGE 15–18)
The final school years are **Seconde**, **Première** and **Terminale**, when the final **baccalauréat** examination is taken. For these final years, your child will be educated at a **lycée**. It is here that final choices will be taken which affect the kind of bac for which your child will prepare, and consequently, the kind of higher education which they will normally continue.

Seconde

More than 60% of pupils currently enter the Seconde in the general/technology classes. This leaves scope for taking final decisions over which type of bac to study for. Only those seeking careers in music or dance, or a technical qualification (**brevet de technologie – BT**) have specifically orientated courses. Those preparing either the BEP of CAP can study a further two years to take a **bac professionnel** before finishing their studies.

Première and Terminale

The choice must now be made which of the variety of bacs your child will study for. The general bac leaves the option open for entry into higher education. Other choices will be required if she or he wishes to pursue a vocational course at university. The courses attended in these final years will depend on the option chosen. There are seven compulsory subjects, physical education, and two optional subjects.

At the end of Première, there are written and oral French tests for bac candidates. The marks from these are included in the overall success or failure of the candidate. The final examinations are taken in summer of Terminale, and results are published very shortly afterwards at around the end of June or beginning of July.

For those who fail the first time, it is possible to retake the bac. As it is the key to any form of success in France, as well as entry to higher education, it is highly advisable to do so!

EDUCATION IN ENGLISH

The opportunity for a child to be educated at a French school can be excellent for their future prospects, ensuring that she or he will be bilingual in the future. However, it may also prove frightening and daunting for a child whose command of French is not sufficient. You must also consider the effect upon their education if you will only be living in France short-term, and will be returning to your native country and education system.

The options open to you are:

1. Boarding school in the UK or the US. This may not even be an option, depending upon your financial situation, your company's willingness to pay fees, and you and your child's attitude to boarding school.

2. Private international schools in France. The same financial criteria may affect your decision, and as well as accessibility to any such schools.

3. French schools with international sections. These are schools within the state system which normally charge a small fee for schooling in English. These schools work towards the 'Option Internationale' of the bac, and teaching is by native English-speakers.

4. French schools which offer high-level English programmes. Extra hours of education in English from native English-speakers.

5. French schools with European sections. These will normally offer some extra education in English, but not necessarily given by a native English-speaker.

The American School of Paris (tel: 01 41 12 82 82, fax: 01 41 06 23 90, *www. asparis.org*) and British Schools of Paris (tel: 01 34 80 45 90, fax: 01 39 76 12 69, *www.ecis.org/bsp*), private schools in the suburbs, each respectively follow the national curriculum of their 'home' countries. They would therefore allow your children to continue within the same educational system as they may have known before, according to your own nationality.

The International Sections of Lycées probably offer the best option for those who want their children to benefit from an Anglo-French education at a very reasonable cost. Currently there are about eight British sections in France, and about six American sections. The general rule (which varies between sections) is about four hours per week of English language and literature, and two hours a week of geography and history. The International Lycée at St Germain-en-Laye is considered to be the best lycée in this section (tel: 01 34 51 62 64, fax: 01 34 51 39 36, e-mail: adm@lycee-international.net).

Within Paris itself, bilingual private education up to 6 years old is offered at the Montessori Schools (tel: 01 45 55 13 27, fax: 01 45 51 25 12, *www.montessori-paris.com*, based at the American Church on quai d'Orsay), the Lennen Bilingual school (up to 12 years old) in the 7th arrondissement (tel: 01 47 05 66 55); the International School of Paris in the 16th arrondissement (from 3–18 years old) tel: 01 42 24 09 54, fax: 01 45 27 15 93, *www.isparis.edu*; and the Ecole Active Bilingue, a group of schools for all ages to be found in the 8th and 16th arrondissements (tel: 01 45 63 47 00, fax: 01 45 63 62 23, *www.eab.fr*).

The international option of the bac is very highly regarded, and roughly equivalent to S-levels within the British education system. It is therefore a good option for those seeking university entry not only in France, but in other countries too.

More information about native English education in France is available from **The English-Language Schools Association France (ELSA-France)**, e-mail: *Association Sis@wanadoo.fr*, and website address: *www.assoc.wanadoo.fr/association.sis.* This website has full information on all schools in France offering English-language education in all categories (state, private, exclusively English-speaking and part-English speaking). ELSA has strong links with the Section Internationale at the Collège and Lycée de Sevres, rue Lecoq, 92310 Sévres. Tel: 01 46 23 96 35. There is an official Anglo-American listing of all schools in France offering education in English on *www.britishcouncil.fr.*

EDUCATIONAL BENEFITS

- **L'aide à la scolarité**. This is available for children at collège. It is means-tested, and limited to those who are already receiving another form of family or housing benefit, or benefit for a handicapped adult.

- **L'allocation de rentrèe scolaire**. This is available for children between six and 18 years old, under the same conditions as above. Each child will automatically be awarded the benefit. The limit of joint income permitted to obtain this benefit rises with the number of children that you have.

Both benefits are administered by the **caisse d'allocations familiales** (*www.caf.fr*).

HIGHER EDUCATION

Students tend to go to a university nearest to their homes, partly to keep down costs by continuing to live at home. Naturally Paris draws a high student population of not only locals but 'foreigners' in all senses of the word, from other parts of France and from other parts of the world, drawn to the city's academically excellent institutions. In 2000, 173,000 foreign students were studying in France.

The only entrance requirement is normally a pass at the bac. As a result, there is generally high competition to enrol on the course of your choice at the university of your choice. The university year runs from October until June.

The French degree structure

◆ **Years 1 and 2 – DEUG (Diplôme d'Etudes Universitaires Générales)**. This is the core curriculum course which must be passed before continuing with further study. Many students repeat this year, and the DEUG on its own is not highly regarded.

◆ **Year 3 – Licence**. This can be passed in most subjects. It is roughly equivalent to a BA or BSc.

◆ **Year 4 – Maîtrise**. Roughly equivalent to an MA.

◆ **Year 5 – DEA (Diplôme d'Etudes Approfondies)**. A preparatory year for a doctorate.

◆ The **Doctorat** is the final stage. There is now a limit of four years for completion of the doctoral thesis.

If there is any doubt over level of your degree, a **lettre d'équivalence** can be requested from the Ministère de l'Enseignement et de la Recherche equating your degree to a French degree level.

In accordance with the European standardisation programme, the French degree structure is being adapted to the '**3-5-8**' or '**LMD**' system, of bac + 3 (Licence), bac + 5 (Maîstre), and bac + 8 (Doctorat). This new system is being introduced progressively, and should be the standard by 2005. The new system will take into account credits earned at other universities, and notably at foreign universities.

Student resident permits

Some Paris colleges and university departments have agreements with the residence permit authorities of the Préfecture de Paris allowing you to submit your application directly to the college administration. In this case, they will pilot you through the application and you will only have to go the Préfecture to collect your carte once it is ready. This applies to students of all nationalities.

If you undertake the process yourself, remember to take copies of everything with you, as well as originals. The same rules apply for student **cartes de séjours** as for all other foreign nationals in France.

1. Citizens of one of the original EU member countries do not require a carte de séjour.

2. Citizens of one of the countries which joined the EU in 2004 do still require a carte de séjour.

3. Non-EU citizens do require a carte de séjour (see below).

Students in the second category should consult their own Embassy for up-to-date information on the documents required, which may include some of the items listed below for non-EC students. You can also consult the website of the Préfecture de Paris on *www.prefecture-de-paris.interieur.gouv.fr.*

Students from other countries
Students from outside the EU, including Americans, require an entry visa before arrival in France. In addition to the basic requirements for Americans applying for a **visa de long séjour** (see Chapter 2), students will also require a letter of admission (**attestation de pré-inscription**) when applying for the first time to a French university, or other similar evidence of enrolment. Academic credentials may be checked by the French consular services in the USA where you apply for your visa. See the US Embassy in France website for further details and advice (*www.amb-use.fr*). Nationals of other countries should check with their nearest French Consular office for formalities which they need to complete.

You must apply for your carte de séjour within 30 days of entering France. You will need to bring originals and copies of the following documents:

1. The original of your valid passport plus copies of the pages indicating the marital status of the applicant, the date limit of the passport, and the visa allowing entry into France. You must bring your **visa de long**

séjour, or **visa de court séjour** marked **étudiant-concours** plus the **attestation de réussite** for the entry exam which you have passed.

2. Your birth certificate or a certified French translation of your birth certificate. If you are married or divorced, you will require either the marriage or divorce certificate, or ID certificate from your own national consulate.

3. Originals plus copies of the **certificat d'immatricula-tion, d'inscription**, or **pré-inscription** for your course at your faculty; or membership of the one of the EU programmes mentioned above; or your internship contract (**convention de stage**). You also need copies of degree certificates, exam results, etc to prove the seriousness of your application, and show your current undertakings.

4. Originals plus copies of proof of residence, as above.

5. Proof of financial resources as above:

    (a) If you are receiving a grant (**bourse**), you will need a statement on letter-headed paper from the grant-making authority stating the duration of the grant, the amount granted, and what studies you are undertaking. This should preferably be stamped by the French consulate which has issued your visa.

    (b) If you are receiving funds from abroad, you need to take as much evidence as possible with you of monthly payments.

    (c) If you are being financed by a third party in

France, you need to supply a certificate and personal and financial documents relating to your sponsor (enquire for further details).

(d) If you intend working part-time, you need to bring your contract or job offer, stating the nature of the position, the number of hours, and the gross salary.

(e) If you are working as an au pair, you need either your approved contract, or your job offer from your family.

6. Three black and white passport-size photos.

There are two principal recommended centres in Paris for non-EU student applications, both open from 15 September to 15 December. Outside of Paris, contact your departmental préfecture.

◆ Cité Internationale Universitaire de Paris, Maison Internationale, 17 boulevard Jourdan, 75014 Paris. RER ligne B station: Cité Universitaire.

◆ Centre des étudiants étranger, 13 rue Miollis, 75015 Paris. M° Ségur or Cambronne.

Student welfare
Students have their own **régime** in the Sécurité sociale, for those between 20 and 28 years old. Students from EU countries will need Form E111 when coming to study in France. Upon arrival they will then need to contact the **Direction des Régimes Spéciaux** of their local university caisse d'assurance maladie.

You must join the student social security régime if you are over 20 and under 28, and/or you are a foreign student; have no rights deriving from a parent, or from your own paid employment; and you are enrolled in an establishment deemed to fall under the student social security régime. Students who receive a French government grant are exempt from the social security fee.

There are also two student **mutuelles** (complementary health insurance schemes) available, from which you should choose one to join: either La Mutuelle des Etudiants (137 bd St Michel, 75005 Paris. Tel: 0810 600 601, *www.lmde.fr*); or La SMEREP (54 bd St Michel, 75005 Paris. Tel: 01 56 54 36 34, *www.smerep.fr*).

Housing and other benefits are means-tested on the basis of the income of the student's parents. All students are eligible for limited housing benefit. However, a distinction is made between those who depend solely on their parents for financial support, and those who work their way through their studies. In fact, those who work are worse off in terms of benefits.

Two of the most important places that you will need to find are the **CROUS (Centre Régional des Oeuvres Universitaires et Scolaires),** and the CIDJ (Centre d'Information et de Documentation Jeunesse), if your university has one. The important Paris CIDJ is at 101 quai Branly, 75015 Paris, beside the Eiffel Tower (tel: 01 44 49 12 00).

The CROUS will issue your student card, which will allow you a wide variety of discounts (eg, travel, museum entrance, etc). The CROUS acts to some extent as a Student Union would in a British university, in terms of the welfare and general information services it offers. The CIDJ has a job centre, travel agency, bookshop and a reference library on social security rights, etc.

The Cité Internationale Universitaire de Paris

The extensive residential campus on the southern edge of Paris with its own sports grounds and RER station is a popular choice for students in higher education. Thirty-seven nations have their own college or maison. The main reception centre at 19 boulevard Jourdan, 75014 Paris can be contacted on 01 44 16 65 54, and the admission office on 01 44 16 64 41 (and 64 68 for the student welcome centre). The College Franco-Britannique (9b, boulevard Jourdan) which can be contacted on 01 44 16 24 00, admits over 200 students of at least third year university level from all over the world, with 50% of the rooms reserved for British students. There are also American and Canadian colleges.

The Grand Ecoles

The Grandes Ecoles are the élite higher education institutions (some of which are private), which consistently produce the leaders of French commerce, industry, politics, and society in general.

Competition for entry is obviously fierce and very selective. Being a foreigner will probably not help your case, unless you have already attended a top-level university in your own country. However, if you do succeed in graduating from one of these schools, a successful professional life will be almost assured, with a very useful set of future contacts.

English-speaking universities in France

The American University of Paris (www.aup.edu)
US Admissions Office, 60 East 42nd Street, Suite 1463, New York 10017. Tel: 212 983 1414, fax: 212 983 04 44, e-mail: *usoffice@aup.edu*.

International Admissions Office, 6 rue du Colonel Combes, 75007 Paris. Tel: 01 40 62 07 20, fax: 01 47 05 34 32, e-mail: *admissions@aup.edu*

Continuing Education and Summer Programmes, 102 rue St Dominique, 75007 Paris. Tel: 01 40 62 06 14, fax: 01 40 62 07 17, e-mail: *ce@aup.edu* or *summer@aup.edu*

The American University of Paris (AUP) is a private university based in central Paris in the 7th arrondisse-ment, near to the American Church community centre. The AUP offers undergraduate courses in a wide variety of subjects, summer programmes and continuing educa-tion which will help you develop skills for the Parisian (and other) job-markets (eg, web design, screen-writing, accounting). All courses are taught in English. The AUP also offers help with accommodation for its students. Candidates may join the university for either the fall of spring semesters. The AUP also offers distance learning courses.

The British Institute of Paris (www.bip.lon.ac.uk)

The British Institute (tel: 01 44 11 73 73, fax: 01 45 50 31 55), housed in the same building as The British Council (the cultural affairs department of the British Embassy *www.britishcouncil.fr*), is situated at 11 rue Constantine overlooking Les Invalides. The Institute is an integral part of the University of London, and offers a BA Honours Degree Course in French Studies, the only British university department offering the chance to learn French in France. The Institute also offers continuing education courses such as translation.

The Open University (www.open.ac.uk)

The British distance-learning university, the **Open University**, has now been operating in France for several years, and has held two degree conferral ceremonies in Paris. All courses are taught in English using proven methods, and cover a wide range of subjects. The obligatory summer schools are also held in France. For further information, write to: Rosemary Pearson, 51 rue de Villiers, 92200 Neuilly-sur-Seine. Tel: 01 47 58 53 73, fax: 01 47 58 55 25, e-mail: *r.pearson@open.ac.uk*.

Other degree courses in Paris

There are an increasing number of **MBA** courses being taught from Paris bases with joint teaching programmes linked to US universities and business schools. These courses are almost all taught at least partially in English. Details of the courses and schools available will be found in most English-language magazines in Paris. The most renowned French Business School is INSEAD (tel: 01 60 72 42 42 *www.insead.fr*) near Fontainebleau, now ranked among the world's leading schools.

Parsons School of Design in central Paris (tel: 01 45 77 39 66, *www.parsons-paris.pair.com*) offers full-time, part-time and evening classes and Bachelor of Fine Arts degrees in fashion design, illustration, computer graphics, etc.

Learning the language

Private language schools and teachers abound in Paris and across France. The quality and value for money that you will receive from these institutions and individuals varies enormously, and you should try to seek local guidance from expatriate groups and colleagues. Sign up early to ensure your place at your preferred school and course. You will normally have a brief test to establish just how much or how little you know. After that you will be 'streamed' into the appropriate class.

Your local **syndicat d'initiative** should be able to provide a list of language schools in your area. Many universities now offer language courses for foreigners. Foreign university students will also normally find that French tuition is included on their timetable.

The best-known Paris language schools for foreigners are the following:

◆ **Alliance Française**, 101 bd Raspail, 75006 Paris. M° Rennes. Tel: 01 45 44 38 28, fax: 01 45 44 89 42, *www.alliancefrancaise.fr*. The flagship of a worldwide network of deservedly renowned French language schools.

◆ **Institut Catholique**, rue d'Assas, 75006 Paris. M° Rennes. The renowned private Catholic University in central Paris (open to people of all and no faiths) has a major centre for French language teaching to foreigners.

◆ **La Sorbonne**, Cours de Civilization et de la Langue Française, 47 rue des Ecoles, 75005 Paris. M° St-Michel. Tel: 01 40 46 22 11, fax: 01 40 46 32 99. Offers courses and diplomas at all levels, including business French.

Cultural learning opportunities

WICE – The Women's Institute of Continuing Education, 20 bd Montparnasse, 75015 Paris. M° Duroc. Tel: 01 45 66 75 50, fax: 01 40 65 96 53, *www.wice-paris.org*. WICE offers everything from art history to creative writing classes and cultural tours. WICE also offers TEFL English-language teaching qualifications required to make a successful entry to the job market as an English teacher. Despite the name, the clientele is not exclusively feminine although women account for about 90% of the 1,000 members from 25 different countries.

Cookery courses

Cookery classes in the capital of cuisine are not cheap (in fact they are anything but that), but your stay in Paris is a once-in-a-lifetime opportunity to learn unique skills. Three of the best are:

◆ **The Ritz-Escoffier School**, 15 place Vendôme, 75041

Paris Cedex 01. Tel: 01 43 16 71 70/71/72, fax: 01 43 16 36 68/69 *www.ritz.com*, at the legendary Paris hotel with prices which will bring tears to your eyes.

♦ **Le Cordon Bleu**, 8 rue Léon Dulhomme, 75015 Paris. Tel: 01 53 68 22 50, fax: 01 48 56 03 96 *www.cordon-bleu.net*. One of the most renowned French cookery schools, with five different 'schools' and a nine-month diploma.

♦ **La Cuisine de Marie-Blanche**, 18 avenue de la Motte-Picquet, 75007 Paris. Tel: 01 45 51 36 34, fax: 01 43 47 38 68, *www.cuisinemb.com*. Learn how to tame your own hungry rabble by saying 'Let them eat cake', from the descendant of one of the eye-witnesses to Marie-Antoinette's infamous one-liner. Courses in English, French and Spanish.

FINDING OUT MORE

♦ **The English-Language Schools Association France (ELSA-France),** e-mail: *AssociationSis@wanadoo.fr*, and website address: *www.assoc.wanadoo.fr/association sis*.

♦ *www.aparc.com*. English-speaking parents' association in the Chantilly region which organises regular English lessons and education in English for children.

♦ **Centre National des Oeuvres Universitaires et Scolaires (CNOUS)**, *www.cnous.fr*. Each university has a regional centre (**CROUS**). The individual websites linked to this central site are the best place to find out all the practical details of student life, from residence permit centres to housing offers.

◆ *www.edufrance.fr*. Multi-language French government website. General information and useful links.

14

Looking at Health and Welfare

For British citizens, it is essential that you obtain a copy of the Department of Work and Pensions pamphlet *Your social security insurance, benefits and health care rights in the European Community* Number SA29. You should also contact the Department of Social Security Overseas Branch, Newcastle upon Tyne, NE98 1YX, to check on the pamphlets that they have available. Separate leaflets are available from the Northern Ireland Social Security Agency International Services at 24–42, Corporation Street, Belfast BT1 3DP. You can find SA29 on-line on the British Embassy website *www.amb-grandebretagne.fr*

French healthcare is considered to be amongst the best in Europe. Critics might retaliate, however, that this is because the French are a nation of hypochondriacs, which at times it is hard to dispute and the cost of sometimes over-generous healthcare has certainly been a bitter pill to swallow in recent years. A number of reforms are currently being debated to curb the French social security debt and bring order to a generous system which is often abused, and is straining to keep up with an ageing population.

In 2002 President Chirac established two health priorities for his new term of office: the fight against cancer, and aid to the handicapped. In 2004, new health service reforms were proposed which are still being debated. They are provoking fierce arguments in some quarters, but they are likely to be adopted.

JOINING THE SOCIAL SECURITY SYSTEM

If you are living and working in France, you are obliged to join the French **Sécurité sociale**, covering pensions, sickness and healthcare, and unemployment. Generally, you will need certified copies of your birth and marriage certificates as for your carte de séjour. Check with your employer and/or your local social security office.

The official telephone information line for the Paris Health Authority, the **Caisse Primaire d'Assurance Maladie de Paris** (CPAM de Paris) is 0820 904 175, and the website is *www.cpam-paris.fr*. The site is in French only, and a little dense in comparison to some of the other official French sites, but it does contain plenty of useful links and hints.

◆ If you are in regular employment in France, you should automatically join the social security system courtesy of your employer. You and your employer make regular contributions to ensure that you and your dependants are adequately covered. This rule applies to all foreigners who have obtained their carte de séjour.

◆ If for any reason the enrolment (**inscription**) to the **Sécu** (as it is generally known for short) is not organised by your employer, you should go to your local **caisse** (each arrondissement and commune has their own local branch). You will need to take with you a piece of official ID, a **relevé d'identité bancaire** also known as a **RIB** (bank account details, available from your bank), and your pay slips. These last documents are essential to show that your employer has been making the necessary contributions on your behalf to the social security service.

◆ If you are in paid employment in France, and are therefore enrolled in the French social security system, your spouse, partner (if they are totally dependent on you financially), your children under 16 years of age, or up to 20 years of age if they are studying, are all covered by your social security payments for standard medical treatment and reimbursement.

◆ If you are self-employed, you pay a percentage of your taxable income as your contribution which can be deducted for income tax purposes. Self-employed workers are not covered in the same way as employed workers by the Sécurité sociale. It is therefore important that you join the appropriate scheme as soon as possible after arriving in France. See Chapter 5 on self-employment.

◆ If you are a UK national sent to work in France for less than 12 months, you will normally remain insured under the UK national insurance scheme. You or your employer should obtain the appropriate forms (E101 and E111) from the DSS Overseas Branch, Newcastle upon Tyne NE98 1YX, before coming to France. These prove that you remain insured under the British system, and entitle you to emergency medical care. (Also see below.)

◆ Employers are obliged to make declarations and payments on behalf of au pairs to the social security administration service (URSSAF). This will provide you with basic rights and coverage.

◆ If you are unemployed and come to France to look for work, see the Chapter 4 on working in France.

◆ If you are student and an EU citizen, you will need to obtain Form E111. See Chapter 13 on education in France for full details.

Introducing the Carte Vitale

The Securité sociale is notoriously slow in issuing numbers, cards known as the **Carte Vitale**, which are also the means of reimbursement. You may have to wait some time until you receive your card demonstrating your eligibility to use state services, and for reimbursement. Medical treatment will only be reimbursed after proof that you have worked 200 hours in the previous three months. This can include time worked in the UK. Form E104 available from the DSS in Newcastle upon Tyne will need to be completed and submitted by your French employer.

In 1999 the **Couverture médicale universelle** guaranteed minimum health care to all 'stable' French residents. Parallel with this move, efforts have been made in recent years to reduce the paperwork involved in the reimbursement process by the introduction of the Carte Vitale which is now issued to all subscribers to a CPAM. Once your rights have been validated (ie, you have joined the system), they remain valid throughout the time that you are a legal French resident. The end-date on your card will simply indicate when the card needs to be renewed and/or brought up to date. Each person in the household over the age of 16 who is registered with the Sécurité sociale, or derives their rights from their spouse, partner or parent, will receive their own individual Carte Vitale.

If your card carries specific prescription charge exemption rights etc, then the end-date indicated will refer to the moment when your rights and needs in this respect will be reconsidered by the Sécu. If you lose this card or it is stolen, or for some reason you never receive it, you have to make a **déclaration sur l'honneur** in writing to your caisse in order to be issued with a new card.

What is the carte vitale and how do you use it?
The Carte Vitale is a personalised record on a credit card sized 'chip' (**puce**), which allows doctors and other health service professionals to register their acts and charges on

a central system. The plan was that in 2002 the brown **feuilles de soins** (see page 307) would disappear and reimbursement would become a paper-less process. However you should not count on this becoming an immediate reality. Generally this is now the case, but some specialists and private doctors are still not equipped with the carte vitale system.

The carte vitale sends the required information through to a central databank which will automatically register the demand for reimbursement for the cost of the transaction, which you must still pay in full.

You should note that the carte vitale is not a form of payment and you are still required to settle the full fee at the end of your appointment and to be reimbursed subsequently. The difference is that you do not have to send the forms through the post to the Sécurité sociale, so there is less paperwork and less chance of lost and unpaid claims.

Updating your carte vitale
You can make updates to the information on your carte vitale. You can do this yourself at one of the 150 (approximately) sites in Paris (eg, hospitals, local caisses, pension withdrawal centres, family support centres and pharmacies) which have computer terminals (**bornes**) which allow you to check the accuracy of the information on your card. They do not give access to medical records.

◆ If you move home, you may well move to a different reimbursement centre/local caisse. You will need to make contact with your new caisse to ask them to update your carte with your new address and perhaps also new bank details.

♦ If you acquire some form of exemption or medical assistance, this should also be registered on your new card.

♦ Children acquire their rights from their parents who are already in the system. New mothers need to present both a demand in writing for the inscription of their children, plus the birth certificate (**extrait d'acte de naissance**) and the **livret de famille** (see page 318), at their local caisse. All reimbursements concerning the children will then be made onto the same bank account as for the mother or father (as you wish).

WORKING ABROAD FOR A FIXED PERIOD

Medical records
If you inform the DWP Contributions Department that you are going to live or work abroad for a limited period (eg, because you or your partner have been seconded), they will automatically inform the National Health Service Central Register. They will amend the Central Index of Patients which helps to determine funding for each Family Health Service Authority (FHSA). The FHSA will in turn withdraw your medical records from your General Practitioner about nine months after your departure. Your records will either be held until you return or re-register with a new doctor, or until they are destroyed. Records are normally held for at least six years.

If you are going abroad for a limited period and plan to return to your current home area, it may be useful to inform your General Practitioner of both your departure and your anticipated return date. This will avoid your records being withdrawn unnecessarily.

Maintaining British social security rights

The DWP pamphlet SA29 explains in detail how to go about maintaining British social security rights whilst working abroad. It is very important that you read this pamphlet and take advice based on the information which it provides. This can affect your eligibility for state benefits upon your return to the UK, and your pension rights later in life.

Voluntary contributions can also be made in some circumstances, but these will not automatically entitle you to French social security benefits. They will simply guarantee your right to apply for British benefits.

IMMUNISATION

Standard immunisations are always worthwhile, although there are no particular dangers associated with life in France. Frequent contact with former French colonies in Africa may possibly mean that certain diseases are more common in France than in the UK or the USA, but the extra risks are minimal. All vaccines are available on prescription in France from chemists' shops (**pharmacies**), and can be administered by qualified doctors. If you arrange immunisations yourself, you can ask your doctor to write you a prescription in order to obtain reimbursement from the Sécurité sociale. However you will generally have to pay a fee to the doctor, so it is best to ask him or her to write the prescription when they administer the immunisation.

GOING TO THE GENERAL PRACTITIONER

In France you are not limited to registering with one general practitioner in your area. You are free to consult as many doctors as you wish, as often as you wish, wherever you wish. The French frequently take advantage of this system to ask for second or even third opinions, but it is not really advisable unless you doubt the competence or approach of your doctor.

Sticking to one doctor allows him or her to know you and your problems better. The government is now actively encouraging doctors and patients to build 'exclusive' relationships, to cut back on the amount of money spent reimbursing multiple doctors' appointment fees. Your chosen GP may also be designated as your **médecin-référent**, which means that he or she will coordinate all your medical cover and also prescribe generic medicines (see below).

Each time you visit the doctor, you will be asked to pay a consultation fee (**honoraire**) currently of €20. The price depends on the system the doctor works within (see page 311). The level at which you will be reimbursed for standard doctors fees is currently 70% for doctors who are **conventionné**. Prices increase for home calls (€30), night calls (up to €40 more, according to the time), Sundays and bank holidays. There are also small charges for medical acts such as cleaning and dressing a wound, administering injections, etc.

For those doctors who now accept the Carte Vitale, an automatic registration of your visit activates an automatic claim for reimbursement from the Sécurité sociale.

GOING TO THE CHEMISTS
At the chemist's shop (**pharmacie**), indicated by a green cross, hand over the prescription (**ordonnance**) to the pharmacist. Once your medicines have been prepared, you will be asked to pay in full. The level of reimbursement for medicines varies from nothing up to 100% if you have obtained an exemption certificate. Chemists' shops provide a rota of weekend cover, which is posted clearly in shop windows along with details of late-opening chemists.

The chemist may advertise and/or ask if you wish to operate the **tiers payant** system. This means that you only pay the one third of the cost of the drugs which is nominally at your charge, with the balance being paid by the Sécurité sociale and your mutuelle. Some chemists are equipped for this system with Carte Vitale card readers. This option is only open to salaried employees within the French social security system, and not to self-employed workers.

Finding the medicines that you need
Most medicines are available in both France, but may be marketed under a different name. It is very worthwhile checking this with your regular pharmacy, or even the drug company, before moving to France. Another good idea is to take the packaging listing the ingredients with you, so that the doctor can check the components against a similar product in the 'Bible' he or she always consults before prescribing.

Over-the-counter drugs are available in more or less the same way as in the UK. Chemists will advise you as to cost and value of the products you require. Paracetamol and aspirin are both known under the same names.

In 1999 the Health Ministry introduced a 'right of substitution' allowing pharmacists to propose (but not impose) generic copies of the medicines prescribed. These medicines must contain all the same compounds and properties as the brand-named medicines marked on your prescription. If you accept these cheaper medicines (the average saving is around 30%), then the actual medicine handed over the counter to you will be noted in writing on the original prescription beside the first-named medicine. Doctors are being encouraged more and more to prescribe cheaper generic drugs.

Parapharmacies

Parapharmacies are not allowed to deliver of sell medicines or prescription drugs. However, they do offer a wide range of homeopathic products, skin creams, etc. Some chemists also maintain a parapharmaceutical department.

Obtaining exemption certificates

If you have a disability or disease which requires regular and/or expensive medication, you may be eligible for an exemption certificate (**prise en charge**). Normally this will cover 100% of all fees associated with treatment, including medicines.

You will need to speak to your general practitioner or hospital specialist to arrange this. It is not an easy process, and can take a long time. There is a list of 30 diseases recognised as automatically offering exemption. The minimum length of period for treatment is now considered to be six months.

You will need thorough medical documentation, a recommendation from a French doctor, and will be summoned for an examination by a local health authority doctor (**médecin conseil**). Exemptions are also sometimes granted for a limited period after an accident and during the convalescence period.

REIMBURSEMENT OF MEDICAL FEES AND PRESCRIPTION CHARGES

The Carte Vitale system includes automatic reimbursement of medical fees and prescription charges.

If you receive a brown **feuille de soin** because the practitioner is not equipped for the Carte Vitale, once you have a complete feuille de soin, fill in the personal details, including social security number and means of payment (direct debit or cheque), and send it to your local **caisse** where your file (**dossier**) is held. Keep a copy of each feuille de soin sent. In either case, after several weeks you will eventually be reimbursed, and will receive a statement of how much you have been reimbursed for each expense.

You will also need to send a completed feuille de soin to your local caisse if you have lost your card, and are waiting for a new one.

The completed feuille de soin should include the details of your doctor's fee, signature and surgery details; and the details of the prescription drugs you have received, including the **vignettes** (stickers) from the drug packaging. Without these vignettes, you will not be reimbursed for the medicines.

Form E111 available from British post offices will provide British citizens with emergency healthcare cover for up to three months from the date of issue. However, the level of cover is limited to emergencies. Reimbursement can take place in either France or the UK. Private health insurance will provide a fuller cover for a visit of several months.

COMPLEMENTARY HEALTH INSURANCE

The remaining part of your expenditure on treatment or medicines can be reimbursed by joining a mutuelle, which is the standard French private health scheme. If you are in paid employment, you will almost always find that you are automatically included in such a scheme. Contributions are deducted each month along with regular social security contributions, and will be indicated on your pay slip.

Almost every trade and profession has its own mutuelle, and it is very worthwhile belonging to such a scheme. Benefits can also include extra sick pay, and the ability to attend private clinics if necessary or you desire. In principle, mutuelles will cover the remaining costs incurred. They will also cover some dental and eye-care costs.

Some mutuelles offer the possibility to link your reimbursements from the Sécu directly to the reimbursement system offered by your mutuelle. For further details of this kind of service, you will need to make enquiries with your own mutuelle. Otherwise, you will need to send each statement of reimbursement from the Sécu to the mutuelle, along with your mutuelle membership details.

Students are required by law to join one of the special student mutuelles. See Chapter 13 for further details.

LOOKING AT HOSPITAL TREATMENT

Every large town has at least one **hôpital conventionné** which acts as the local general hospital, and includes the casualty unit (**urgences**). You have a free choice as to whether to enter a public hospital (providing you do not arrive in emergency!) or a private clinic. However, there are certain differences as regards reimbursement for the cost of your healthcare.

Private hospital treatment will only be reimbursed by the Sécurité sociale at the same rate as treatment in a hôpital conventionné. If you chose a private clinic, you will be given a form which must be validated by your local health authority centre, where your file is held. Once this has been validated, you hand this back to the clinic at your admission.

Your local caisse d'assurance maladie will settle the largest part of your hospital bill (80%) if you are in a public hospital. Remember that private clinics will charge more for their services, and that you will only be reimbursed on the basis of a stay in a public hospital. The outstanding 20% (or more for private treatment) is at your cost. Hospital treatment is thus the moment that you will most appreciate financially the benefits of a mutuelle.

In all cases you will be asked to pay the **forfait journalier** (about €11), which is basically a 'board and lodging' fee. You will normally also be offered the chance to hire your own telephone, and sometimes also a TV. Rooms are normally shared, except for those cases which require isolation.

There are numerous situations where your entire medical bill (ie, not just the usual 80%), except the forfait journalier, will be paid entirely for you by your local caisse. For instance:

◆ important surgery

◆ if you are in hospital more than 31 days

◆ delivery of a baby (for 12 days) – nor are you obliged to pay the forfait journalier

◆ if your admission is due to a work accident – once again, the forfait journalier is not charged

◆ if you are receiving invalidity payments or benefit due to a work accident

◆ if you are suffering from a serious illness which requires expensive medical care (as recognised by your local caisse).

You may also find that certain minor operations and clinical tests will take place during the course of one day, in which case you will be assigned a bed and admitted only for the day (**hôpital du jour**).

DENTAL AND EYE CARE

The same rules apply for visits to the **dentiste** or the **opthalmologiste** (optician) as apply to visiting a general practitioner. The optician will simply provide the prescription for your glasses or contact lenses, and you must then go to one of the many specialist shops in order to choose your frames or lenses. Conventionné dentists are reimbursed at the same levels as doctors' fees in the same category.

Points to remember

1. It is very important to check if the medical practitioners and services you use – doctor, dentist, optician, hospital, physiotherapist, etc – are **conventionné**. There is nothing to stop you using private medicine, but you must be able to bear the cost.

2. About 20% of doctors are **non-conventionné**. Their fees are reimbursed much less by the Securité sociale and mutuelles. Practitioners who are **conventionné à honoraires libres** charge variable prices. The Securité sociale will reimburse at their conventionné fixed rate, and the mutuelle normally covers the rest of the cost. For instance, if your non-conventionné doctor à honoraires libres charges you €35 for a consultation, the Sécu will reimburse 70% of €20, not 70% of €35.

3. Make sure that all practitioners who do not accept the carte vitale complete a **feuille de soin** and return this to you after each consultation. Also make sure that pharmacists similarly complete their part of the feuille, and attach the **vignettes** from the medicine boxes.

HEALTH IN THE WORKPLACE

The French commitment to healthcare includes the company's doctor (**médecin de travail**). You will be expected to undergo a medical examination by this doctor, and paid for by the firm:

♦ when you join the company
♦ once a year thereafter
♦ after a prolonged absence due to illness
♦ after pregnancy leave.

You also have the right to ask to see this doctor on request, and you may also be obliged to see the doctor at the request of your company. These doctors also carry out spot-checks on your working conditions.

Smoking in the office

In 1992 smoking was banned in public areas (eg, cafés and restaurants) and in open work areas and shared offices, except in designated areas. Smoking is extremely popular in France, and this law is often brazenly flouted. In some companies, it is strictly applied. If you find yourself in a smoking environment and you object, speak to your company's human resource division first to try to reach an amicable resolution to the problem. If this has no effect, speak to your médecin de travail.

Sick leave and sick pay

Under French law, absence due to illness during the first year of your contract is not paid leave. Application of this law is, however, often at the discretion of the firm.

If you are obliged to take time off work due to illness, ask the doctor for a sick note (**arrêt de travail**). You should complete and sign this paper, and send one copy to your employer, two copies to the Securité sociale, and keep one copy for yourself.

The note will specify the length of absence permitted, and will also designate the hours in which you may go out to buy provisions, etc. This is from 10h00–12h00 in the morning and from 16h00–18h00 in the afternoon. If you intend to recuperate from your sickness elsewhere than your home, then you must have the prior agreement of your local caisse. If you are admitted to a hospital, you must also include a copy of the **bulletin d'entrée** given to you when you are admitted. **You must send off this note to your employer and your caisse within 48 hours.**

Be warned – the Securité sociale regularly undertake random investigations to see if you are obeying the terms of the note. If you are not there when the inspector calls, the Securité sociale can and will refuse to reimburse the firm for part of your salary during your absence. You could also face disciplinary proceedings. You are obliged to provide all details regarding the place where you can be visited during your arrêt de travail. This includes providing entry codes to your building. The government intends to introduce much stricter controls of sick notes and sick leave.

Your employer will continue to pay you during your absence, but will recover part of the cost from your Caisse d'Assurance Maladie. Your entitlement depends upon having completed a certain number of hours of work. If your inability to work lasts less than six months, your eligibility will depend upon your having worked 200 hours in the last three months. If your inability is more serious and requires a longer period off work, eligibility for sick pay requires you to have worked at least 12 months, with at least 200 hours worked in the last three months.

Accidents in the workplace

If you have an accident at work or travelling to work, you should inform your employer within 24 hours. You must then ensure that the following steps are taken:

(a) **By your employer** – your employer must declare the accident at your own caisse within 48 hours; give you a form certifying the accident, which will exempt you from paying medical fees in advance; and send an **attestation de salaire** to your caisse if you are signed off work due to the accident.

(b) **By your doctor** – the doctor who treats you should issue a medical certificate indicating your state of health and the consequences of the accident; send sheets 1 and 2 within 24 hours to your local caisse, and give you sheets 3 and 4 of the declaration.

(c) **By you yourself** – send sheet 4 (**certificat d'arrêt de travail**) to your employer; and take sheet 3 of the medical certificate to every subsequent doctor's appointment, etc.

Sick pay is subject to income tax, and basically you will receive half your normal daily pay. Maternity pay or monies paid as a result of a work accident are not subject to income tax. Payments are made every 14 days.

FAMILY MATTERS

Pregnancy healthcare

If you are a British citizen and pregnant at the time of moving to France, you should speak to your doctor and local health authority to find out what steps you need to take to ensure your health and benefit entitlements.

You must declare your pregnancy before the end of the third month to your Caisse d'Assurance Maladie, and to the **Caisse d'Allocations Familiales** or **CAF** (family benefit centre). To do this you must hand in the **premier examen médical paréntal** form duly signed by your doctor. You will receive a **carnet de maternité** with vouchers for the services to which you are entitled.

The services to which you are entitled free of charge are:

1. Pre-natal and post-natal examinations.

2. Eight pre-natal sessions to help you prepare for the delivery.

3. Twelve days' free hospital treatment in a **conventionné** hospital or clinic, or one which is **agrée** (approved).

4. From the first day of the sixth month of pregnancy, all medical expenses (whether related to the pregnancy or not) are reimbursed by the caisse at 100% (except certain types of drugs).

These rights are limited by the number of hours worked and the amount of money you have paid, or your husband or partner has paid, in the preceding months. You will have to pay as usual for all the services you receive, but will receive reimbursement at 100%. Vouchers should be stuck to the feuille de soins each time that you send in a claim for reimbursement, if that system is still in operation.

The current cost is €160 for a delivery by a midwife (**sage-femme**). Extra costs are incurred for a night-time delivery, for Sundays and bank holidays. All costs are reimbursed at 100%.

Maternity leave pay

Once again, the number of hours and level of contributions made is one of the deciding factors in whether you receive paid maternity leave. You must also have been enrolled in the Sécurité sociale at least 10 months by the expected date of delivery of your baby.

To obtain maternity pay, you must send the **attestation de salaire** (salary certificate) signed by your employer to the Caisse d'Assurance Maladie as soon as you begin your maternity leave. You must then send a similar form to the caisse at the end of your maternity leave. The pay is calculated on the basis of your salary for three months before you stopped work, and works out at 84% of your daily wage. At the end of your maternity leave, you must also send a certificate from your employer to your local caisse stating that you have returned to work.

If you are already receiving maternity allowance when you leave the UK, you may be able to persuade your British social security office to carry on providing that benefit.

Maternity leave
For a first or second child, the normal leave period is six weeks before delivery and ten weeks afterwards. From the third child onwards, it is eight weeks before delivery and 18 weeks afterwards. For twins, it is 12 weeks before delivery and 22 weeks afterwards; and for triplets (or more!) it is 24 weeks before delivery and 22 weeks afterwards. In the case of premature delivery, the total leave period is not reduced. In medical necessity, a doctor may prescribe an extra two weeks.

Paternity leave
The new and popular paternity leave is reimbursed in exactly the same way as maternity leave pay. Employers are obliged to accept requests for paternity leave.

You automatically have the right to three days' leave when your child is born. To apply for paternity leave as well, you need to send a registered letter to your employer with receipt (**lettre recommandé avec accusé de réception** – see Chapter 12) at least one month before the start date of the paternity leave requested. A model letter to your employer can be found on *www.social.gouv.fr/famille-enfance*. A second registered letter, either from you or your employer, must be sent to your caisse, together with a salary certificate (**attestation de salaire**) and a copy of the birth certificate (**extrait d'acte de naissance**), or of your updated livret de famille with details of your new child, or of an official statement from you recognising fatherhood of the child (**acte de reconnaissance**).

You may take up to 11 days, but leave must be taken in one go (ie, not a few days here or there). Weekends are included in the time calculated. It must be taken within four months of the birth. For multiple births paternity leave entitlement rises to 18 days.

Registering the birth

You **must** register the birth of your new child *within three working days*, ie, if your child is born on a Thursday, you have until the following Tuesday at the latest. Otherwise, you cannot register your child's birth without making an application to the courts. The registration should take place at the mairie of the place where your child was born, and the following documents are required:

◆ The **déclaration de naissance** completed by the hospital, doctor, or midwife (sage-femme).

◆ A piece of official identity (carte de séjour, driving licence, passport) for the person registering the birth.

◆ The mother's **carnet de maternité** (see page 315).

◆ The **livret de famille** if you have one. You will only have this if you were married in France.

◆ Your passports (if you and your wife have separate passports).

◆ You should also register your child's birth at your own embassy to ensure the nationality rights of the child for the future. Contact the consular services to find out how to do this.

Once you have registered the birth, you need to send a copy of the birth certificate (**extrait de certificat de naissance**) or the **livret de famille** to your local caisse. You should also add one of your 100% exemption vouchers. The caisse will you send a guide for medical 'surveillance' of your child up until the sixth birthday. You will also receive vouchers corresponding to the obligatory examinations which must be undertaken. These should be taken to the examining doctor on each occasion together with the **carnet de santé** (personal health notebook) of the child.

Maintaining foreign citizenship rights

The information below was published in 2000 by the American Embassy in Paris and the Paris-based magazine *Living in France, www.parisfranceguide.com.*

Regulations change frequently, and it is important that you check with your own embassy as to the requirements for the correct registration of the nationality status of your children.

For **American** citizens, registration is by appointment-only at the American Embassy (tel: 01 43 12 46 71). You will need to request a registration pack which must be completed before the appointment and bring the originals or certified copies of the following documents, and also your child:

(a) French birth certificate, **extrait de l'acte de naissance intégrale.**

(b) Evidence of parent(s) US citizenship (eg, passport, naturalization certificate).

(c) Parents' marriage certificate plus livret de famille if the wedding took place in France.

(d) If either of the parents has been previously married, either the decree of dissolution or divorce, or the death certificate of the previous spouse.

(e) Two recent passport-size photographs of the child for his/her passport.

(f) Fees in cash or travellers cheques – check the exact amount required when you make your appointment.

If the child has only one parent with US citizenship, the parent must have lived in the US for at least five years, for two of which they were over the age of 14.

A child born in France with two **Australian** parents has automatic Australian citizenship. Registration should occur either at birth or upon demand of a passport. Children with only one Australian parent need to apply to the immigration department of the Australian Embassy.

British parents are not obliged to register their new-born children at the embassy. A child may have a British passport providing at least one parent is British, and both parents agree in writing. Remember that all British citizens of no matter what age are now required to have their own passport, and children may no longer be registered on their parents' passports.

Any child born with at least one parent who is a **Canadian** citizen is entitled to Canadian citizenship. Certificates of Canadian citizenship can be obtained at the Paris embassy.

Support groups for English-speaking mothers
There are two principal Paris-based support groups for English-speaking mothers:

1. MESSAGE (*www.messageparis.fr, e-mail: info@messageParis.org*). A network of English-speaking mothers and future mothers in and around Paris. Meetings and activities for mothers and children, specialising in early parenting.
2. The Junior Service League of Paris (JSLP), tel: 01 47 20 00 03, and 01 46 21 55 72. A wide-ranging women's social welfare network and group including health and child welfare, and training courses for childminders.

These organisations, and regional consulates, will be able to put you in touch with regional associations.

Child benefit and family allowance
The current level of family allowance is €112.59 per month for two children, €256.83 for three children, €401.08 for four children, and then increases by €144.25 per child for more than four children. For children aged 11–16, the amounts are increased by €31.67 per child, and for those aged 16–21 (still at the charge of their parents), the amount is increased by €56.21 per child. However if you only have two children, these increases only apply for the second child.

To apply for these benefits, you need to register at your local Centre d'Allocations Familiales (CAF). If your child is born in France, and you have declared the pregnancy (see above), the CAF should contact you automatically. Details of state assistance to which you may be entitled can be found on *www.caf.fr*. In January 1998, the Socialist government introduced means testing for **allocations familiales**. This takes into account the salaries of both parents if they are working.

A number of other benefits are available from the CAF under certain conditions for parents who are forced to give up work to look after their children:

- ◆ **L'allocation de présence parentale**. Valid initially for four months and for up a total of one year, the APP is available to parents to care for sick, handicapped or disabled children.

- ◆ **L'allocation parentale d'éducation**. Valid if you have given up your employment to look after your child up to the age of three years.

- ◆ **L'AFEAMA (aide à la famille pour l'emploi d'une assistante maternelle agrée)**. The level of aid offered depends on the total family income. The level of support is reduced from the age of three years, when the child could enter a public school.

One Parent Benefit and Child Benefit from the British authorities normally ceases if you move abroad permanently. However, if you or your child stays in the UK, you can receive these benefits. Any UK insurance contributions you have paid *may* help in persuading the French authorities to pay you the French **allocations**. More information is available from, Department of Work and Pensions Child Benefit Directorate, (Washington), Newcastle upon Tyne NE88 1BR. Tel: 0870 010 0547 (in the UK), or +44 870 from abroad. E-mail: *Child. Benefit@dwp.gsi.gov.uk.*

SEXUALLY TRANSMITTED DISEASES

Your nearest hospital will be able to put you in touch with services and clinics for venereal disease. Information in English on HIV and AIDS-related issues is available from FACTS (see Figure 16). For free AIDS information ring the SIDA information service on 0800 840 800 (24 hours a day, seven days a week).

HELP WITH DISABILITY

There are numerous support groups in France to help disabled or handicapped people and those who care for them. Your doctor should be able to direct you towards the appropriate association. You should also apply to the **Bureau de l'Aide Sociale** of your local mairie for a Disabled Person's Card which will entitle you to certain discounts and assistance.

If you are receiving Severe Disablement Allowance in the UK and you want to go to another EU country, including France, you must contact the Pensions and Overseas Benefits Directorate, Department of Work and Pensions, International Pension Centre, Tyneview Park, Whitley Road, Benton, Newcastle upon Tyne NE98 1BA. The decision as to whether you continue to receive this allowance will depend upon your age, how disabled you are, and how long you have lived in the UK.

If you are receiving any form of disability working allowance or carer's allowance, and you move to France, you will not be able to continue receiving British support. Visiting France may also affect your UK allowance. Contact your local benefits authority to see what help they can offer in transferring your rights gained by British national insurance contributions to the appropriate French authorities.

Services of interest for those with disabilities or handicaps who are living in France include:

♦ **The English Language Library for the Blind** (35 rue Lemercier, 75017 Paris. Tel: 01 42 93 47 57, *www.ell-b.online.fr* Tuesday–Thursday 09h00–17h00) supplies a wide variety of recorded books on cassette in return for an annual subscription.

♦ France Telecom provides a range of products called **'Arc-en-Ciel'** (rainbow) which are designed to facilitate communication for the disabled. These include telephones with flashing lights for those with sight disabilities, and a system known as the **boîtier Dialogue** which allows communication via Minitel for the hard-of hearing or speech-impaired at an increased speed. Ask at France Telecom agencies for details.

♦ The RATP provides details of RER and métro stations and bus lines which easy access for passengers with disabilities. More details can be found on their website *www.ratp.fr*.

♦ The French national railways service, SNCF, offer a variety of travel discounts and arrangements for disabled travellers. These include first class travel at second class tariffs. In some cases the accompanying person will be entitled to travel free. **To qualify for these advantages, apply at the bureau de l'aide sociale of your local mairie for the appropriate card**. Similar offers may be offered by other travel companies, so do check.

♦ FAVA (tel: 01 42 45 17 91) is the Franco-American Volunteers Association for the mentally retarded, providing programmes for children and adults.

SERVICES FOR ENGLISH-SPEAKING PATIENTS

Many French doctors do speak some English. But unless you are reasonably fluent in French and familiar with medical terms, you could experience difficulties, especially if the illness or problem is serious. Help can be found at the following places:

♦ English-language consulates have lists of English-speaking doctors.

♦ Private health insurance companies and travellers' associations (eg, American Express, Automobile Association) often have help packs they can provide to their customers before they leave.

♦ The American Hospital in Paris, 63 boulevard Victor-Hugo, 92202 Neuilly-sur-Seine Cedex. Tel: 01 46 41 25 25. Emergency service number 01 47 47 70 15, patient access department 01 46 41 27 27. This expensive hospital may be accessible to you via your mutuelle, but otherwise do not count on receiving much reimbursement from the Sécu for access to this hospital.

◆ The Hertford-British Hospital, 3 rue Barbé, 92300 Levallois-Perret. Tel: 01 46 39 22 26, 01 46 39 22 22 for emergencies, fax: 01 46 39 22 26. A full range of treatment available in a small modern hospital within the French social security system with English and English-speaking staff.

◆ The English-language group of Alcoholics Anonymous can be contacted on 01 46 34 59 65.

◆ A cancer support group is based at the American Hospital and can be contacted on 01 46 41 25 25.

◆ FACTS – English-language support for those testing HIV positive and people with AIDS. Tel: 01 44 93 16 32.

◆ SPRINT (tel: 02 33 21 48 16 or 01 34 86 93 41) is an association of English-speaking therapists for children with special needs.

FINDING OUT MORE

◆ **British citizens** should check the two relevant government websites, Department of Work and Pensions (*www.dwp.gov.uk*); and Department of Health (*www.doh.gov.uk/travel advice*). The NI Contributions Office International Services Helpline is 0845 915 4811 (+ 44 191 225 4811 from outside the UK), e-mail: *internationalservices.ir.sbg@ir.gsi.gov.uk*. The DWP International Pension Centre (covering all benefits) can be contacted on 0191 218 7777 (+ 44 191 outside the UK), e-mail: *tvp.customer-care@dwp.gsi.gov.uk*.

- *www.cmats.fr*. The national site of the French health authority, with links to your local health authority websites and addresses. Click on your region and enter your town name to find your nearest office. Site in French only.

- *www.caf.fr*. The family benefits unit, for everything from maternity and paternity leave information to child benefits, to housing benefits. Site in French only.

- *www.securite-sociale.fr*. This website acts mainly as a springboard for more detailed health agency sites. All of these sites are in French only. The Centre des Relations Internationales of the Sécurité sociale is at 175 rue de Bercy, 75586 Paris cedex 12 (next to the Gare de Lyon). Tel: 01 40 19 53 19.

Travel guides for disabled and handicapped travellers are available in the UK from:

- RADAR, 12 City Forum, 250 City Road, London EC1V 8AF. Tel: (020) 7250 3222.

- Tripscope, The Courtyard, Evelyn Rd, London W4 5JL. Tel: (020) 8994 9294.

- Mobility International, 2, Colombo St, London SE1 1JX. Tel: (020) 7403 5688.

15 SAMU (ambulance service)

17 Police

18 Sapeurs-Pompiers (fire brigade and ambulance service)

0800 23 13 13 Free drug information service
0800 05 41 41 Free child abuse helpline
0800 306 306 Free helpline for the homeless
0800 840 840 Free AIDS information service in French

01 46 21 46 46 SOS Help
English-language telephone crisis line.
Every day 15h00–23h00

01 44 93 16 69 FACTS helpline
English-language telephone helpline for AIDS and HIV
information and support groups.
Monday and Wednesday 18h00–22h00

Figure 16. Emergency telephone numbers in France.

15

Travelling Around Paris

INTRODUCING PARISIAN PUBLIC TRANSPORT

The Paris extensive public transport system is controlled by the **RATP, Régie autonome des transports parisiens** (*www.ratp.fr*) – also known to Parisians during the regular strikes as 'Rentre-Avec-Tes-Pieds', 'Go home on foot'. In spite of the French national hobby of striking, the RATP services offer an excellent public service with **métro** stations at an average distance of approximately 500m apart in central Paris, the **RER (Réseau Express Régional)** offering fast links from the furthest suburbs into the heart of Paris and between central Paris locations, a dense network of buses and also a small number of night-buses, plus fast links to the Paris airports at Orly and Roissy. In addition to these services, local **SNCF** (French national railways, **Société Nationale de Chemins de Fer**) also provide commuter services from the suburbs to all the main Paris stations, where there are interchanges on to the métro or RER.

Maps of the bus, RER and métro systems are available free in métro stations at the ticket office, and at tourist offices. A recorded 24-hour multilanguage (including English) telephone information line on all services operated by the RATP is available on 08 92 68 41 14. In 2001 the RATP launched a new campaign to inform and enable passengers with special needs and limited mobility to use the public transport system. Several buses and métros and RER stations are now equipped with entries/exits for wheelchairs. This access plan can be down-loaded from the excellent fully bilingual RATP website which is linked to the Paris Tourist Office website and has many excellent links.

USING THE UNDERGROUND

The métro

Learning the practicalities
1. In central Paris stations are close together, and trains run from 05h30 until 01h30. Several lines fork at particular stations. To determine the final destination of the train, check the electronic indicators on the platform and the front of the train as it arrives. Generally the métro is clearly marked, well lit, quiet and clean. The basic structure of the métro is a series

of concentric circles with spokes at intervals, enabling you to change from one line to another.

2. One ticket is good for the length of any one trip, providing you have bought the correct ticket. It is cheaper to buy a book of ten tickets (**carnet**) than to buy tickets individually. Tickets can either be bought at the ticket offices (**guichets**) or from automatic vending machines accepting either coins or credit cards.

3. In métro ticket halls and sometimes on the platforms (**quais**), you will find local street maps with alphabetical street indexes, and major monuments (eg, schools, churches, government offices, post offices) will all be indicated. You will also find the métro exits indicated on these **plans du quartier** so that you can take the best exit.

Enjoying your journey

The Parisian underground system, the métro, is one of the best in the world. Founded in 1900 in time for the Universal Exhibition, many of the original wrought iron métro entrances by the architect Guimard are considered works of art, such as the Place des Abbesses and Porte Dauphine. With their orange torch-lamps, yellow name-plates with swirling Art Nouveau script in green picking out the discoloured green copper, these métro exits are one of the most enduring symbols of romantic and exuberant *Belle Epoque* Paris.

Stations built in the 1970s and 1980s Parisian reconstructions, notably Châtelet and Montparnasse, are vast warrens; one wrong turn or change of line (**correspondance**), and you are lost for 15–20 minutes on moving walkways and a search for the **sortie** (exit) which can feel like a TV challenge game show.

To celebrate the centenary of the métro in 2000, a new métro exit was designed for Palais-Royal (in front of the Comédie-Française) with hundreds of glowing colours. Direct access from the Palais-Royal métro leads you into the Carrousel du Louvre and a short-cut to the underground entrance to the Louvre beside the inverted pyramid, thus avoiding the spiralling crowds on the square above.

Many central Paris métro stations have themed decorations linked to their location: the Revolutionary Declaration of Rights at Concorde; at Louvre-Rivoli, treasures from the Louvre line the platform; from Passy to Bir-Hakeim you have a wonderful view of the Eiffel Tower as you cross over the river; whilst you are plunged into submarine copper cleanliness at Arts et Métiers, where the décor celebrates the neighbouring renowned higher education colleges for engineers and architects.

The brand new automated line 14 from St Lazare to the new Bibliotheque-Nationale-François-Mitterrand is a state-of-the art masterpiece, with crowd safety doors, spacious stations, lifts, underground gardens, and the chance to ride in the traditional driver's place at the head of the driverless trains. This line sweeps under Paris and the Seine in only 15 minutes, and it is being extended to Tolbiac in the 13th arrondissement.

RER or Rapid Regional Transit

The RER (**Réseau Express Régional**) is a more recent system with underground trains running deeper than the métro. It is an express system with fewer central Paris stops, but which reaches much further out into the Paris suburbs. Fares vary according to distance, and the RER runs from 05h30 until a little after midnight. A number of central métro stations have intersections with the RER, although the RER and métro stations do not always have the same name (eg, Opéra métro = Auber RER).

There are now five RER lines (A–E), and each one forks at least once if not twice. You will also find 'fast' trains not stopping at all suburban stations. Electronic boards on the platforms indicate both the final destination and stations where the train will stop. They also indicate if it is a short or long train, so that you can position yourself on the platform accordingly, as well as the waiting time for the train.

To transit from one system to another, you need to pass through dividing barriers. If you have a travel pass (eg, **Carte Orange**) you will be able to make the transition without any problem. There is no difference between métro and RER tickets.

To exit from any RER station, you must either use the same ticket you used to get into the system (at which point it becomes obsolete if it is a single ticket); or use a new ticket if you have managed to lose your original ticket. If you have lost your ticket, you may have difficulty leaving the system at main stations (eg, Châtelet, La Défense), as both full-length barriers and ticket controllers will prevent the only other possible methods – squeezing through with a friend, or crawling under/jumping over the barriers.

TAKING LOCAL TRAINS

The French state railway company (**SNCF**) runs local services with frequent stops in the suburbs (**banlieues**) or Paris. These operate at roughly the same times as the RER and métro. Regular green bus/métro/RER tickets are not valid on the SNCF local lines, and you must purchase yellow tickets the same size as the green tickets, but purchased from the **guichets** or vending machines. These tickets will indicate your final destination on both tickets if you buy a return ticket.

Before boarding the train, you must validate (**composte**) the ticket, as with all SNCF tickets. To do this, insert the corner of the ticket into one of the orange machines at the head of the platform, and when the green arrow lights up and you hear a clunk, one corner of the ticket will be automatically removed and date stamped on the reverse side. The ticket is now valid and you can safely board the train. You must repeat this process with your return ticket before joining the train.

TAKING THE BUS

There is an extensive bus network in Paris, and controversial new bus lanes across the city have increased their efficiency. Inside each bus there is a chart of the route and the stops, with information on how many tickets are needed for each distance travelled. Timetables are posted at bus stops, and most bus stops (**arrêt de bus**) also have simple plans du quartier. Certain lines run until 0h30 in the morning, but mostly the last bus is about 21h00. Partial services stopping part-way on the bus route are indicated by a line through the final destination. The major stops on a bus route are also indicated on the sides of the buses.

Bus and métro tickets are identical. However, they are more expensive when purchased from the bus driver. You should punch the ticket in the machine provided to validate it (**composter**) when getting on to the bus, unless you have purchased a travel pass (see page 336).

Once you are on the bus, to request the driver to stop use the red buttons. If you have to fight your way out of the bus because of overcrowding, and the doors close and the driver is preparing to pull away, just shout '**la porte, s'il vous plaît**'. You will normally find a volunteer chorus also chimes in at this point. Remember to board the bus at the front and leave at the rear (if possible), unless it is an extended bus with three sets of doors.

There are a number of night-buses (**noctambus**) which serve Paris, leaving from the Place du Châtelet every hour on the half-hour (eg, 01h30, 02h30), until the métro opens once again at 05h30. You can use your **Carte Orange** pass on these buses, but you cannot use ordinary bus tickets. Individual tickets cost €2.60 and can be purchased from the driver.

Travelling across Paris by bus may not always be the quickest way to travel, but it does allow you to familiarise yourselves with the sights and the city. Try the **Number 67** bus from the Place Pigalle at the foot of Montmartre, down alongside the Louvre, along the Seine river bank, across the Île St Louis, and down into the 5th arrondissement. The **Number 72** bus from Porte St-Cloud to the Hôtel de Ville sticks to the right river bank to give you great views of the Eiffel Tower, Place de la Concorde, the Musée d'Orsay, Notre-Dame, and finally the Hôtel de Ville.

The Montmartre **trolley bus** (**Montmartrobus**) leaving from Pigalle, especially adapted to the steep hill, winds it way through the village to the mairie, and a similar bus is now planned for the narrow streets of the Marais. Also in Montmartre is Paris's only **funiculaire railway** to the terrace of the Sacré-Coeur. The **Bat-o-bus** is a summer seasonal bus service on the Seine running through central Paris. Cheaper than the **bateaux-mouches** that glide by with their multilingual commentaries (which you can always hear in any case), the Bat-o-Bus is a very pleasant way to enjoy a day-time Paris river cruise at a reasonable price. Boarding points are dotted along both river banks.

Choosing your travel pass

All of these services are operated by the RATP and regular transport passes and tickets can be used. A single RATP ticket (**billet**) currently costs €1.40, and a carnet (10 tickets) costs €10.50.

If you intend using public transport on a regular basis, or even for occasional short periods from one day to one week, the most economical and convenient way to use the system is to buy a pass. A free pamphlet in French outlining the passes available and current prices is available at all métro stations.

1. The **Carte Intégrale** is an annual travel pass for bus, train and underground services, in the zones chosen. The card is personal, and can be replaced should it be lost or stolen. You can pay in one lump sum, or by monthly standing order. Some major stations sell this card, but otherwise it can only be purchased by post. Current prices range from €493.90/year for zones 1 and 2 (central Paris), to €1,340.90/year for those living in zone 8 in the furthest commuter towns. The card operates via a chip (**puce**) and you simply 'badge' your way through the entry barriers without inserting the card into the barrier.

2. The **Carte Imagine 'R'** is an annual travel pass for travellers aged under 26 and reserved for school and higher education students, valid in the selected zones Monday–Friday, and throughout the Île de France at weekends and public holidays. As with the Carte Intégrale, it can be paid for in one lump sum or by monthly instalments. For zones 1 and 2 the annual cost is €259.10, up to €777.80/year for zones 1–8.

3. The **Carte Orange** is the **Paris Travelcard** covering bus, métro and RER. Price varies according to the number of zones you wish to include. Zones 1 and 2 cover the whole of central Paris, up to the end of almost all métro lines, but the business district of La Défense is in zone 3. Check at your local station to see which zone you live in. The current monthly cost for zones 1 and 2 is €48.60, and for zones 1–3 it is €64.20.

If you go outside your zone, you have to buy a ticket for the whole journey – you cannot simply buy an extra-ticket to 'add on' to your Carte Orange. When you buy your Carte for the first time, take one passport-size photo with you, and ask for a **coupon orange**. Stick the photo to this, fill in your name and address, and write the number of the coupon on to the white ticket printed with the month and the date. Otherwise, the Carte Orange is invalid and you could face a heavy fine. You will be supplied with a small holder for the coupon and the carte, and you can ask for a free métro map at the same time to insert into the back of the holder. Always remember to take back your ticket once you have passed through the métro or RER barriers. Never put your ticket into the punching machines on buses, but do show the pass to the driver.

4. The **carte hebdomadaire**, which is used in the same way as the Carte Orange, is valid for one week from Monday to Sunday. For zones 1 and 2, the cost is €15.40/week, and for zones 1–3 it is €20.30.

5. The **carte mobilis** is a one-day travelcard, which can be adapted to cover certain zones and not others. For zones 1 and 2 the cost is €5.20, and for zones 1–3 the cost is €6.95. This ticket should be validated (composté). The **ticket jeune** for travellers under 26 is a weekend travelcard for Saturday and Sunday, and public holidays. The cost for zones 1 and 2 is €3.20.

Numbers 1 and 3 above are reimbursed by almost all employers at 50%. Most employers will require you to hand over your monthly tickets at the end of their validity as proof of purchase and use. Families with three or more children are entitled to reduced-rate travel by requesting a **Carte famille nombreuse**. Ask at métro stations for details.

There are a number of other passes available for tourists each year which give unlimited travel for a period of days. Ask about these at any métro stations, or at your hotel or welcome centre. You can also find details on the bilingual phone line listed on page 330.

TRAVELLING TO AND FROM THE AIRPORTS

If you use public transport to travel to either Orly or Roissy, you must either have the travel pass covering the correct number of zones (1–4 for Orly, 1–5 for Roissy), or buy the necessary ticket(s). RER Ligne B goes to both Orly (via the Orlyval shuttle), and Roissy Charles de Gaulle. The Orlyval train is not included in any travel pass, and the cost from Paris to Orly is €8.80. A new high-speed rail link from Roissy to the Gare de l'Est and Gare du Nord is under discussion, but its future is still not decided.

Buses to the airports run from the following places:

◆ The RATP Roissybus from rue Scribe beside the Opéra-Garnier. A single ticket costs €8.20.

◆ Air France buses from Place de l'Etoile (beside the Arc de Triomphe), and Porte Maillot (beside the Palais des Congrés) also serve Roissy. Tickets are purchased on the bus.

- The RATP Orlybus leaves from Denfert-Rochereau métro. The cost of a one-way ticket is €5.70.

- Air France also operates buses to Orly leaving from Invalides métro in central Paris.

TAKING THE TRAM

At the moment only two small inter-suburban lines link northern Paris and western Paris. However, work has now begun on the first Parisian trams which will run from Balard in 15th arrondissement, via the outer reaches of the 14th, to Porte d'Italie in the 13th arrondissement in 2005–2006. Some suburban trams are already in operation.

AVOIDING PROBLEMS WITH PUBLIC TRANSPORT

1. Travel passes must be shown with the accompanying coupon (eg, Orange), with your photo and name. The number on your coupon should be written on the appropriate line on the pass. Failure to do so can lead to a heavy on-the-spot fine.

2. Cartes Oranges can be purchased from the 20th day of the month, valid for the following month. Avoid long delays by buying your ticket in advance of the 1st of the month.

3. Travel passes are personal and not transferable. Ticket controllers (sometimes accompanied by the police) often wait discreetly around the corner from ticket barriers and in strategic corridors. Everybody is controlled, whether you are in suit and tie or jeans and jumper, old or young.

4. Do not put Cartes Oranges, Intégrales, or Imagine 'R' into the validating machines on buses. Otherwise they become invalid!

5. Certain stations are more dangerous than others. Take great care at all the major train stations, and especially Gare du Nord and Gare de l'Est; Châtelet-Les-Halles and Montparnasse on the RER, especially in the long corridors; métro ligne 4 from Strasbourg-St-Denis to the end of the line, Porte de Clignancourt; Pigalle to Porte de la Chapelle; Place de Clichy to the northern ends of ligne 13 and to Nation on ligne 2; and Republique. These stations should be used with caution after nightfall.

6. Many stations have lifts, including some of the key tourist spots at Montmartre. Take care at these stations. The lifts are preferable to taking the stairs, even if you feel threatened, as the journey time is much shorter.

7. Pick-pocketing is rife in the métro and RER. Always be vigilant, even in 'safe' areas like the 7th arrondissement. **Never** leave your baggage unattended or ask a stranger to guard it for you, even for a moment. This rule especially applies at the main train stations.

8. RER trains are often double-decker. There is plenty of room to move around within trains if you feel threatened. On buses, if for any reason you feel unsafe, stay near the front and the driver. The RATP have their own uniformed security service, complete with guard-dogs. You may also see police and uniformed soldiers with rifles in central Paris stations.

The police and military presences are part of the **Vigipirate** anti-terrorist campaign, but also have a very successful effect reducing crime in the underground system.

9. There are alarm buttons on the platforms of all métros and RERs and in many corridors, and within the trains themselves. These have direct links to the ticket offices at stations, and to the train driver. Most central Paris stations have France Telecom card phones on their platforms and at their exits. These can be operated using ordinary French phone cards, and calls to the emergency services are free.

10. The RATP Lost Property Office (**Bureau des Objets Trouvés**) is to be found at 36 rue des Morillons, 75015. M° Convention. Tel: 01 40 30 52 00. The office is open 08h30–17h00 Monday and Wednesday; 08h30–20h00 Tuesday and Thursday (except in July and August when the hours change to 08h00–17h00); 08h30–17h30 on Fridays; and closed at weekends and bank holidays.

'What are they talking about?'

Phrases you will often hear announced over the métro loud-speakers include:

- '*Les pickpockets sont susceptible d'agir dans cette station. Veuillez veillir à vos affaires personnelles*' – Pickpockets are at large in this station. Take care of your personal belongings.

- '*Suite à un mouvement social, le service est très pertubé/ interrompu sur la ligne 1 entre Etoile et Bastille/sur toute la ligne'* – As a result of strike action, the service is very disrupted/has ceased on Line 1 between Etoile and Bastille/on the whole line.

♦ '*Suite à un incident voyageur à St Germain des Prés, le service est momentanément suspendu entre...*' – Following an incident involving a passenger at St Germain des Prés, the service is temporarily suspended.

♦ '*Suite à une manifestation, les stations Franklin Roosevelt et Champs-Elysées Clemenceau sont fermées au public. Les correspondances sont assurées.*' – As a result of a demonstration, these stations are closed to the public (ie no entries or exits). You can still change trains here if you are already in the underground.

TAKING TAXIS

In Paris, like everywhere else in the world, taxis are harder to find in the rush hour or bad weather. You can normally find a taxi by simply hailing one down on a busy main street, or by going to a **Stationnement de Taxi** (taxi rank). You will often find taxis waiting for fares outside nightclubs, well-known hotels or theatres. Taxis now use the new bus lanes, thus increasing their advantage over individual cars.

In Paris, when the sign on top of the cab is not lit up, the taxi is occupied. When it is lit, the taxi is for hire. If you have ordered the taxi, the meter will be running when the taxi arrives, as you pay for the service from the moment the driver has accepted the call to collect you. Make sure if you catch a taxi in the street that the previous fare has been cleared from the meter. Day and night rates should be displayed, and many taxi drivers have standard rates for a trip to the airports near Paris. Tipping is generally 10%.

Finally, bear in mind that all taxis will take three passengers, but very few will accept four passengers without prior request by telephone. Extra charges are made for large amounts of luggage, including perhaps the 'excess baggage' of a fourth passenger, if you do manage to squeeze them in!

DRIVING

Without a doubt the Place de l'Etoile with its centrepiece, the Arc de Triomphe, is the most notorious symbol of one of the world's best-known bad habits, Parisian driving. Even with a four-fold transport service, bad-tempered, bad-mannered Parisians are still addicted to driving to work every day, if only so that they can complain about pollution and traffic jams before, during and after their journeys, especially during transport strikes. Given the congestion in Paris and the difficulty of finding parking space, you would be well advised to stick to using public transport in Paris.

Parking in Paris is **spécial** in the French sense of the word. Many people would say that the best advice would be bring along a can-opener to manoeuvre yourself in and out of the available slots, or to escape from the mess somebody else has made of your neat parking. A residents' parking permit (**vignette de stationnement résidentiel**) can be obtained from your local town hall, which gives you the right to preferential parking rates and access. If you receive a parking fine, you need to buy the appropriate fiscal stamp (**timbre fiscal**) at a tobacconists, affix the stamp and send the payment. Failure to do so in the specified time limit will lead to an increased fine. If your car is towed away, you will need to make enquiries at the nearest commissariat to find out to which car pound (**fourrière**) it has been taken.

Driving papers

All drivers must always carry their driving licence with when driving, as well as the original registration document, and the car insurance documents. You must be at least 18 years old to drive in France. The annual car tax (**vignette**) has been abolished for individuals, but still applies to company cars.

British drivers in France

Officially, it is no longer necessary to exchange British driving licences (**permis de conduire**) for a French licence.

Applications for international driving licences, if necessary, (valid for three years) should be made at your local préfecture. You should note, however, that international licences are not valid in the bearer's country of residence, and are intended for visitors. British citizens visiting France can drive with a UK driving licence.

American drivers in France

US visitors who stay in France less than 90 days can drive in France with a valid US licence although it is advisable to carry a translation of their licence. French residents (who have either a carte de séjour or carte de résident) can drive in France for up to one year from the start date of their residence permit. In this case either a 'sworn' translation or an international driver's licence is also obligatory. American students may drive with an American licence throughout the duration of their studies.

Thirteen American states have official agreements with France which allow holders of state licences to exchange their licences for French licences. These states are: Colorado, Connecticut, Delaware, Florida, Illinois, Kansas, Kentucky, Michigan, Ohio, New Hampshire, Pennsylvania, South Carolina and Virginia. This agreement allows you up to one year to exchange your American licence for a French **permis de conduire**, after which time the exchange is no longer possible. In practice, you should allow up to three months for the successful exchange of licences. The whole process takes place at the Préfecture de Police on Île de la Cité (M° Cité) and needs to be completed before the end of the first year of residence.

To exchange your licence you need to obtain and complete the necessary form from the préfecture; to provide your US driver's licence with a notarised translation into French; a proof of your current address (rental agreement or EDF or France Telecom bill); a photocopy of both sides of your carte de séjour; and two passport-size photographs. As with any French administrative application, make sure you have originals and copies available of all of these documents.

If you hold a US licence from another state, you must take the two-part French driving test (part-written, part practical) after lessons from a recognised French driving school which will allow you to fulfil the obligation to take the test in a dual-control car. Some concessions are made for the fact that your knowledge of French may be limited when you take the practical test, and a translator may be allowed to accompany you.

Replacing a lost licence

If you lose your licence or it is stolen, you must report it at the police station nearest to where the incident happened. They will give you a receipt valid for two months, which acts as a temporary licence. During that period go to your local préfecture and request a new licence. Take with you:

- the receipt of your declaration of loss or theft
- a piece of official identity
- the completed form requesting a duplicate licence
- a proof of residency (eg, tenancy agreement, electricity bill, etc)
- three passport-size photos.

It can take three to six weeks to obtain your new licence. You will also have to pay the appropriate fee.

Lost or stolen US driving licences can only be replaced by the Department of Motor Vehicles in the driver's home state.

IMPORTING A CAR

You can import a car for up to six months in one year without completing customs formalities. A new or used car on which VAT (TVA in France) has already been paid in another EU country can be imported in to France by a

French resident free of French VAT.

Otherwise, VAT is payable *immediately* upon entry into France. You can pay at the point of importation or at your local tax office. You will then be issued with a customs certificate (**Certificat de Douane 846A**) permitting you to register the vehicle in France. The same form will also be required even if VAT has already been paid, to prove that this obligation has been met.

Tourists (anyone staying no more than 90 days) can bring a car or motorbike into France duty-free and retain their foreign number plates but must display a USA driving disk beside the licence plates. Cars brought in for more than three months need French licence plates, which requires registering the car.

US temporary residents who hold a **carte de séjour temporaire** are exempted from customs duties if they can show:

(a) that they will stay in France less than one year
(b) they have a permanent residence outside France
(c) that they have lived outside of France for at least one year
(d) that they have owned the vehicle for at least six months.

Long-term residents are not entitled to exemption from customs duties on imported vehicles, and the car must carry French licence plates and be registered in France, as well as ensuring the full payment of all duties on the vehicle in the country of export.

REGISTERING A CAR IN FRANCE

Registering an imported car

Imported vehicles must be registered in France within three months of entry. To do this, you must contact the local **Direction Régionale de l'Industrie, de la Recherche et de l'Environnement (DRIRE)**. After the local vehicle inspection centre (**Inspection des Mines**) has checked that your car meets French construction and use regulations, you will receive a certificate from DRIRE which will allow you to apply for the registration certificate (**Certificat d'Immatriculation** – more normally known as a **carte grise**). This happens at the préfecture, or the Préfecture de Police, or local mairie in Paris. They will provide a checklist of documents required, which are:

1. Proof of origin of the vehicle or copy of the certificate of sale.

2. The foreign registration document.

3. The customs certificate 846A (see above).

4. A manufacturer's certificate of construction. This is available from a local car dealer, the French importer, or the manufacturer. *Officially* it is no longer required, but it may be asked for. It can also be very expensive. The point of the document is to prove that the vehicle meets European safety standards.

5. A completed request for a registration card form (**Demande de Certificat d'Immatriculation d'un Véhicule**), available from the préfecture, or the Préfecture de Police, or the local mairie in Paris. This document should be accompanied by your carte de séjour or passport and proof of residence.

6. A technical test certificate if your vehicle is more than four years old. All vintage vehicles and those over four years old are subject to regular testing every two years.

Once you finally receive your car registration, new number plates must be installed within 48 hours. They can be made up and fitted at local garages for a small fee. The last two numbers of your new registration will refer always to the département in which the car is registered.

Registering a new car

You have 15 days in which to register a newly purchased car. You will need a new form to apply for a new **carte grise**, the certificate of sale, the technical certificate from the **Inspections des Mines**, a piece of official identity (eg, carte de séjour), and a proof of residency less than three months old (eg, electricity or telephone bill in your name).

Registering a second-hand car

Once again, you have 15 days in which to register. Vehicles less than 10 years old cost the same to register as new vehicles; those which are more than 10 years old cost half as much to register. You will need ID and proof of residence (as above), and the **carte grise barrée** (old registration document of the car) supplied by the former owner. Cars more than four years old must also have the necessary technical certificate dating from less than six months before the purchase. You also need a **certificat de situation administrative** supplied by the seller.

Moving home

Even if you stay in the same département, you must change the address on your carte grise. This is free, and can be done immediately at the local mairie or préfecture, by presenting a new proof of residence and your carte grise. If you fail to do this, you could face a fine.

Replacing your carte grise

If you lose your carte or it is stolen, you must report it to the police. You will be issued with a temporary document which will allow you to use your car. It will also allow you to apply for a new carte. You will need an official piece of identity, a proof of residency, the receipt of your police statement of loss, the form requesting a duplicate carte, and the necessary technical certificate for vehicles more than four years old.

Selling your car

If you decide to sell your car once you have moved to France, you must supply the following documents to the buyers before the sale is complete and legal:

1. The **certificat de vente**. It is your responsibility to obtain this from the préfecture or sous-préfecture.

2. The '**carte grise barrée**' (ie, 'crossed-out'). You must write across the carte in indelible ink '**vendue le ____**' (sold on ____) and fill in the date. You must then sign the amended carte.

3. If the car is more than four years old, a technical certificate dated less than six months before the date of the sale proving that the car is roadworthy (see above).

4. A **certificat de situation administrative**. To obtain this, go to your local préfecture with your carte grise. You will need to submit the registration number of the vehicle, the model, and the power of the engine. The certificat will certify that there are no outstanding fines relating to the vehicle.

Within 15 days of the sale of the car, you must hand in the second copy of the certificat de vente at the préfecture at which it was previously registered. Restrictions apply on the sale of cars imported duty-free which are regulated by the French Customs Office.

Insurance

Fully comprehensive insurance is advisable to cover the costs of breakdown or accidents. Third-party motor insurance for unlimited liability is compulsory in France. You will need to shop around to find the best policies and prices. Third-party insurance is required for the import of cars whether they are owned or not, and if you opt to take out a policy before arrival you must have proof ready for French Customs at the point of entry (land or sea). The Customs Offices themselves offer temporary insurance for up to 30 days at these same points of entry.

Fuel

Garages are placed at intervals of 24km along all motorways, and are to be found across the city centre.

Many of the Parisian and suburban garages are self-service. **Faites le plein, s'il vous plaît** means 'Fill her up, please', if you do find yourself being served.

Leaded petrol is now sold only in one grade (**essence super**). Unleaded is sold in two grades: **essence sans plomb**, and **super sans plomb**. The minimum quantity that you can buy is five litres. Diesel (**gazole**) is cheaper and readily available. A favourite tactic in French disputes to pressurise the government is to block access to petrol refineries, and if possible, Paris itself. The result is always panic buying, and long queues at the pumps. If trouble seems to be looming, then plan ahead if possible.

Road rules

The most important thing you do need to remember is that in France you drive on the right! Also important is the fact that in built-up areas, you must give way to traffic coming from the right – the famous **priorité à droit** rule. In less built-up areas, traffic on main roads has priority over traffic from side roads. The exception to the rule of priority is at roundabouts. Traffic entering the roundabout has priority. **Except** when signs such as **Cédez le passage** (give way) or **Vous n'avez pas la priorité** are displayed.

Health and safety precautions

- Seat belts are obligatory in France, including in the rear of the car if they are installed. You can face an on-the-spot fine if you disobey this rule.

- Random tests are made for drink-driving in France, which is a major killer on the roads. The legal limit is now 80mg alcohol per 100ml of blood – not much more than one glass of wine. You may face an on-the-spot fine, a court appearance, or a driving ban if you are found guilty.

♦ Speed limits are reduced in bad weather. Generally on toll motorways (**autoroutes à péage**) the maximum speed is 130kph, and 110kph in bad weather. The minimum speed in the outside (overtaking) lane is 80kph during daylight on flat roads with good visibility. For dual carriageways and toll-free motorways, the limit is 110kph; for other 'departmental' roads the limit is 90kph; and for roads in built up areas the limit is 50kph. The limit on ring roads is 80kph.

♦ The government has introduced an ever-increasing number of automatic and manual radar speed-traps. Tickets are issued automatically, on the basis of a 5% margin of error in the speed recorded. Fines should be paid promptly to avoid increases, and in addition French licence holders may find that they will lose several points from their licence. Repeat offenders could find themselves losing their French licence, at least for a limited period. Fines are also being issued now for offences such as using hand-held mobile phones whilst driving. Generally, there is now a very strong emphasis on applying road rules and regulations.

♦ Cars made in the UK and Ireland must adjust their headlights in order not to dazzle on-coming traffic. Headlight converters made from pre-cut black masking tape must be fitted over the headlights. If another driver flashes his headlights at you it is to indicate that he has priority and that you should give way.

◆ If you break down, try to move the car to the side of the road and flash your hazard warning lights. The red warning triangle should be placed 30m behind your car (100m on motorways). Emergency phones (**postes d'appel d'urgence**) are at 4km intervals on main roads, and every 2km on motorways.

◆ If you have an accident, you should call the police immediately by dialling 17. The ambulance service will also be alerted if necessary. You and the other parties must complete and exchange an accident statement form (**constat à l'amiable**) and exchange insurance details. If possible, persuade witnesses (**temoins**) to remain and make statements.

Pollution controls

Pollution is a major problem in Paris. To combat this problem, regulations are enforced each year (or threatened), whereby you can only drive on alternate days. This depends on the last two numbers before the letters in a number plate. On one day, only even numbers (**pairs**) will be allowed to drive; the next day it will be the turn of the uneven numbers (**impairs**). Listen out for warnings on the TV and radio. Certain areas of Paris are now regularly reserved for pedestrians, cyclists and rollerbladers, and this is a growing tendency in Paris. See below for more details.

TWO-WHEELED TRANSPORT

Cyclists (and taxis) now share the bus lanes which run the length and breadth of the city with protective barriers to stop encroachments from cars, vans and lorries. Cross-country biking is also a popular sport at weekends and on vacation. On Sundays, the quais of the Seine and the

Canal St Martin are reserved for cyclists. The Bois de Boulogne and the Bois de Vincennes respectively to the west and the east of the city centre also provide plenty of good space for fans of open-air pedal-powered propulsion with regular weekend closings to four-wheel traffic.

If you have your own bike, you can take it on the RER lines A and B in the carriages marked with bike signs at weekends, and on weekdays from 09h00–16h30, and after 19h00 (ie, not in rush-hour). Métro ligne 1 can also be used on Sundays up until 16h30, although Louvre-Rivoli and La Défense are not accessible. For more information call Maison Roue Libre on 01 53 46 43 77.

FINDING OUT MORE

♦ **The French Travel Centre**, 178 Piccadilly, London W1V OAL. Tel: 0891 244123, fax: (020) 7493 6594, *www.franceguide.com* and *www.fr-holidaystore.co.uk*. Open Monday–Friday 10h00–18h00, Saturday 10h00–17h00 and French Railways Ltd, The Rail Europe Travel Centre, 179 Piccadilly. Tube: Green Park or Piccadilly Circus. **Take a look at the franceguide site for lots of handy hints on driving in France**. There are also links for disabled travellers, and a broad general help section.

♦ *www.equipement.gouv.fr* – the transport ministry website.

♦ *www.voyages-sncf.com*. The popular multilingual website for checking long-distance train times and ordering tickets. These can either be sent to your home or collected at the station.

- *www.ratp.fr*. The excellent multilingual website for the Paris transport authority, with suggestions for day-trips, amusing the children, etc, plus all the usual travel information you would expect.

- *www.eurostar.com* (within Europe) or *www.eurostar-tickets.com* (USA and Canada only). Both sites offer times and tickets, but the North American site offers discounted tickets for these travellers.

- *www.eurotunnel.com*. Bilingual site for the underground-overground option.

- English-speaking helpline for **Motorail**: in France, 0892 35 35 39, outside France +33 892 35 35 39.

- *www.bison-fute.equipement.gouv.fr*. The transport ministry's excellent French-only site with travel updates, road works and closures, and school holidays dates (ie, when not to travel).

- *www.eurolines.com* and *www.hoverspeed.com*. Coach travel to France. The Hoverspeed site offers both ferry and coach information.

- *www.brittany-ferries.co.uk*, and *www.poferries.com*. Cross-channel ferries to the UK and Ireland.

- *www.airfrance.com*; *www.britishairways.com*; *www.flyb-mi.com* (British Midland). For regular flights to Paris and major French cities.

16

Shopping in Paris

There are perhaps four major cities in the world which symbolise the art of shopping: London, Milan, Paris and New York, the four poles of the fashion world. But as man and woman do not live on labels alone, you need to think about the needs of the everyday household before you get down to what many consider to be 'the real thing'.

FOOD SHOPPING

Almost every arrondissement and commune in and around Paris has its own market, offering fresh produce from fruit and vegetables, meat, cheese, to household products and clothes (although these will not always be reasonably priced in markets). Shopping at a French market is a real experience, lots of fun and a good way to brush up your language skills whilst choosing your produce.

Market streets will normally always include the household suppliers for your daily dietary needs: the **boulangerie** (bakery), where you can also buy **pâtisserie** (cakes); the **boucherie** (butchers), the **charcuterie** (cold and smoked meats, and pies), and the **poissonnerie** (fish shop); the **épicerie** (grocers store); the **fromagerie** (cheese shop); the **cave à vins** (wine shop/off-licence); and probably at least one **confiserie** (chocolate/sweet shop).

Remember that France works on the metric system, with 1 pound = approximately 0.45 kg. If you tell a butcher or cheese merchant how many people you wish to serve, she or he will normally propose what they think is the usual amount. Normally shopkeepers will serve you your items, and then ask, **et avec ça?/ça sera tout?** – and with that?/ will that be all? If you have nothing more to buy, then the answer is simply **C'est tout merci**.

At the charcuterie if you are buying ham, etc, you will be asked **combien de tranches?** (how many slices). At the fromagerie, the shopkeeper will probably show you either the whole cheese or a ready-cut piece and ask you to choose the size of portion (**morceau**) that you want for hard cheeses. Soft cheeses such as Camembert are normally sold either in halves or whole; and certain small and rarer cheeses (eg, goats cheese, **chèvres**) are only sold whole.

At the bakers if you buy a baguette, you will be asked if you want it **coupé en deux?** (cut in half?). If you buy a small loaf of bread the question will be **tranché?** (sliced?) If you do ask the baker to slice the loaf, it will be produced using a professional machine, presented in plastic with a seal, and with a small surcharge. Finally, if you buy flowers either at the market or in a **fleuriste**, you will be asked if they are a gift (in which case they will be gift-wrapped automatically) or for the home – **c'est pour offrir ou pour la maison**?

Your concierge and/or your neighbours will be able to tell you where to find your nearest market. Some of the best known are:

♦ avenue de Président Wilson (16th), rue Cler (7th) and rue Poncelet (17th) – all excellent markets, especially renowned for being the places where 'ladies who lunch' come to buy their provisions. In rue Poncelet, treat yourself to coffee and central European goodies at **Stübli**, and throw caution regarding your waistline to the wind.

♦ rue Montorgueil (1st and 2nd) – one of the most beautiful market streets with a fine selection of foods and the clientele the **plus-hype** of all Parisian markets. Shopping here is often more like attending a fashion parade as the local 'cool crowd' pick out the best produce or watch you doing the same from the café terraces. Check out the former royal choclate shop **Stohrer** for some of the best chocolate in Paris.

♦ rue Lepic (18th) – the original Montmartre street market, home to *Amélie of Montmartre*, a favourite and bustling venue for the local stars and fashion crowd who have flocked to the Butte since Christian Dior launched the New Look here in the 1940s. One of the most 'authentic' Parisian street markets.

♦ boulevard Raspail (6th) and boulevard des Batignolles (8th and 17th) are both organic food markets, the places to buy 'green greens' but also free-range eggs, meat, cheese, etc.

What do you do if you do not have the time, facility or inclination to shop at the market? Supermarkets are not lacking and there is nothing particularly special about the way in which French supermarkets function – everything is pretty self-explanatory, even if you do not speak French. There are normally check-outs (**caisse**) for deliveries (**livraisons**), but these will be charged below a minimum spend.

The major hypermarkets are to be found outside Paris itself. The most well-known hypermarkets are **Auchan** and **Carrefour**, both of which also diversify into clothing, computers and even package holidays. However, they do not offer some of the other services which are now found in British counterparts. The **Picard** chain of shops specialise in offering frozen (**surgelé**) food, and are to be found across central Paris. There are also several e-shopping alternatives such as *ooshop.fr* and *telemarket.fr*.

Details of expat grocery stores and services for the homesick and also for special occasions such as Thanksgiving can be found easily found in FUSAC. The three most famous food stores in Paris – not for everyday shopping unless you like to stretch your budget! – are **La Grande Epciérie** at Le Bon Marché in the 7th; and **Hédiard** and **Fauchon** behind the Madeleine church in the 8th. All of these are luxury stores, but at affordable prices

– in small doses! **A consommer avec modération** as the French say. Note that the word 'cheap' does not exist in French, only the phrase **pas cher,** which means 'not expensive'!

DISCOVERING DEPARTMENT STORES

The five principal department Parisian department stores (**grands magasins**) offering everything from household items to clothes and in some cases branches are also to be found distributed across Paris in the main shopping areas. In most cases the flagship shops in the city centre have now been reproduced elsewhere in the suburbs or in other city shopping centres:

◆ **Bazar de l'Hôtel de Ville**, rue de Rivoli, 75004 Paris. *www.bhv.fr*. M° Hôtel de Ville. The **BHV** as it is usually known is one of the great department stores, specialising in home furnishings and most especially in the DIY paradise (or hell, depending on how you feel about it) in the basement. For those of us who cringe at the sight of a hammer and a nail, the new **Bricolo café** in the basement offers the chance for basic DIY lessons whilst you take a coffee break.

◆ **Galeries Lafayettes**, boulevard Haussman, 75009 Paris.*www.galerieslafayette.com*. M° Chaussée d'Antin/ RER Opéra. Also above the Montparnasse station in the 15th. The boulevard Haussman branch is the best with an excellent choice of clothes and a huge food section.

◆ **La Samaritaine**, rue de Rivoli, 75001 Paris. *www.lasa-maritaine.com*. M° Louvre-Rivoli. Recently renovated, the Art Nouveau masterpiece with a trendy terrace restaurant Strong on household items and clothes.

◆ **Le Bon Marché**, 75007 Paris. *www.lebonmarche.fr* M° Sévres-Babylone. Right next to the métro, so impossible to miss. Trendy and chic like the neighbourhood it serves, with frequent theme promotions.

◆ **Printemps**, boulevard Haussman, 75009 Paris. *www.printemps.com* M° Havre-Caumartin/RER Opéra. The rival to Galeries Lafayettes. The dome is best seen at Christmas when the tree is in place. Free fashion shows during the Fashion Weeks, and a very **hype** menswear department.

All of these stores have discount card schemes, etc and both Galeries Lafayettes and Printemps in particular are full of concessionary mini-shops from all the major designers.

SHOPPING FOR THE HOME

If your budget does not stretch to shopping in one of these shops, home furnishings can also be found at **Conforama** next door to La Samaritaine on the river-bank of the Seine. **Castorama** at the Place de Clichy (*www.castorama.fr*) is another DIY/garden centre favourite if you cannot face another afternoon spent wandering around the basement of BHV like a lost soul. You should also check out Leroy Merlin (*www.leroymerlin.fr*), and Mr Bricolage , 'Mr DIY' (*www.mr-bricolage.fr*). Habitat is on avenue Wagram and boulevard de la Madeleine (*www.habitat.fr*) and Ikea (*www.ikea.fr*) has four shops in the inner suburbs.

For plug adaptors (**adaptatuers**) try the local hardware stores (**drogueries**) or go to the accessories department of the major hi-fi and electrical appliance supplier **Darty** (avenue des Ternes, Forum des Halles, Madeleine and boulevard Rochechouart). **FNAC**, the all-purpose music/ book/computer/ticket agencies also stock plug adaptors. **Surcouf** on avenue Daumesnil in the 12th is a noisy computer warehouse shop surrounded by IT discount shops. Remember that French keyboards are different to English ones. If you can make the change, it would be as well to move over to a French keyboard so that you can apply the accents where necessary when you write your correspondence.

Interior design and fashionable home furnishing stores abound in Paris, and you would be well-advised to check the specialist press and also *A nous Paris* and *Zurban* who provide weekly updates on the latest and greatest. Areas like Abbesses, Oberkampf or Ménilmontant (the trendy districts) obviously offer the best chances of finding something really original. The **Conran** shops in Paris can be found behind Le Bon Marché in the 7th or at La Madeleine in the 9th.

For plants and garden equipment, go to **Castorama**. If you are looking for more choice, go to **Truffaut** on the Left Bank of the Seine in the 13th arrondissement. On the Île de la Cité, the flower market in front of the préfecture is one of the most well-known addresses in Paris. The other place to browse is on the Right Bank of the Seine at the **quai de Gesvre** and **quai de la Megisserie**. The latter is also known for specialising in selling pets of all shapes and sizes, and their own 'home furnishings'.

SHOPPING FOR CLOTHES

Whole books have been written on the topic, and several weekly columns appear in English detailing the latest places to be seen buying things to be seen wearing. Every magazine and newspaper has its fashion section, and you will quickly catch on to the places that match your budget and style.

The Champs-Elysées remains a popular place to shop, but the real action takes place on rue de Rivoli from la Samaritaine down to Hôtel de Ville, and also the Forum des Halles. Fashion victims can head off to whichever district best reflects their taste, be it hippy chic in the north-east of Paris or ultra-chic in the 'golden triangle' around avenue Montaigne or down in St Germain des Prés.

	Men's suits	Men's shirts	Men's shoes
UK/USA	36 38 40 42 44 46 48	14 14.5 15 15.5 16 16.5 17	7.5 8 9 10 11 12
France	46 48 50 52 54 56 58	36 37 38 39/40 41 42 43	41 42 43 44 45 46
	Dress sizes	**Women's shoes**	**Women's tights/stockings**
UK	8 10 12 14 16 18	3 4 5 6 7 8	8 8.5 9 9.5 10 10.5
USA	8 10 12 14 16	5 6 7 8 9 10	8 8.5 9 9.5 10 10.5
France	36 38 40 42 44 46	36 37 38 39 40 41	0 1 2 3 4 5

Figure 17. Clothes size conversions.

SHOPPING FOR THE CHILDREN

The major department stores all have good children's departments, as do chains such as **Prisunic** or **Monoprix** where kids and adult clothing are also available. One of the most famous children's shops – and not the cheapest – is **Au nain bleau**, 408 rue St Honoré, 75008 Paris. M° Madeleine. **Toys'R'us** can be found in the La Défense shopping centre. Probably the best way to find good children's shops, however, is through word-of-mouth from other parents. The two key guides once again are *Zurban* and *A nous Paris* for the most up-to-date news.

BARGAIN HUNTING IN THE SALES

The **soldes** as they are known are regulated to make sure that sales start across France on the same day, thus stopping late starting towns suffering from shopped-out consumer disinterest. The main sales are still the New Year sales in early-mid January, and there are also summer sales.

Obviously the best bargains go first, but this will only be the first mark-down (**démarque**). There will probably be second and third mark downs (each should be indicated with the original price on the sale ticket). Sale items are not normally refundable or exchangeable. Items may be marked at any stage in the year as being reduced (**remise de** X%/X€), but the use of the term 'solde' is now strictly controlled. As a result 'promotions' advertised as **prix promotionel** (sales by another name) have limits placed on their time-span and financial impact, to avoid under-cutting the market.

BARGAIN HUNTING AT FLEA MARKETS

The three most well-known flea markets (**marchés aux puces**) are:

1. **Porte de Clignancourt** 75018 Paris (métro of the same name) – Saturdays, Sundays and Mondays. A vast sprawling market of clothes, antiques, furniture, books – you name it, you will probably find it at

Clignancourt. The market is a popular venue with tourists and pickpockets, so be careful that you do not end up finding your lost items being sold somewhere further on. Real bargains are rare here.

2. **Porte de Vanves** 75014 Paris (métro of the same name). Household items in the mornings and clothes in the afternoons at weekends.

3. **Porte de Montreuil** 75020, avenue de la Porte de Montreuil. Mainly household items.

In recent years, there has been an explosion in the number of local **brocantes** (antiques fairs) and **vide-greniers** (car-boot sales). These are always local initiatives, so keep an eye out for posters. The antique fairs are run by professionals, but you might find a bargain or two at the car-boot sales.

Paris is one of the acknowledged capitals of second-hand/ antique clothing shops. Keep an eye out for **dépôts-ventes** dealers where you can put your clothes in to be sold with the shopkeepers keeping a commission on the sale if and when it happens. This system also applies to furniture. The specialist clothes shops are once again to be found in areas such as Batignolles or Oberkampf, but you should check guides such as the *Time Out* guide for the best tips in English, or magazines such as *Nova* or *Zurban* for tips in French.

(17)

Discovering Parisian Sporting Life

Paris is campaigning vigorously to win the bid to host the 2012 Olympic Games, having lost their 2008 bid. Parisians, like Londoners, New Yorkers, and the inhabitants of most major western cities, have a sporting life divided between participating (gently or vigorously) and spectating (regularly or occasionally). The geography of France offers the chance to practise almost any sport on a regular basis, and living in the capital is not a handicap to this rule. However, the importance of certain spectator sports and events is still central to the French and especially Parisians.

KEEPING FIT

Joining a gym

◆ The most well-known chain of gyms in Paris is **ClubMed Gym** (*www.clubmedgym.fr*), with current annual subscription rates ranging from €726–826/ year. Membership of the club entitles you to use any of the clubs across Paris and indeed outside the Paris region also. All the clubs offer cardio-training equipment, weight-training facilities, sport counsellors on hand for advice and training programmes, and classes for all levels. Some are open on Sundays, and all are packed early evening during the week at the end of office hours. The club in the 15th arrondissement also has a large swimming pool. Many **comités d'entreprise** subsidise membership for the firm's workers.

◆ The cheaper rival to Gymnase Club is **Gymnasium** offering about the same number of gyms and working on the same principles. In the 11th, 17th ,18th and 19th arrondissements, the **Cercles de la Forme** (*www.cercle-maillot-bolivar.com*) also offer another good alternative to the main chains.

◆ The luxury muscle factories are the **Waou Clubs**, also run by ClubMed Gym. An annual subscription here will set you back €1,146. There are fewer Waou Clubs, but the quality of the facilities and service is higher. At the exclusive end of the market, there is also the **Ritz Health Club** (tel: 01 43 16 30 60) if your blood pressure can take the membership fee, and **Les Thermes** at the star-studded **Royal Monceau Hotel** on avenue Hoche.

◆ A full list of all the Paris gyms, whether part of the chains, exclusive haunts, or small local gyms, can be found on *www.infogym.com*.

Joining a sports club or centre

If you want to try or practise a number of different sporting disciplines, and also meet new people, the best idea would be to join a sports club. The most well-known clubs are:

1. **The Standard Athletic Club (SAC)**, route Forestière du Pavé de Meudon, 92360 Meudon la Forêt. Tel: 01 46 26 16 09, fax: 01 45 07 87 63, *www.standac.com*. Private British club with a large international membership on the edge of Paris. Eight tennis courts, two squash courts, a swimming pool, sports fields with football, rugby, cricket and hockey teams; golf section, snooker, fully stocked bar and large clubhouse facilities and home to many social events. Car necessary for access.

2. **Aquaboulevard**, 4–6 rue Louis Armand, 75015 Paris. Tel: 01 40 60 10 00, fax: 01 40 60 18 39. M° Balard. Just on the edge of Paris, the great sports centre with centrepiece swimming pools and slides etc, accessible on day passes. Packed in warm weather. An artificial beach is among the attractions, but like most beaches you have to fight your way onto it when the sun shines. This site is part of the **Forest Hill** group of private members-only sports centres around the edge of Paris in the inner suburbs (*www.aquaboulevard.com* for full details of all sites).

Swimming in Paris

Paris has over 30 municipal swimming pools, but also quite a number of private pools. The municipal pools tend to open early in the morning and then close for school classes during the day. At the weekends you will still need to go early to avoid the crowds. At a municipal pool you are normally required to wearing a swimming cap (**bonnet de bain**).

Amongst the most popular pools in Paris are:

◆ **La Butte aux Cailles**, 5 place Paul-Verlaine, 75013 Paris. Tel: 01 45 89 60 05 – a listed masterpiece.

◆ **La Piscine Pontoise**, 19 rue Pontoise, 75005 Paris. Tel: 01 55 42 77 88 – at the centre of the trendy private **Quartier Latin** sports centre.

◆ **La Piscine Suzanne Berlioz des Halles**, Forum des Halles, 75001 Paris. Tel: 01 42 36 98 44 – the Olympic-size temple of the bodies beautiful. Often packed but stays open late.

◆ Three pools roll open their roofs in fine weather: **Piscine Hébert**, 2 rue des Fillettes, 75018 Paris. Tel: 01 42 76 78 24; **Piscine Georges-Hermant**, 4 rue David d'Angers, 75019 Paris. Tel: 01 42 02 45 10; and **Piscine Georges-Vallerey**, 148 avenue Gambetta, 75020 Paris. Tel: 01 40 31 15 20.

◆ A new 'suspended' pool floating on the Seine is due to open in the 13th in 2006, opposite Bercy.

Cricket, rugby and soccer

You can find current contact details for the **British Rugby Club of Paris** on the website *www.britishinfrance.com*. You need to check for contact details as team captains come and go. The **SAC** fields several cricket teams, and other teams are to be found at the **Thoiry Cricket Club** at the Château de Thoiry. Details of this association are also available on the same website.

Football fans who want to follow the local team will need to discover the Parc des Princes stadium at Porte St Cloud, home to the **Paris-St Germain (PSG)** club. The club has a high media coverage but a low score average despite being First Division players. More details of the club, including ticket sales, on *www.PSG.fr* or tel: 0825 075 078. For those who want to play as well as watch football, the SAC fields several teams in a local tournament division. Otherwise, to kick around a ball with your pals, head for Les Invalides in summer, or the wide open spaces of the two Bois to the east and the west.

Both football and rugby fans will want to find their way to the **Stade de France** (RER station of the same name) to the north of the city centre. The masterpiece built for the 1998 World Cup can be visited when matches are not being played.

Dance classes

Probably not what everybody might think of as sport, but certainly an excellent way to keep in shape. The most well-known place to try is the **Centre de Danse du Marais**, 41 rue du Temple, 75004 Paris. Tel: 01 42 72 15 42, fax: 01 42

77 71 57, *www.paris-danse.com*. Every conceivable type of dance course seems to be on offer from jazz to classical to contemporary to belly-dancing. Always packed out. The Tex-Mex diner in the courtyard is a cool hang-out and the café-theatre at the end of the courtyard is a favourite for one-man shows. Music lessons also available.

Rollerblading in Paris

The number of French bladers is estimated at about four million. Most Friday nights throughout the year, an enormous free rally of bladers – up to 22,000! known as **Friday Night Fever** – rollers through Paris by night over variable courses of around 20–25km (for experienced rollers only), leaving Place d'Italie at 22h00, and returning there at about 01h00. The event is under the protection of the special cycle and roller-blade units of the Paris Police Force, and is one of the major social events in Paris for bladers.

A Beginners Mega-Blade (**Rollers and Coquillages**) leaves from Boulevard Bourdon at Bastille every Sunday at about 14h00 (tel: 01 44 54 07 44). These 'junior' events for the less-experienced also attract up to 10,000 people, and last about 3–4 hours. For more information check the following website and its links: *www.paris.roller.online.fr*. **The Paris Rollerblade Association** (which has information in English) can also be contacted at Pari Roller, 62 rue Dulong, 75017 Paris. Tel: 01 43 36 89 81.

In the summer the banks of the Seine between Place de la Concorde and the Louvre are closed on Sundays for pedestrians, cyclists and bladers. The Canal St Martin is also reserved for the same clientele every Sunday.

Playing a round of golf

Obviously the main golf courses are outside the city limits, with strong concentrations to the north near Chantilly. The **Fédération Française de Golf** (tel: 01 44 17 63 00) can provide you with further details of Paris courses and clubs. The SAC also has a golf section which could be a good way for English-speakers to discover the Parisian courses. British expatriates might also try contacting the Royal Society of St George (cf. *www.britishinfrance.com*) who organise regular golf tournaments.

THE SPORTING YEAR

The great sporting events of the Parisian year fall into two categories. Popular events include the **Paris Marathon** each spring, and the final lap of the **Tour de France** cycling race each July. The popular viewing grounds are the Champs-Elysées, but traffic will be bad across the city on both days.

The indoor **tennis** championships at **Bercy** remain reasonably accessible if you simply organise yourself well enough in advance to obtain tickets. They draw the great names of tennis, so they are well worth the effort. However, when it comes to the summer exterior event at **Roland-Garros** on the edge of the 16th arrondissement, you really need to apply very early and quickly for tickets and/or be prepared to pay for the best tickets, or find the right company to invite you.

Roland-Garros falls into the same category of event as the great Parisian horse races. Half of the skill of the game is spent in obtaining entry to the best seats; a quarter of the skill is expended in being seen in those seats; and whatever you feel you can muster for the rest goes towards enjoying the event. Roland-Garros, like the **Prix de Diane at Chantilly** (normally about the third Sunday in June); or the **Prix de l'Arc de Triomphe at Longchamps** (first Sunday in October, M° Porte d'Auteuil then free shuttle-bus), forms part of the Parisian 'season'.

Longchamps draws a huge British contingent of week-enders, and many local residents will turn up with the cars laden with food and set up picnics in the car parks leading up the edge of the racetrack. Much the same happens at dainty Chantilly, through the woods and at 'the bottom of the garden' of the fabulous château. Whereas Long-champs definitely has airs of going to the Derby at Epsom, Chantilly is the French Ascot. Both days out are good fun for all the family, with bands and plenty of space for kids to let off steam. The race tracks at **Maisons-Lafitte** and **St Cloud** are less pretentious, and the trotting races at the **Hippodrome de Vincennes** in the Bois are a popular venue for **nocturnes** (evening sessions) when you can have dinner whilst watching the races.

(18)

Catering for the Kids

For generations, the French worked on the basis that 'children should be seen but not heard': well-behaved, polite, and demonstrating no form of exuberance. The reality is of course very different! The French education system creates extensive periods (Wednesdays, weekends and long school holidays) when parents face the question, what can you do to keep your **mômes** (kids) out of mischief and amused? The answers are not lacking in and around Paris, and the most up-to-date answers can be found each week in the two principal weekly Paris lifestyle guides, *A nous Paris*, found free in métro stations each Tuesday, and *Zurban*, available at kiosks every Wednesday. There are also special supplements to the major newspapers and magazines timed to coincide with the school holidays.

The suggestions in this chapter are only a selection of the more well-known examples, and you should check the supplements and journals for new ideas. The website *www.ratp.fr* is also another good source of ideas. For ease of use, they have been organised by general geographical proximity.

NORTHERN PARIS

◆ **Parc de la Villette**, 211 avenue Jean Jaures, 75019 Paris. M° Porte de la Villette or Porte de Pantin. Tel: 01 40 03 75 03, *www.villette.com*. The great cultural activity centre built on the north-eastern edge of Paris with the **Cités de Science**, **de la Musique**, **d'Industrie**, and a special **Cité des Enfants**. Excellently laid out including bilingual exhibition areas. Heavily orientated for children. Giant 360 cinema (**la Géode**) with natural history films, and an open-air cinema for summer evenings. Lots of lawns designated to be played on by children and adults, and a good place for kids to let off steam after a movie, an exhibition or a workshop.

◆ **Jardin sauvage de St Vincent**, rue St Vincent, 75018 Paris. M° Larmarck-Caulaincourt. Tel: 01 43 28 47 63. In the heart of old Montmartre just behind the Sacré-Coeur, a place to learn about plants, their uses, and generally about ecology.

◆ **Parc Asterix**, BP8, 60128 Plailly. Tel: 03 44 62 33 96, fax: 03 44 62 32 94, *www.parcasterix.com* (bilingual site). Before EuroDisney arrived this was the main Paris theme park. No prizes for guessing what the storyline is ... Accommodation available. To the north of Paris by car.

♦ **Musée de l'Air et de l'Espace**, (93) Le Bourget. Tel: 01 49 92 71 99. Almost 200 different flying machines on display at Paris's original airport, and a newly-refurbished planetarium with an 8m diameter and 3,500 stars.

EASTERN PARIS

♦ **Bois de Vincennes**. The huge forest has a multitude of resources to amuse the children. The main **Paris Zoo** is at 53 avenue de St Maurice, 75012 Paris. M° St Mandé or Porte Dorée. Tel: 01 44 75 20 10, and just beside it is the boating **Lac Daumesnil**. Further to the east stands the original **château de Vincennes**, with its huge keep and seventeenth-century apartments, open to the public and looking just the way a castle should (M° Château de Vincennes). Only a few yards away lies the **Parc floral de Paris**, (Esplanade du château, route de la Pyramide, 75012 Paris. M° Château de Vincennes. Tel: 01 43 43 92 95, *www.parcfloraldeparis.com*), a huge activity park for families on the edge of the forest with picnic areas, plenty of space to play and a wide variety of activities. Beyond the Parc floral lie yet more boating lakes, and across the forest at Joinville-le-Pont lies **La ferme de Paris** (route de pesage, tel: 01 43 28 47 63) with real animals in fields for the infant Parisians to discover. The Bois also boasts sports grounds, and hundreds of acres of forests.

♦ **Parc de Bercy** M° Cour St Emilion or Bercy. The latest arrival on the Parisian park scene, especially planned for children, with a labyrinth, vines, a vegetable garden tended by local children, exhibition areas, and a free-for-all area for families to play on leading up to the terrace overlooking the Seine with its sculptures representing other nations. A really excellent park leading up to the Bercy indoor sports complex, and leading down to the great multi-screen cinema complex at St Emilion.

◆ **Disneyland Paris**, Marne la Vallée. Tel: 01 60 30 60 30, *www.disneylandparis.com* (bilingual site). The big one! RER (and even TGV and Eurostar) direct to Mickey's Magic Kingdom. All the fun of Disney fare. Many different day passes available, plus accommodation and restaurants, regular **spectacles** (shows).

◆ **Sea Life Paris-Val d'Europe**, Centre Commerciale Internationale Val d'Europe, 14 cours de Danube, Serris, Marne La Vallée. Tel: 01 60 42 33 66, *www.sealife.fr* (bilingual site). A vast aquarium beneath the shopping centre, with sharks swimming around the transparent tube you have to take to complete your journey once you begin!

SOUTHERN PARIS

◆ **Jardin des Plantes**, 57 rue Cuvier, 75005 Paris. M° Jussieu or Austerlitz. Tel: 01 40 79 37 94. Paris's botanical gardens, with a small menagerie to introduce the kids to animal as well as plant life. Herb and flower gardens and exhibition areas.

◆ **Jardin du Luxembourg**, boulevard St Michel, 75006 Paris. RER Luxembourg. Special children's treats amongst the neat lawns and flower-beds, including ponies and puppets.

- **Parc Georges Brassens**, rue des Morillons, 75015 Paris. M° Convention. Children's playgrounds and vegetable gardens tended by the pupils of the school leading onto the park.

- **Château de Fontainebleau**. Tel: 01 60 71 50 70. Four free game guides are given away to children when they visit the château with their parents to help them enjoy their visit.

- **Parc du Domaine de Courson**, Courson-Monteloup (91). Tel: 01 64 58 90 12. You will need a car to reach this palatial park, but when you do, you can picnic in the park before exploring it on your own or at certain seasons accompanied by students from the local landscape architectural school.

The new town of Sénart is also planning a vast aquarium for some time in the next few years as part of its development projects. See also **Aquaboulevard** in Chapter 17 (page 370).

WESTERN PARIS

- **Bois de Boulogne**. The children of the west are not lacking in amusements either, thanks to their own forest. The most famous site is the **Jardin d'acclimatation**, Bois de Boulogne, 75116 Paris. M° Sablons. Tel: 01 40 67 90 82, *www.jardindacclimatation.fr*. Open every day, and free for children under three, with entry fees for older children and adults. Radio-controlled boats, merry-go-rounds, mini-motorbikes, puppet shows, a circus and a mini-farm are all on offer. Over at La Muette on the edge of the Bois lie the **Jardin de**

Ranelagh, another popular play area, leading up to the two lakes. The **Lac Inférieur** is the real boating lake with an island in the middle and a regular ferry. All around you will find plenty of open space in which to sunbathe, picnic, play games, etc, and the forests run way out to the west. Also try out the **serres** (greenhouses) d'Auteuil in avenue de la Porte d'Auteuil, opposite the famous Roland-Garros tennis club. Huge nineteenth-century greenhouses reminiscent of Kew Gardens in London offer a variety of fascinating plants.

◆ **Parc de St Cloud.** The grounds of the former royal palace now provide another favourite Parisian escape overlooking the Seine above the Pont de Sevres.

◆ **Château de Thoiry Safari Park,** 78770 Thoiry. Tel: 01 34 87 40 67, *www.thoiry.tm.fr* (bilingual site) – With an American Lady of the Manor, British cricket teams, and wild animals roaming free in the safari park, this has to be one of the most exotic places within easy striking distance of Paris!

◆ **Espace Rambouillet,** route de Clairfontaine, (78) Rambouillet. Tel: 01 34 83 05 00. A natural park to the west of Paris leading up to the presidential country retreat. If lions and tigers are not your preferred animal option, try the regular forest inhabitants such as deer in Rambouillet.

CENTRAL PARIS

Children in central Paris are perhaps the most spoilt for choice of all Parisian youngsters. Two favourites, one old and one new, are:

◆ **Parc Monceau**, 75008 and 017, M° Monceau. Sandpits, swings, a mini-lake and eighteenth-century follies. A classic Parisian play area and extremely popular – but keep off the grass!

◆ **La Tour Jean-sans-Peur**, rue Etienne-Marcel, 75002 Paris. M° Etienne-Marcel. Tel: 01 40 26 20 28. The last vestige of a medieval fortified palace built in 1411, recently restored and opened to the public, 'the place to play at knights in the very heart of Paris', with a special learning-game path for children.

CHILDREN'S WORKSHOPS

Every school vacation period sees a flurry of impressive activity from the hundreds of Parisian museums, from the great château at Versailles or the Louvre to the smaller specialist museums, in order to lay on workshops for young Parisians from the ages of about four upwards (depending on the museums and facilities available). Both *Zurban* and *A nous Paris* review these workshops very regularly, so you should definitely check these two publications for ideas on how to constructively amuse your children.

Theatres groups and dance schools also offer workshops, and many establishments offer workshops throughout the year. The **Académie américaine de la danse**, 5 rue Rousselet, 75007 Paris. M° Vaneau. Tel: 01 47 34 36 22 offers bilingual classes for children aged four and over. The great **Opéra-Garnier** offers back-stage tours to children aged five and over, and the chance to design and create costumes (tel: 01 40 01 22 46). If your child has picked a good basic grasp of French then the choices of workshops will be much wider, although a number of museums, etc offer bilingual classes.

Details of French language classes for children at Paris museums can be found on the excellent bilingual website *www.monum.fr* or by calling 01 44 61 20 00. The main English-language bookshops (Brentanos, and WH Smith) also offer special kids' book clubs and activities. Call in at the stores for further details.

SPORTS, SCOUTING AND GUIDING

Many of the sports clubs and associations listed in Chapter 17 offer junior sides. Depending on your children's level of French, they might also enrol for a city-sponsored holiday sports course (from the age of seven) at one of the 23 **centres d'initiative sportive** across Paris, offering tennis, diving, judo, canoeing, etc. British Brownie and Guide packs can be found in Maisons-Lafitte, Bougival, and at the British Schools of Paris (senior and junior). For more details check *www.britishinfrance.com*. British Scouts have packs at Bougival and Maisons-Lafitte, Chantilly and Fontainebleau. American packs are based at the American School of Paris, and also Marymount School (tel: 01 46 24 10 51).

SANTA'S LITTLE HELPERS IN PARIS...

Paris at Christmas is a magical city. Taking the kids to see the lights and the shop windows is a fun way of building up to the day. Take in the Champs-Elysées in the early evening with their elegant lights, and perhaps the avenues George V and Montaigne also. But the essential visits are to the animated window displays of the **grands magasins**, **Printemps** and **Galeries Lafayettes** (boulevard Haussman), **La Samaritaine**, and **Le Bon Marché**, all of which rival each other in animation, decoration and imagination.

(19)

Meeting People in Paris

Making new friends with whom you can share your experiences and to whom you can turn to and also offer help is not always easy. The French as a rule are reserved, and take time to get to know newcomers whether foreign or French alike. As a foreigner, you will most likely also suffer from a lack of common experience initially, whether in understanding catchphrases or favourite television programmes; not to mention not having experienced life in **la France profonde** (the deep backwaters of France), nor having been through the French education system.

Although some French people may admire a total embrace of their culture, many would find it puzzling and ill-advised. The French and especially Parisians believe strongly in **networking**, whether through social, business or culturally-identified groups. Paris is composed essentially of exiles who do not hesitate to call on fellow Auvergnats, Bretons or Corsicans to help them out when they first arrive. Sticking together, at least at first, is normal for the French, so why should expatriates be any different?

Anglophone is a word used in French to describe anybody who is English mother-tongue, a slightly more global term than Anglo-Saxon which is principally reserved for the Americans and the British. Nonetheless, the principal English communities in and around Paris are the American and British, followed by the Irish and Canadian, and a small but visible Australasian community.

COMMUNITY CENTRES IN AND AROUND PARIS

Anglophone community centres are mainly linked to the churches. You will find information regarding childcare, youth groups, housing, employment, support lines and social organisations.

◆ **The American Church**, 65 quai d'Orsay, 75007 Paris. M° Invalides/Alma-Marceau. Tel: 01 40 62 05 00, *www.acparis.org*. The focal point for Anglophone community activities in Paris, with strong links to groups as diverse as Alcoholics Anonymous, the American University of Paris, and the Montessori Schools. Extensive housing and employment advertising service. The Information Centre operated by the 'Women of the American Church' (*www.woac.net*) offers advice and information on almost any practical topic for newcomers and local residents. The church is open every day.

- **The American Cathedral**, 23 avenue George V, 75008 Paris. M° Alma-Marceau/George V. Tel: 01 53 23 84 00, *www.us.net/amcathedral-paris*. The Episcopalian British-designed and built masterpiece just off the Champs-Elysées. Home to the Junior Service League, housing and employment ads, and extensive community and arts groups. There is a pay counselling service and one of the best church choirs in Paris.

- **St George's Anglican Church**, 7 rue Auguste-Vacquerie, 75116 Paris. M°/RER Charles-de-Gaulle-Etoile, Kléber, George V. Tel: 01 47 20 22 51, *www.stgeorgesparis.com*. A thriving diverse communities, 50% British, 50% 'rest of the world'. High Anglican worship, excellent music and thriving Sunday school and crèche. Useful community notice-board.

- **St Joseph's RC Church**, avenue Hoche, 75008 Paris. M°/RER Charles-de-Gaulle-Etoile. Tel: 0 42 27 28 56, *www.stjoeparis.org*. RC Church served by Irish priests caring for English-speaking Roman Catholics. Large and diverse congregation on Sundays. Sunday school, catechism in English, American Catholic Women's Group all on offer. Useful community notice-board.

- **St Michael's English Church**, 5 rue d'Aguesseau, 75008 Paris. M° Concorde. Tel: 01 47 42 70 88, *www.stmichaelsparis.free.fr*. This packed Evangelical Anglican church offers modern worship in English. Strong youth/student section, many groups and activities for all ages.

- **The Scots Kirk**, tel: 01 48 78 47 94, *www.scotskirkparis.com*. The rebuilt Kirk is home to a friendly and dynamic community who will introduce you to the Caledonians of Paris.

- **St Peter's Church, Chantilly**, 7a avenue de Bouteiller, 60500 Chantilly. Tel: 03 44 58 53 22, *www.stpeterschantilly.info*. The modern church centre attached to the historic church has an English language library, groups for men and women, and an active British Scout group.

- **Holy Trinity Church**, 15 avenue Carnot, 78600 Maisons-Lafitte. Tel: 01 39 62 34 97. Home to a busy community of Anglophone locals and offering a full range of family activities, from mother and toddler groups to Scouts and Guides.

- **St Mark's Church**, 31 rue du Pont Colbert, 78000 Versailles. Tel: 01 39 02 79 45. A modern Evangelican Anglican church providing a community focal point to the west of Paris.

- **The Great Synagogue of Paris** is to be found at 44 rue de la Victoire, 75009 Paris. M° Opéra or Le Peletier. Tel: 01 45 26 95 36. Other synagogues can be found across Paris the suburbs.

- The main **Paris Mosque** is to be found at 2 place Puits de l'Ermite, 75005 Paris. M° Monge. Tel: 01 45 35 97 33. Includes renowned gardens, tea rooms and hammams.

COMMUNITY COMMUNICATION
- *France-USA Contacts,* 26 rue Bénard, 75014 Paris. Tel: 01 56 53 55 54, fax: 01 56 53 54 55, *www.fusac.fr*; US office: France Contacts, POBox 115, Cooper Station,

New York, NY 10276. Tel: 212 777 5553, fax: 212 777 5554. Free indispensable magazine available at over 50 Anglo-owned or friendly restaurants, shops, pubs, churches etc, across Paris. Excellent jobs section, useful housing and an excellent guide to what's on in bars, restaurants, etc.

◆ *The Paris Voice*, 7 rue Papillon, 75009 Paris. Tel: 01 47 70 45 05, fax: 01 47 70 47 72, *www.parisvoice.com*. Jobs and housing ads at the end but also offering well-informed news and reviews. Free at the same points as FUSAC.

◆ *Time Out in Pariscope*, 100 rue du Faubourg St Antoine, 75012 Paris. Tel: 01 44 87 00 45, fax: 01 44 73 90 60, *www.timeout.com/paris*. Excellent English language quarterly free listings guide, available at the same distribution points as FUSAC. Their annual guide is probably the best on the market for day tripping, nightlife, etc.

◆ *International Welcome to Paris Insiders Guide*, BP 232, 92205 Neuilly Cedex. Fax: 01 47 22 31 60/45 02, e-mail: *ameline.dominique@wanadoo.fr*. Annual free publication available at churches, consulates and major Anglophone associations. Packed pocket-size English-language handbook.

COMMUNITY EVENTS

◆ **Bloom where you are planted**. At the American Church on quai d'Orsay every year in the first weeks of October. Three one-day sessions for new expats. Hugely popular and informative.

- **Annual church bazaars/rummage sales**. In the run-up to Christmas the main sales are at the American Cathedral, St George's and St Michael's churches.

COMMUNITY RESOURCES

- **The American Library of Paris**, 10 rue du Général-Camou, 75007 Paris. Tel: 01 53 59 12 60. *www.americanlibraryinParis.org*. M° Ecole-Militaire/Alma-Marceau. Open Tuesday–Saturday 1000–19h00. Membership library open to all, with regular events.

- **Brentanos**, 37 avenue de l'Opéra, 75001 Paris. Tel: 01 42 61 52 50, fax: 01 42 61 07 61, *www.brentanos.fr*. The main American bookstore just by the Opéra-Garnier. Also sells American stationery and has book clubs for adults and children.

- **Children's English Learning Centre**, 33 rue de Fleurus, 75006 Paris. M° Rennes. Tel: 01 45 44 11 66, fax: 01 45 44 08 07. Exactly what it says it is. Offers adult conversation/social groups and also kids' holiday activities. A good place to know next to the Alliance Française.

- **Galignani's**, 224 rue de Rivoli, 75001 Paris. Tel: 01 42 60 76 07. The original British bookshop in Paris still has a large English-language section. Busy but refined (Mme Chirac is a regular).

- **WH Smith**, 248 rue de Rivoli, 75001 Paris. M° Concorde. Tel: 01 44 77 88 99, fax: 01 42 96 83 71, *www.whsmith.fr*. The English bookshop in Paris at the Place de la Concorde.

- **The Abbey Bookshop** (Canadian, second-hand), 29 rue de la Parchemenerie, 75005 Paris. M° St-Michel.

- **San Francisco Book Company** (second-hand), 17 rue Monsieur le Prince, 75006 Paris. M° Odéon.

- **Shakespeare & Co**, 37 rue de la Bûcherie, 75005 Paris. M° St-Michel. The famous second-hand English-language bookshop in Paris, picking up where Joyce and the 'Lost Generation' left off.

- **Tea and Tattered Pages**, (second-hand), 24 rue Mayet, 75006 Paris. M° Duroc.

- **Village Voice**, 6 rue Princesse, 75006 Paris. M° Mabillon.

INTERNATIONAL ASSOCIATIONS

A large number of Anglophone associations are open to all nationalities.

- **British and Commonwealth Women's Association**, 8 rue de Belloy, 75116 Paris. Tel: 01 47 20 50 91, *www.bcwa.org*.

- **Le WIC de Paris/Women's International Club**. Tel: 01 34 46 01 14.

Parents with children in Anglophone or bilingual educational establishments will also find that Parents Associations events also provide a good opportunity to meet and make friends.

American associations
- **Association of American Residents Overseas**. Tel: 01 47

20 24 15, *e-mail:aaro@aaro.org.*

◆ **Association of American Wives of Europeans**. Tel: 01 40 70 11 80, *www.aaweParis.org.*

◆ **American Women's Group in Paris**. Tel: 01 42 73 28 72, *www.awgparis.org.*

◆ Details of all the various societies and associations can be found on the US embassy website *www.amb-usa.fr* in the Consular section for Americans in France.

Australian associations
◆ **Association France-Australie**, c/o Australian Embassy. Tel: 01 45 75 19 20, *www.austgov.fr.*

◆ **Association Culturelle Franco-Australienne**. Tel: 01 46 03 01 92.

British associations (*www.britishinfrance.com*)
The 60 British and Franco-British associations cover all aspects of life. A free annual digest is available at churches, consulates, etc. Their website also gives contacts and full details of the member associations.

Canadian associations
◆ **Canadian Women's Group**, 5 rue de Constantine, 75007 Paris. Tel: 01 44 43 21 03, e-mail: *afcp_cwgp@yahoo.fr,* based at the Canadian Cultural Centre.

◆ **Canadian Club of Paris**, c/o The Abbey Bookshop. Tel: 01 46 33 16 24.

Irish associations
◆ **Collège des Irlandais**, 5 rue des Irlandais, 75005 Paris.

Tel: 01 45 35 59 79, *www.centreculturelirlandais.com*.
The Irish Cultural Centre in the former seminary. Has
its own chapel (popular with the Irish community) and
gardens.

◆ **Federation of Irish Societies**. Tel: 01 48 76 62 09.

◆ **Association of Irish Women in France**, 24 rue de
Grenelle, 75007 Paris. Tel: 01 42 22 51 08.

◆ The city's Irish bars also provide good networking
points. See FUSAC for addresses and events. The
occasional free magazine *Irish Eyes* is another important means of contact. This can be found in the same
places as FUSAC, etc.

Partying in Paris

Partying in Paris is a well accepted tradition. Whether you are an inveterate night-owl and **fêtard** (party-goer) or just an occasional dabbler on the social scene, you need to have a basic grip of what to expect in order to 'pass the first post'. You will soon establish your own rhythms and favourite haunts. Even if the latter turn out to be pretty 'classic' by Parisian standards, there is no shame in that; after all, they would not be well known if they were not worth going to.

FRENCH DINNER PARTIES

Dinner parties in France are normally held at about 20h00–21h00. Written invitations should be acknowledged by written replies. Normally, a French dinner consists of the following elements:

- Starter (**entrée**) normally accompanied by white wine.

- Main course (**plat**) accompanied by red wine, unless white wine is appropriate.

- Cheese *before* dessert, served either by itself or with a light salad.

- Dessert perhaps accompanied by a special dessert wine (**sauterne**).

- Coffee, served at the table. This may or may not be followed by liqueurs.

It is not advisable to take wine as a gift for your hostess. French people are generally knowledgeable about wine, and will normally have carefully selected what they wish to serve with a particular meal. If you take a gift of wine, it should be good quality and French. Non-French wine is viewed, at best, with caution. Gifts of wine will almost certainly be placed in the store, and served on a later occasion.

A bottle of Champagne is a good present, which need not be expensive. This can also be laid down in a cellar, or chilled during dinner and served with dessert. Flowers are cumbersome for a hostess when she is about to serve dinner. For foreigners, bringing a product or gift from your country is an original idea, and provides a talking point at the table. A small box of good chocolates is also another popular gift, which can be purchased from specialist shops, or even at the **boulangerie.**

If you do not wish to drink alcohol, mineral water is almost always available at French tables and in all restaurants. Smoking is very prevalent in France, and rules regarding smoking at the table, and even between courses, will vary according to the hosts and the company you keep. As with many table manners, it is very much a game of 'Follow my leader'. If you object to somebody smoking beside you, a discreet request rather than a loud haughty lecture will achieve the effect you require.

You may well find a rack or block beside your plate, which is a knife or fork rest. In France, it is quite common to keep the same cutlery throughout several courses. Bread is normally in plentiful supply on French tables, and should be broken with your hands, not cut with a knife. Butter is not normally served with bread.

Whilst business associates may well be invited to dinner, there is rarely 'shop talk' at the table. Conversation is more likely to revolve around new films, exhibitions, current events, and probably you as a foreigner in France. French dinner parties, like any other, can either be insufferably formal or very relaxed. If you do not know the rest of the party well, remember that the French are generally conservative and dress accordingly. The fading custom of sending thank you notes is nonetheless greatly appreciated, and will probably ensure your popularity with your new friends.

Formality and etiquette are part of the French fascination with rules and regulations. If you are worried about making gaffs (**faux pas**), then invest in one of the many etiquette guides available.

PARTIES

Cocktail parties usually begin about 19h00, and will last for a couple of hours. Informality over the time of arrival may not be matched by informality over dress, and you should try to find out roughly what is expected of you.

If you decide to organise a more traditional British-style party, do not expect your French guests to bring a bottle with them. In France, the host traditionally provides all the requirements for an evening's entertainment. One way to get around this is to call a party a **soirée à l'anglaise**, literally a British evening, and gently explain the bring-a-bottle concept to your French guests. You should warn both neighbours and the concierge that you will be organising a party, and post polite notes in French in the entrance hall of your building apologising in advance for any inconvenience caused.

Encourage your guests to leave quietly, and be careful about the level of noise. The police may be asked to intervene at rowdy parties after 22h00. Your neighbours will normally be forgiving if you make an excuse such as 'It's my birthday'. However – remember you only have one birthday a year!

THE PARISIAN PARTY YEAR PLAN

September

La rentrée scolaire (return to school) remains the real starting point of the year. University students start next month. Around the middle of the month you have two antipathetic cultural events: **Les Journées du Patrimoine/**

'**Portes-Ouvertes**' when you can visit the embassies and state palaces normally closed to the public; and the **Technoparade**, which is Paris's limp response to the Love Parade in Berlin. Just to add to the mayhem, the fashion pack flies in for a week of shows and showing-off.

October

Le Prix de l'Arc de Triomphe at Longchamps, the greatest horserace of the year equivalent to the Derby, takes place on the first Sunday. **Halloween** is now popular in Paris with plenty of costume parties in clubs, bars and private homes. Trick or Treat is not really accepted practice. Half-term holidays for Toussaint fall at the end of the month. A popular new innovation in October is **La Nuit Blanche**, when the Mairie de Paris organises events, concerts and 'happenings' across the city.

November

November 1 is **Toussaint**, All Saints Day, 11 November is **Armistice Day**. These are both national holidays when shops and businesses are shut. There is a wreath-laying ceremony at the Arc de Triomphe at 11am by the President, and a service at Notre-Dame for the British community in the afternoon. The third Thursday is **Beaujolais Nouveau**, the festival of a wine too young to drink, except that the more you drink the better it tastes. Parties in bars across Paris, the most famous being in rue du Marché St Honoré in the 1st.

December

Only **Christmas Day** is a bank holiday in France, and you can legitimately be expected to work on the 26th. The

French tradition is a grand family dinner on Christmas Eve, then off to Midnight Mass, and presents after Mass or early next morning. New Year's Eve is also known as **St Sylvestre**. **Le réveillon** (name for an evening banquet used at Christmas and New Year) is a special occasion for yet more gluttony. Avoid the Champs-Elysées and Place de la Concorde at these times. Greetings cards are normally sent to wish Happy New Year rather than Christmas, and can be sent between mid-December and the end of January.

January

New Year's Day is a national holiday. January 6 is the **Fête des Rois**. The tradition is to buy a galette of pastry and almonds at the boulangerie, invite family and friends to share it with you, and the person who finds the gift (**fève**) in their slice of cake is the king/queen for the day and wears the supplied paper crown. The youngest person is expected to crawl under the table to announce the distribution of slices.

February, March and April

Chandeleurs, (Candlemas, 2 February) is the French pancake (**crêpes**) day. The half-term holidays (**vacances scolaires**) are a popular ski season in February. Both **Mardi Gras** (Shrove Tuesday) and Ash Wednesday (**Cendres**) depend on the date of Easter. Paris does not hold a carnival unlike other some other cities in France. **Good Friday** is not a holiday in France, but **Easter Monday** is.

May

The favourite month of the year! Three national holidays: 1st **Labour day/May Day (Fête du travail)**; 8th **Victory in Europe Day (Fête de la Victoire)**; and **Ascension Day** (depends on Easter). If the dates work out, you can find yourself with three long weekends. On Labour Day, the popular tradition is to give a sprig of Lily of the Valley (**un brin du muguet**) to friends and family for good luck. The last Sunday in May is the French **Mother's Day (Fêtes des Mères)**.

June

Officially the **Pentecôte**, (Whit Monday) bank holiday has now been abolished, but the situation is unclear. June 21 is the **Fête de la Musique**, with free open-air concerts across Paris. The main venue is at République with top-name billing. Check the press for listings. **Gay Pride** on the third Saturday normally draws a huge crowd, so be ready for traffic problems. The **Prix de Diane** at Chantilly, the equivalent to Ascot Gold Cup day, is at about the same time as the **Roland Garros** tennis championships equivalent to Wimbledon or Flushing Meadow.

July and August

Bastille Day on 14 July is the French National Holiday (**fête nationale**). The parties begin on the 13th in the evening, with parties at the fire stations (**bals de pompiers**). On the 14th there is a grand military parade in the morning and a spectacular **son et lumière** firework display in the evening at the Eiffel Tower. The **fête de l'Assomption** on August 15th is celebrated as a national holiday. It is traditionally one of the hottest and quietest times of the year in Paris. There is an open-air mass in front of Notre-Dame, but most Parisians are by now travelling to or from the coast. If you don't have that luck, you can try out the other Parisian novelty, **Paris plage**, the artificial beach on the banks of Seine in the city centre. The hugely popular urban beach replaces the traffic on the riverbank roads, and includes sand and sun-loungers, a swimming pool, palm trees, games and picnic areas, and free evening concerts and activities.

EATING OUT IN RESTAURANTS

Finding good restaurants which offer value for money can be difficult. The best Paris restaurant guide in English is the annual *Time Out* guide, but all major newspapers and entertainment guides have regular weekly updates, depending on the style of meal you are looking for. For business lunches note that both *Le Figaro économie, Les Echos* and *La Tribune* all include restaurant reviews both for business lunches and for general guidance.

Generally, restaurants offer a choice between meals at a fixed price chosen from a menu or **formule**, or allow you to choose from the whole menu, which is known as eating **à la carte**. The formule is normally more economical, and generally involves a selection of the dishes offered in the menu. It may be a starter (**entrée**) and main course (**plat**), or a main course and dessert, or all three. A small jug of wine (**pichet**) is also sometimes included. Alternatively, you can ask for a jug of tap water (**une carafe d'eau**) which is free. Mineral water must be paid for. **NB:** Some restaurants will only offer a lunchtime set menu (**formule du midi**). Be careful to check this before you set out for the

restaurant in the evenings, especially if you are on a
limited budget.

The menu should always indicate if service is included
(**service compris**). This may effect your decision as to
whether to leave tip, especially in expensive restaurants. If
you order a meat dish, depending on the meat you will be
asked how you liked it cooked – **quelle cuisson?**

- **saignant** – rare
- **à point** – medium rare
- **bien cuit** – well-done.

The French like their meat cooked very rare compared to
the Americans and British, so you should perhaps over-
compensate if you do not like rare meat.

Foreign and regional food

The choice of restaurants available will depend on your
location. Non-French food is widely available, and as in
the UK the choice reflects France's colonial past.
Vietnamese and North African food (**couscous**) are
popular, and Chinese and Italian food is widely available.
Indian food is rarer, although in Paris once again you
should go to the Passage Brady near Strasbourg-St Denis.
British cooking is still eyed with suspicion and/or mirth in
France, and there are no truly British restaurants.

What you will find in France is a great choice of
restaurants offering regional specialities. Some of these
are now universal, and you will find **boeuf bourguignonne**
(Burgundy beef stew), for instance, available everywhere.

Fast food and take-aways

Fast food is widely available in France, and major international chains have outlets in most principal towns and cities. Chinese and Indian take-aways are still not common, but home-delivery services are widespread. Some restaurants do offer **plats à emporter**, but this involves ordering your food at the restaurant and squeezing up to the counter while you wait. Alternatively go to a **traiteur** who offers Italian or Chinese/Vietnamese/Thai (the three tend to be mixed together) dishes sold by the portion.

Gastronomic Paris

◆ **Chinese**. The two Paris Chinatowns (but including plenty of Vietnamese and Thai) are in Belleville (19th and 20th) and Place d'Italie (13th).

◆ **St Germain des Près**, the **Marais, Bastille**. A mix of intimate and trendy restaurants of varying quality. **Brasserie Lipp** at St Germain remains an institution, and **Chez Paul** in rue de Charonne is full-hearted French fare with lashings of Gallic arrogance from the staff.

◆ **Chartiers**, rue du Faubourg Montmartre. The original French canteen, in an original nineteenth-century interior. The food is good but basic, prices are reasonable, and the atmosphere guaranteed.

◆ **The great classics**. **La Tour d'Argent**, quai de la Tournelle (for very special occasions and if you have a silver tower of your own to pay the bill); the **Jules Verne** restaurant on top of the Eiffel Tower (three months' waiting list for a table, the sky is the limit for the price range ... save it for really special occasions).

CAFÉS AND PUBS

Cafés are one of the great traditions of French society, ranging from the high-brow literary **salons** of St Germain des Prés in Paris to scruffy street-corners, and encompassing every style in between.

Drinking at the counter (**comptoir**) is cheaper than at a table (**en salle**) or on a terrace (**en terrasse**). The same rules apply in cafés to ordering alcohol as to ordering coffee or tea. Exploring the local cafés and finding one that suits you, where you can while away half an hour with the newspaper, a book or friends for the price of a coffee, is another of the joys of France.

Those cafés which display a red tabac sign also double as tobacconists, offering a wide range of products at the cigarette counter (eg, phone cards or fiscal stamps). Many also offer a **service restauration** at least at lunchtime, with sandwiches and hot meals available. Some of the terms for these meals you will need to know include:

- **Croque-monsieur** – ham and cheese toasted sandwich

- **Croque-madame** – as above, but with a fried egg served on top

- **Chèvre-chaud** – hot goat's cheese normally served on toast, with a small mixed salad. Either a starter or a main course

- **Francfort-frites** – Frankfurter sausage and chips. Sausages such as **saucisse de Toulouse,** are more like a Cumberland sausage and will be served with other vegetables and a sauce.

- **Garnis avec...** – served with: chips **(frites),** mashed potato **(pommes vapeur),** fried/roast potatoes **(pommes sautés),** pasta **(pâtes).**

- **Salade** – Be careful here. In French this means both lettuce, which may be all you receive, or for instance, you may receive a **salade de tomates** (a plate of sliced tomatoes). A **salade mixte** will be a side-salad of lettuce plus perhaps chicory **(endives)** and tomatoes. Salads which are served as main courses will normally have a list of their ingredients.

- **Omelettes** are normally also available in variety of styles and content.

In Paris, some cafés also become centres of nightlife. This café scene is dominated by two brothers, the frères Costes, who own **Café Beaubourg** outside the Pompidou Centre. Now they have gone one better and taken over the top floor of the centre itself with **Chez Georges**, a 'sweetie darling' paradise with stunning views across Paris. They also have **Café Marly** at the Louvre (the best summer terrace in Paris) **L'Esplanade** opposite Les Invalides, and **La Grande Armée** next to the Arc de Triomphe. All Costes cafés offer high but not unaffordable prices; great locations; fantastic modern décor; sultry staff clad in black; and plenty of star gazing. The ultimate is now the **Hôtel Costes** round the corner from Place Vendôme, where Mick Jagger celebrated his 50th birthday, and the resident DJ has produced three highly-successful albums of lounge music. The courtyard restaurant is bliss in summer, even if the majority of the people hanging around it are hell.

A selection of other cafés/bars and districts to know are:

◆ **Abbesses** – **Le Sancerre** and **Le Chinon** in rue des Abbesses, and **La Fourmi** in rue des Martyrs.

◆ **Oberkampf** – **Le Café Charbon**, the **Mecano Bar**, and all the bars in between on rue Oberkampf, although you should also check out neighbouring rue Jean-Pierre Timbaud.

◆ **Marais** – The **Café Trésor** in rue du Trésor for trendy night-owls; and **Le Petit Fer à Cheval** for its on rue Vieille du Temple for its interior and **La Belle Hortense** bookshop-wine bar opposite. The **rue des Archives** is the centre of the gay district, stretching from Les Halles to Bastille.

◆ **Bastille** – An embarrassment of riches. Check out the rue de Charonne, rue de Lappe and Faubourg St Antoine. The **Barrio Latino** is the place everybody wants to be, but snug little hideouts like the **Bar sans nom** are really the places where the seductive atmosphere is at.

◆ **St Germain des Près** – The great literary cafés are to be found next to the church, but try heading round to **La Palette** on rue de Seine for a great interior and exterior in fine weather. Round the corner in rue Mazarin is **L'Alcazar's AZ Bar**, is now one of Paris's top lounge bar, above the restaurant.

- ◆ **Latin Quarter** – At one end head for the **Place de Contrescarpe** off the rue Mouffetard with its cafés, or if you prefer lusher surroundings try the chic **Closerie de Lilas** at Port-Royal.

- ◆ **Canal St Martin** – On the quai Jemmapes and quai de Valmy from the Hôpital St Louis down towards République. To check out the local Bobos, try the **Antoine & Lili** café on a Sunday.

There are over 60 Irish pubs across France in the principal cities, most notably Paris.

The cost of a glass of wine will depend on its size and quality. The standard French person will drink a half-pint (**demie**) of whatever is on tap (**pression**). This is one local custom you should take up quickly! Spirits are generally more expensive.

CABARETS AND CLUBS

The French have been famous for generations for their cabarets and nightclubs. In Paris, the **Folies-Bergères**, the **Lido**, the **Crazy Horse** and the **Moulin-Rouge** continue to offer high-class, but expensive, entertainment, with a champagne dinner and a grand musical show. Smaller cabarets are also very popular, allowing singers and comedians to perform in a more intimate atmosphere.

Nightclubs, almost by definition, fall in and out of fashion very rapidly and regularly. You should check the style of a club by using a guide, or by asking somebody whom you know already goes to the club. Styles vary widely, even at the same club, depending on the day of the week. The trendiest Paris nightclubs have a very exclusive door policy, so swot up in advance on what to wear and how to act.

At the time of writing, the nightclub scene is thriving in Paris, although it is now a lot more industrial than it used to be. One-night events are becoming more and more popular with DJs jetting in from the US and the UK. Flyers can be found in the trendy bars (ie where 'people like us' hang out); so find the bars and you will find the info. Otherwise listen to the daily updates on Radio FG, read *Nova* magazine, shave your head and grow a goatee beard (unless you are a woman ...), and you should soon fit in at most of the top nightclubs. *Time Out in Pariscope* provides an objective view separating the hot from the hype in Paris nightlife.

French nightlife gets going much later than in the UK. Bars generally close at 02h00, and nightclubs will generally start to fill up from about 01h00, and then stay open until dawn. The entry price may include one drink (**une consommation**), but after that be prepared for high prices.

Paris clubs are not grouped together but can be found in a number of different areas; including:

- ◆ **Champs-Elysées**. The extravagant predominantly gay **Queen**, and the exclusive **VIP Room** and **L'Etoile** head the local hit-list. **Nirvana** is a very trendy bar with a basement nightclub, and **Manray** often feels more like a club than a restaurant.

- **Left Bank**. In **St Germain**, the trendy **WAGG** beneath the **Alcazar** restaurant completes the Conran bar and restaurant emporium. In **Montparnasse**, the **Redlight** and neighbouring **Amnesia** are currently two of the hottest clubs. Nearby, the **Dancing de La Coupole** has undergone a transformation as a new favoured Saturday-night venue. Along the banks of Seine, you will also find floating nightclubs at the **Bibliothèque Nationale**.

- **Montmartre** – The **Follies Pigalle** remains one of the temples of Paris nightlife and extravaganza. Across the road, the **Divan du Monde** and **Elysées Montmartre** are popular one-night venues. **La Boule Noire** beneath **La Cigale** is also another address to note.

- **Central Paris** – **Le Cabaret** (Le Cab') at Palais-Royal is another sought-after restaurant and club experience. **Les Bains** has lost some of its cachet, but making it past the selection at the door remains a mythic experience.

THE PERFORMING ARTS

France is traditionally very generous in state patronage of the arts. The result is a rich variety in the performing arts, with Paris naturally being centre stage. Tourist information centres will be able to tell you what forthcoming productions and events are planned in your own area.

Music

Paris naturally has a high concentration of fine concert halls, such as the **Salle Pleyel**, but the wealth of fine churches provides a secondary source of concert venues. Among the most popular church venues are the Eglise St

Séverin in the 5th, and La Madeleine in the 8th.

The Anglophone expatriate communities are very well served by semi-professional musicians in and around Paris. Many touring British choirs stop off in Paris and sing in one of the city's great churches, and details of these visits can always be found at the Anglophone community centres. The main popular music concert venues are Bercy, **Le Bataclan** (11th), **La Cigale** (18th), and **L'Olympia** (9th). Tickets and listings ca be found at both the Virgin Megastores and the main FNAC stores.

Opera and ballet

Opera flourishes in Paris, not only in the new **Opéra-Bastill**, but also at the **Opéra-Comique** in Place Boïeldieu, and sometimes also at the old Paris Opéra (the **Palais Garnier**), and in other theatres such as the **Theâtre Chatelet**. Both traditional and modern operas are included in their repertoires. The Paris Ballet is now housed at the grand **Opéra-Garnier**, and provides a full programme each season. Visiting ballets also regularly appear in Paris.

Theatre

The theatre in Paris especially thrives, with many small theatres offering the chance for new actors and productions to appear before the public. The most famous French theatre is the **Comedie-Française**, which now has three theatres.

There are also occasional performances in English in Paris, at the following addresses and by different companies:

- The **Shakespeare Garden** in the Bois de Boulogne. An open-air summer season with a company from the UK. Tel: 01 42 27 39 54.

- **Théâtre de Nesle**, 8 rue de Nesle, 75006 Paris. Tel: 01 46 34 61 04. A small cellar theatre with regular productions in English, including children's shows.

- **Sudden Theatre**, 14bis, rue St Isaure, 76018 Paris. Tel: 01 42 62 35 00. A repertory theatre providing a welcome to English language companies and their followers.

- **Dear Conjunction**. Tel: 01 42 85 09 57. Justifiably the Anglo community's favourite company. American and English Paris resident professionals, alternate performances in English and French. Broad range of material performed at various venues. Watch the Anglo press for details and follow the crowd.

- **The International Players**. Tel: 01 39 62 79 64 (see also *www.britishinfrance.com*). Musical productions from Gilbert and Sullivan to *Grease*, with popular pantomimes at Christmas. Normally performs in 'Angloland' Le Vesinet. Generally high standard and a good night out.

- **Paris theatres with productions in English**. The **Bouffes du Nord** (10th), **MC93** in Bobigny (93), and **Les Amandiers** at Nanterre (92) all occasionally have productions in English, normally of very high quality by visiting directors or companies.

Going to the cinema

Cinema is one of the great passions of the French, which they consider to be the '7th art'. Paris has two film festivals sponsored by the city. Other festivals take place throughout the year linked to particular themes, and there is also an American Film Festival at Deauville and a British film festival at Dinard.

Films in English with French sub-titles are widely shown and are marked **v.o. (version originale)**. **V.F. (version française)** means that films have been dubbed. **Premières** (first nights) are great occasions, but there are plenty of **avants-premières** now which are advertised in the press. Wednesday is the day that new films come out in France, and is worth avoiding at cinemas if you want a quiet night out. Late-night showings are available at various cinemas across Paris, such as the **UGC Ciné-Cité** in Les Halles or the **Pathé-Wepler** at Place de Clichy. For cinema times check *Pariscope, Officiel & Spectacles* or *Zurban*. The latter also has details of cinema passes which are available.

Essential reading

Weekly entertainment guides coincide with new films every Wednesday. General news magazines come out on Thursdays. The newspapers publish their critiques on different days. Amongst the best guides are:

◆ **In English**:
 Time Out quarterly magazines
 The Free Voice
 FUSAC (listings only)

Where (monthly subscription magazine, tel: 01 43 12 56 56).

◆ **In French**:
Pariscope
Zurban
A nous Paris
Officiels & Spectacles
Nova
Aden (weekly supplement of *Le Monde*)
Libération (each day)
Le Figaroscope (weekly supplement of *Le Figaro*)
and the Paris supplement to *L'Express.*

Zurban is probably the best observer of what is going on, and *A nous Paris* in its new format is still more subjective in its views. *Where* offers a good variety of restaurant reviews and feature articles, but *Time Out* remains the best guide in English.

BIRTHS, MARRIAGES AND DEATHS

Although these are not leisure activities, it is appropriate to know a few of the social customs of the hatched, matched and despatched 'business' which still thrives in republican France so that you do not make any blunders. Obviously there is no Court Circular page in French newspapers, but both *Le Figaro* and *Le Monde* carry social announcements, as well as *Libération* to a lesser extent. The choice of paper depends entirely on the class pretensions and politics of those concerned.

Births

Births (**naissances**) are often announced not only by cards but also by a small advertisement in one of the papers named above. Typically, a birth announcement will be roughly translated as, 'Marie and Pierre are pleased to announce the arrival of their new sister Jeanne' followed by the name and address of the parents.

Infant baptisms are heavily on the decline in France. For Catholic families, they normally take place during the Parish Mass on Sunday mornings, and will be followed by a family lunch. Coloured sugared almonds (**dragees**) are often distributed, pink for girls and blue for boys.

Marriages

No religious wedding ceremony may take place in France until a civil marriage has first been performed by the mayor at the town hall. This applies to all religions and denominations. If a large religious ceremony is to follow, then normally only close family and friends will attend the wedding at the **mairie**. However, many people choose to stick to civil marriage. Being invited to be a **témoin** (witness) is an honour equivalent to being a bridesmaid or usher.

Wedding lists are very popular in France, and are an easy way of dealing with the problem of presents. The style of the wedding is of course entirely personal to the couple, and may range from the unusual to the strictly traditional. A traditional Catholic wedding will normally take place in the course of a Nuptial Mass in the bride's home parish.

As with British weddings, French weddings can be the occasion for a great show of finery. As ever in France, be careful to find out as much about the dress code expected as possible. The wedding invitation may well read like a genealogy of the couple, with grandparents and parents of both sides listed.

The car procession from the church or mairie to the reception is often the occasion for a fanfare of car horns. The French tradition in wedding receptions is the opposite of the British. Everybody is invited after the wedding to the **vin d'honneur**, to toast the couple's health and happiness. However after that the reception is limited, ranging from a seated dinner (**dîner placée**), to a **soirée dansante** (dance).

Deaths

Generally you will receive a **faire-part** (card announcing a death), including the same genealogical list as you would find on a wedding invitation, only longer. For instance, a faire-part announcing the death of a grandmother would begin with her spouse, include any surviving brothers and sisters and their spouses, and then move on to mention each child and their children, sometimes each by name.

The French are very attached to the tradition of writing to express condolence. The faire-part will announce when and where the funeral is to take place, if donations should be made in place of flowers or wreathes (**ni fleurs ni couronnes**), and whether it is a 'family only' affair (**dans la plus stricte intimité**).

At a French Requiem Mass, each mourner will be invited to take part in the ritual absolution of the coffin, the **absolut,** as a final farewell. This is not obligatory if it contradicts your own faith. If you do wish to participate, move at the instruction of the undertaker, and then 'follow the leader'. Burial is still much the most common end for French men and women, and cremations are rare.

Escaping From Paris

So – you've read the book, found the job, moved your home, enrolled for your courses, shopped till you dropped, partied like there was no tomorrow. What do you do next? The realistic answer is take a break and head out of Paris before it finally drives you crazy. It is a fantastic place to live, but escaping from the city is essential for your mental health. Thankfully it is not hard to do either due to the excellent French transport system.

WHEN SHOULD YOU GO?

The best idea is of course to take a long weekend. With the number and dates of the French bank holidays, this is not too difficult. French bank holidays 'belong' to the date, and are not transferred, for example, if Christmas Day falls on a Saturday, then it is observed on that day and no time off is given in lieu of the weekend celebrations.

However when a **fête** falls on a Thursday or Tuesday, the bridge day is often taken as a holiday by French residents to make a long weekend. (See Figure 18.) The term for this is **faire le pont**, literally to make the bridge. When bank holidays are close together (eg Ascension, or Toussaint and Armistice) you will also find that many people will go away between the two fêtes to avoid using up too many holidays.

Obviously this creates peak season rates and travel problems, so you need to plan in advance. Friday nights (after 5pm) and Monday mornings are also to be avoided.

Date	Occasion
1 January	New Year's Day (**Jour de l'An**)
March/April	Easter Day and Easter Monday (**Pâcques**) **NB: Good Friday is not a holiday in France**
1 May	Labour Day (**Fête du Travail**)
8 May	Liberation Day (**Fête de la Libération**)
May	Ascension Day (**l'Ascension**) **NB: Date depends on the date of Easter**
14 July	National/Bastille Day (**Fête Nationale**)
15 August	Assumption day (**l'Assomption**)
1 November	All Saints Day (**Toussaint**)
8 November	Remembrance Day (**Fête de la Victoire 1918**)
11 November	Armistice Day
25 December	Christmas Day (**Noël**) **NB: 26 December is not a holiday in France**

Figure 18. Public holidays in France.

WHERE TO GO

Your finances or planning might not allow you to take a whole weekend off, or you might simply wish to take a breather from the Parisian rat-race. There is no shortage of options to choose from for this purpose. The following is just a few suggestions to help you start to explore the nearby regions:

To the north

◆ **Châteaux**. Less than one hour by train from Paris is **Chantilly**, the fairytale château at the centre of a forest, equestrian museum and racecourse. Across the forest lies **Pierrefonds**, another picture-postcard nineteenth-century folly, whilst royal **Compiegne** was a favourite of Louis XV and Napoléon III.

◆ **Cathedrals**. Both only one hour direct from Paris by train lie **Amiens**, with one of the most stunning Gothic masterpieces in France dominating the pretty town, and **Beauvais**, the unfinished highest Gothic cathedral in the world.

◆ **Towns**. **Senlis** (for which you need a car) is one of the prettiest and most historic former cities in the Val d'Oise with its tiny cobbled streets, ruined château, ramparts and cathedral. **Lille** is the great metropolis of the north, with a strong Flemish feel. Beautifully restored in the old city centre, excellent restaurants, terrific shopping, a good range of bars, and fine architecture are all combined with new museums in the nearby towns connected by the city's own métro system. The city centre boasts a fine opera house, theatres, and the most important art gallery outside of

Paris (**musée des beaux-arts**). You could happily spend a weekend in Lille and come back to Paris feeling much the better for it. English guide books and pamphlets readily available at the Tourist Office.

To the west

◆ **Châteaux**. With direct rail and RER links to central Paris, **Versailles** has a distinctly different feel to it than Paris. If you can't face the crowds at the château, then wander far from them in the surrounding parks, and visit the **Trianon** or Marie-Antoinette's mock farm. Another alternative is to head up to **St Germain-en-Laye** on the RER, visit the castle and wander along the terrace and back through the woods. Two hours direct from Paris by train lies **Tours**, the capital of the Loire valley. From here you could hire a car to visit the Renaissance châteaux which fill the valley, or if you want a quiet weekend stop off in **Amboise** or **Blois**. If you head into Normandy, then try the **Château de la Roche-Guyon** if you have a car, Rommel's HQ during the Second World War.

◆ **Cathedrals**. One hour from Montparnasse are the world-renowned medieval splendours of the stained glass windows (**vitraux**) of **Chartres Cathedral**. You should try to pick a sunny day to best appreciate the windows. **Rouen**, the attractive capital of Normandy, is dominated by its city-centre cathedral and a cluster of other Renaissance churches, only one hour by train from St Lazare.

◆ **Beaches and gardens**. From May to September, a direct rail link is made from St Lazare to the Calvados coast of Normandy. **Cabourg** (the home of Marcel Proust) and **Houlgate** are more laid-back resorts with big sandy beaches, but the jet-set head for **Deauville**, which is packed in summer months. If you have a car, you could try Monet's home at **Giverny**, but peace and quiet are not assured. Nearby is the museum of American Impressionists. The **D-Day beaches** and **cemeteries** are also within easy reach of **Caen** and **Bayeux** and its famous tapestry.

To the south

◆ **Châteaux**. The train from Gare de Lyon will take you in about one hour to **Fontainebleau**, the great royal château in the forests to the south of Paris. You need a car to reach **Vaux-le-Vicomte** but it is worth it to see the château that inspired Louis XIV's jealousy and the creation of Versailles.

◆ **Towns**. **Provins** is a medieval masterpiece, and feels a million miles from the bustle of Paris. Two hours south of Paris by TGV from the Gare de Lyon is **Dijon**, the pretty and historic capital of Burgundy, with regular tours of the local vineyards leaving from the city centre.

An excellent pocket guide of day-trips using local train and RER services in the Île de France is, *An Hour from Paris*, by British Parisienne Annabel Sims (Pallas Athene, 2002). The book describes in detail everything you need to know for a perfectly planned day out in the Paris countryside. If you go further afield, the best guides are still the Green Michelin guides.

All the French regions have tourist offices in the centre of Paris (generally **La Maison de** ...). Check the *Pages Jaunes* for exact details, choose your destination, pack your bags and **bon weekend et bon voyage!**

Index

Printed in Great Britain by
Amazon.co.uk, Ltd.,
Marston Gate.